Weapons of Democracy

NEW STUDIES IN AMERICAN INTELLECTUAL AND CULTURAL HISTORY

Jeffrey Sklansky, Series Editor

Weapons of Democracy

Propaganda, Progressivism, and
American Public Opinion

JONATHAN AUERBACH

Johns Hopkins University Press
Baltimore

Johns Hopkins University Press
2715 North Charles Street
Baltimore, Maryland 21218-4363
www.press.jhu.edu

Library of Congress Cataloging-in-Publication Data

Auerbach, Jonathan, 1954–
Weapons of democracy : propaganda, progressivism, and American public
opinion / Jonathan Auerbach.
pages cm. — (New studies in American intellectual and cultural history)
Includes bibliographical references and index.
ISBN 978-1-4214-1736-3 (hardcover : alk. paper) — ISBN 978-1-4214-
1737-0 (electronic) — ISBN 1-4214-1736-7 (hardcover : alk. paper) —
ISBN 1-4214-1737-5 (electronic)   1. Public opinion—United States—
History.   2. Propaganda—United States—History.   3. Progressivism
(United States politics)—History.   4. Communication in politics—
United States—History.   I. Title.
HN90.P8A94 2015
303.3'80973—dc23   2014041145

A catalog record for this book is available from the British Library.

*Special discounts are available for bulk purchases of this book.
For more information, please contact Special Sales at 410-516-6936
or specialsales@press.jhu.edu.*

Johns Hopkins University Press uses environmentally friendly
book materials, including recycled text paper that is composed of
at least 30 percent post-consumer waste, whenever possible.

For my students,
with all due respect

One by one the State has gained the weapons of democracy.

—*George Creel, 1914*

Contents

Acknowledgments

I am happy to give thanks for the support offered by various friends and colleagues as I drafted this book, including Neil Fraistat, Sue Curry Jansen, Ted Leinwand, Bob Levine, Jan Stievermann, and Orrin Wang. They are excellent interlocutors all, as were audiences at the Heidelberg Center for American Studies and at the Universities of Debrecen and Szeged in Hungary, where I was a Fulbright senior specialist in 2014.

At key stages in the writing I benefited from sage advice from Russ Castronovo and Gordon Hunter. I also am deeply grateful for the feedback given to me by a pair of historian colleagues, Saverio Giovacchini and Jim Gilbert, who both read the manuscript from cover to cover.

In Bob Brugger at Johns Hopkins University Press I was fortunate to find an editor sympathetic to my brand of intellectual history based on close textual reading. His enthusiasm was a great source of encouragement as I rounded the bend toward the finish line. I also appreciate the invaluable suggestions for the final draft offered by the anonymous reader for the press.

Various archivists and reference librarians offered crucial support along the way, including Richard Peuser at the National Archives, Patricia J. Herron at the University of Maryland, and the National Agricultural Library's Wayne Olson and Perry Ma, who helped procure a high-resolution image of the wartime allegorical figure "Public Opinion." Finally, I thank the Graduate School, University of Maryland, for a Research and Scholarship Award, which enabled me to complete the book.

Weapons of Democracy

Introduction

Soon after the end of the First World War, political commentator Walter Lippmann declared a "crisis" in Western democracy. Lippmann's stark pronouncement gave voice to a set of misgivings that had been troubling American social reformers since the late nineteenth century. Rather than blame the usual suspects—bad policies and dishonest politicians—Lippmann offered a more unexpected and surprising diagnosis. He located this crisis in "news," in how information is produced, circulated, and received in a society dominated by mass media. Calling such social intelligence an "unregulated private enterprise" (as opposed to being directed by the state), Lippmann worried that citizens could no longer be expected to hold accurate and informed beliefs about the world. Other Progressives proposed a myriad of additional reasons for this crisis: stultifying educational practices; the numbing effects of industrial labor; rampant corruption in party politics; the inordinate power of unrestrained monopolies; and the nation's growing heterogeneity, including an influx of unassimilated immigrants.

All valid if partial, these explanations shared a concern about the viability of public opinion, the process by which "we the people" in a constitutional democracy actively participate in their own governance via voting and via debating views in print and in person. If a unitary public is nothing but a mere "phantom," as Lippmann concluded a few years after his earlier pronouncement, then opinions en masse could all too easily be made or unmade *for* people, not *by* them. Lippmann ominously called this opinion-making process "the manufacture of consent."[1]

A more familiar term for such large-scale persuasion would be *propaganda*. Propaganda is a dark word that commonly conjures up the nightmarish thought control of totalitarian regimes, whose cynical manipulation of the masses aims to turn citizens into powerless dupes. But propaganda was not always held in such disrepute. In 1622, to counter the widening influence of the Reformation, Pope Gregory XV established the Congregatione de Propaganda Fide, a group of cardinals dedicated to the worldwide dissemination of the true faith, a transmission of doctrine aided by the Vatican's post office. This religious meaning held sway until the French Revolution, when the word migrated to more secular political institutions. The concept was invoked both by radicals eager to advance the reign of reason and, more frequently, by anti-revolutionaries to refer to the widespread circulation of the dangerous ideas of universal equality and liberty. During the following century the word was used positively in a host of contexts to advocate for more particular causes, including, in the United States, agitation for women's suffrage, educational reform, and environmental conservation, and even in reference to Hegelianism, when William James in 1882 alluded to an "able set of propagandists" espousing this brand of philosophy.[2]

Only during and in the immediate aftermath of the First World War did the term take on its more familiar meaning of pernicious falsehood, so that propaganda primarily became associated with the evil work of one's enemy. In other words, the notion of propaganda as inherently manipulative and deceitful derived directly from the practice of wartime propaganda itself, specifically the charges and countercharges made between Germany and its adversaries, including various justifications for belligerence and accusations of atrocities perpetrated against innocent civilians. These wholly negative connotations were confirmed a few decades later when the Nazi Reich relied heavily on propaganda to promote genocide and conquest.

While the global violence of the twentieth century marked a turning point in how propaganda was understood and exercised, it would be misleading to assume some sharp division between benign modes of mass advocacy before the First World War and sinister ones after. The Anglo-American liberal tradition of John Locke and his followers posits a clear distinction between coercion and persuasion.[3] But in practice such a strict demarcation is difficult to maintain. From the late 1800s, American reformers struggled to distinguish between modes of influence that encouraged citizens to partake in the life of the polis and those that more directly organized their beliefs, attitudes, and values for them. Propaganda practice therefore must be examined in relation to culturally specific proximate institutions, such as religion, education, advertising, literature, journalism, and public diplomacy.

This book will emphasize how propaganda during the Progressive Era was closely linked to teaching, preaching, selling, and other modes of suasion aimed at helping to shape "public opinion," a phrase constantly evoked and discussed by the press, politicians, and a host of commentators during this period. Progressives' preoccupation with the public would seem to derive from the desire for reform; in order to get citizens on your side to institute change, you have to solicit and pay attention to their views.[4] But public opinion was not simply some preexisting content waiting to be tapped; more than a means to an end, it was rather a contested, slippery terrain continually constituted and reconstituted by Progressive discourse itself: not an epiphenomenon or precondition to renewal, but its very ground. In this regard, propaganda became at once part of the problem as well as a potential solution—a way to control and direct an uncertain, disparate citizenry, but also possibly to mobilize and guide it toward a greater common good.

As a normative concept or ideal, "public opinion" needs to be carefully distinguished from a more familiar, more recent offshoot—"public opinion polling." With the rise in the 1930s of empirically based methods to gather data about the attitudes of individuals, public opinion has commonly been treated as a statistical aggregation of personal views, purporting to reflect and express what citizens believe but without any attempt to understand how these beliefs came to be held or shared. Polling in the four months leading up to the March 2003 US-led invasion of Iraq, for instance, revealed dramatic spikes up and down in the percentage of Americans favoring military intervention. The numbers skewed depending on whether the question of war was asked as a simple binary (yes-no), or whether respondents were given multiple, more nuanced options (factoring in the weapons inspectors), or whether respondents listened to President George W. Bush's January 28 State of the Union address (more Republicans than Democrats), which laid out the case for invasion.

Numbers were also skewed by the process of incessant polling itself, which like mainstream media coverage during this period helped to produce a feedback loop that amplified the drumbeat of war, reinforcing the Bush administration's prevailing version of events. Fears about weapons of mass destruction were inflamed by these weapons of mass democracy, so to speak. A Gallup poll could register the distressing fact that a majority of Americans believed falsely that Iraq was responsible for 9/11, but this kind of empirical survey was inadequate to explain the reasons for such a profound misperception.[5] Public opinion, in the limited sense of tallying views, avoids the deeper question that Robert C. Binkley bluntly posed in the 1920s, along the lines of Lippmann: "How can such a thing as a public be conceived as entertaining such a thing as an opinion?"[6] Public opinion, as construed by Binkley's query, cannot be reduced to mere data gathering, but rather depends on a more complex, more open-ended process of social formation and circulation. Understanding how opinion is actively shaped—not simply registered—in and by a public (or multiple publics) remains of enduring importance for assessing the problems and promises of American democracy today. One hundred years ago, it was this thorny question that crucially stirred and disturbed reformers and politicians just as Progressivism (in both practice and ideology) was beginning to take hold at the start of the twentieth century.

A trio of essays published near the end of the nineteenth century from several vantage points illustrates these growing concerns about public opinion. The first was published in 1887 by the young scholar Woodrow Wilson, who examined the new field of administration; the second was in 1888 by an even younger John Dewey, who discussed the relation between democracy and ethics; and the third in 1899 was by Dewey's friend and colleague George Herbert Mead, who analyzed the connection between publicity and social reform.[7]

Writing in a newly established academic journal, Wilson in his pioneering essay scrutinized the emerging study of governmental administration, a discipline that would seem to have little to do with public opinion.[8] The article was especially prescient in relation to a pair of interrelated episodes linked to Wilson's subsequent presidency, twenty-five years down the road, the first instance a fictional demonstration of administrative mastery (see chapter 1) and the second, in the midst of war, an episode all too real (chapters 2 and 3).

Why, Wilson opens his essay, has the topic of administration come so belatedly to the attention of political scientists, especially in the United States, when in fact "it is getting harder to *run* a constitution than to frame one" (200, emphasis in original)? In a by now familiar move, Wilson offers an exceptionalist answer to this question: "on this side of the sea we . . . had known no great difficulties of government," living in a "new country, in which there was room" (anticipating Frederick Jackson Turner's frontier thesis), which freed us from worrying about the "plans and methods of administration" (203). But given the increasing complexity of the apparatus of the federal government, including the state's increasing regulation of corporations, Wilson argues, the United States is now at a disadvantage compared to its European counterparts when it comes to modernizing a creaky civil service into a more efficient administrative machine.

What prevents such reform? Here is where the American public suddenly enters Wilson's argument. Because democracies cherish "popular sovereignty," they "enthrone" a "multitudinous monarch called public opinion" (207), whose wishes must be obeyed. But Wilson finds "nowadays" that "the many, the people" are "selfish, ignorant, timid, stubborn, or foolish with the selfishness, the ignorances, the timidities, or the follies of several thousand persons,—albeit there are hundreds who are wise." Reform in the face of such mass ignorance is impossible, and therefore "[w]hoever would effect a change in a modern constitutional government must first educate his fellow-citizens to want *some* change. That done, he must persuade them to want the particular change he wants. He must first make public opinion willing to listen and then see to it that it listen to the right things. He must stir it up to search for an opinion, and then manage to put the right opinion in its way" (208, emphasis in original). Such an assessment, surprising in its bluntness, obscures the matter of agency: who is the executive "he" demanding such change in the first place, and how can this all-knowing individual, in a kind of circular reasoning, cleverly offer up a "right" opinion to a stirred-up public opinion, curiously already reified ("it"), to stumble upon, as if by accident?

In the second section of the article, Wilson emphasizes how the field of administration, understood as a "business," must be kept separate from "the hurry and strife of politics"; it is this effort to keep bureaucracy apolitical, above the fray of faction, that is usually taken to be the most important dimension of Wilson's argument. For example, even though he admits that "the study of administration" might seem to overlap with "the study of the proper distribution of constitutional authority" (213), he goes on to clarify that if this distribution is based on sound principles of trust, then "large powers and unhampered discretion" become invulnerable to abuse. In the very assumption of these "indispensible conditions of responsibility" (ibid.), the office of an administrative organizer becomes immune to power's corrupting tendencies. And yet despite his best efforts to distinguish between administrative authority and political power, the two tend to merge when Wilson returns near the end of the article to "public opinion," which he now confesses is not simply an obstacle to reform but "the fundamental problem" of his entire study.

The conventional view of American democracy, Wilson realizes, is that "public opinion" must serve as the "authoritative critic" superintending the conduct of administration, assuring that everything is on the up and up. But such a traditional faith in popular sovereignty, he argues, risks too many meddling busybodies spoiling the soup: the "cook must be trusted with a large discretion as to the management of the fires and ovens" (214). The danger, he reiterates, is that "public opinion," even if "indispensible," cannot be left to its own ignorant devices, but must be instructed and improved to render it as "efficient" as administration itself. Such a pedagogy makes it "necessary to organize democracy" (216); the accusation that this process might be "un-American" and lead to the creation of "a domineering, illiberal officialism" (216) misconstrues what is at stake, Wilson insists. Surely, Americans know how to usefully borrow foreign methods, systems, and tools without becoming foreign themselves. But this patriotic gesture toward exceptionalism at the close of the essay is something of a distraction. More to the point is another set of questions raised by Wilson's analysis but never directly acknowledged or addressed: Who is in charge of educating the public, how are these teachers appointed, and how could this proto-Progressive effort to "organize democracy" not carry its own political implications?

While Wilson at age thirty was making a name for himself in political science with the publication of this landmark article and other essays, Dewey at twenty-nine was establishing himself as an American philosopher of the first rank. The connection between Professors Wilson and Dewey is not as odd as it might first sound. Both were intensely engaged with probing an emerging crisis in American governance, even though they approached the topic from different angles. Dewey's "The Ethics of Democracy," in fact, was triggered by his response to reading a work more clearly in Wilson's bailiwick, Sir Henry Maine's influential *Popular Government* (1885).[9] The British jurist's conservative argument, as Dewey cited and summarized it, essentially amounted to a hatchet job directed against America's political system. For Maine, democracy is a form of government (simply one among others) in which sovereignty depends on the rule of the many, which is a "black omen" (228) precisely because such a reliance on numerical aggregation can produce a unified "common will" (229) only through artificial manufacture, either by party or by corruption. As a result, Maine contended, individual citizens in a majoritarian democracy remain "fragments of political power" (230) with little or nothing to bind them together beyond sheer numbers.

Such an argument, Dewey vigorously responded, rests on a categorically false set of a priori assumptions, starting with the presupposition, also central to social contract theory, that "men in their natural state are non-social units," a "mere mass" that Dewey likens to "a heap of grains of sand needing factitious mortar to put them into [a] semblance of order" (231). Insisting that "the non-social individual is an abstraction arrived at by imagining what man would be if all his human qualities were taken away" (232), Dewey instead posits democracy not as a "problem in arithmetic" (233) but rather more broadly as "a form of society": a "real whole" with a "unity of will" that is precisely what makes it an organism. What Maine treated as a geopolitical concept, a democratically run nation-state, Dewey prefers to regard in terms of social theory. From this perspective, a vote "is not an impersonal counting of one; it is a manifestation of some tendency of the social organism through a member of that organism." This somewhat metaphysical notion ("some tendency") emboldens Dewey to claim that when a man comes to vote "he carries with him in his voting all the influence that he should have, and if he deserves twice as much as another man, it is safe to say that he decides twice as many votes as that other man" (233).

By the phrase "safe to say" Dewey might well be whistling in the dark at this stage in his argument, because while he positively asserts an "influence" commensurate with the social value of one citizen as opposed to another, he does not specify the means by which that deserved influence can be felt or registered outside the ballot box. If, for Dewey, the numerical outcome of votes counts less than the very act of casting a ballot, that is, "the process by which the majority is formed" (234), then he still needs to show beyond mere voting how the multitude comes to organize into a common body. What is the status of a minority that by Dewey's reasoning still must be part of an organic whole, even if not sharing the majority's "tentative opinion" (235), as he gingerly calls it? Where is influence or practical power located in a democracy, and how does it work? Between a self-regulating organic whole (akin to Ralph Waldo Emerson's transcendental "over-soul") and concrete election results, Dewey gives us little to go on.

As in Wilson's article, when a Mack truck threatens to drive a gaping hole in the argument, it is best to invoke American exceptionalism. Dewey does so at this stage in his essay by comparing French, German, English, and American theories of sovereignty, concluding (naturally) that the American theory is the best because it comes closest to realizing the truth that "every man is a priest of God" (237). Instead of a close analysis of how a democracy operates, Dewey substitutes a normative ideal, and an explicitly utopian one at that. In moving from the political to the theological by way of the sociological, he can then reintroduce America as a nation whose democratic "consciousness" (238) now has certain ethical consequences. Against Plato's utopian ideal of a wise aristocracy showing the ruled what they can best do, Dewey embraces a mode of governance that emphasizes an individualism not of numbers (as in laissez-faire liberalism), but rather "of freedom, of responsibility, of initiative to and for the ethical ideal" (244). Dewey understands these ideals precisely in relation to Emerson almost to the point of direct quotation: "in every individual there lives an infinite and universal possibility; that of being a king and priest" (246). While he touches on "industrial equality" (246) near the end of his essay, he "subordinate[s]" the concerns of socialism to wider "human relations" (247) in order to stress how "the economic and industrial life is *in itself* ethical" (248, emphasis in original).

How could such an extravagantly wishful understanding of American democracy ever be activated or put into practice? There is actually an answer to that question, because shortly after Dewey published this essay, he began to work on a

project known as *Thought News*, a philosophical newspaper dedicated to conveying "thought" to a general reading public. The three-year project was the brain-
child of Franklin Ford, a former editor of the business digest *Bradstreet's*. With
the help of university professors, Ford proposed to convert and expand the digest
to form the basis for what he called "The Intelligence Triangle," a centralized
national clearinghouse that, in anticipation of Google, would give its audience
absolutely all information about everything. Composed with Dewey's help, Ford's
1893 "Draft of Action" laid out the rationale for such a scheme, which would be
advertised (perhaps tongue in cheek, although perhaps not) with the slogan "Buy
Your Facts at Ford's." Insisting that in American society "the journalist gains the
central position in life," Ford argued that only such a figure could tap into the
social organism of the whole nation, which simply needed limitless facts, clearly
presented and widely disseminated, to realize its infinite democratic potential.[10]

With the support of Dewey's student Robert Ezra Park (a former journalist)
and his philosophy colleague George Herbert Mead, Dewey and Ford enthusiastically promoted the project in the University of Michigan's student newspaper.
Thought News would be a subscription publication ("$1.50 per volume") like no
other: "It is believed there is room, in the flood of opinion, for one journal which
shall not go beyond the fact; which shall report thought rather than dress it up
in the garments of the past, which instead of dwelling at length upon the merely
individual processes that accompany the facts, shall set forth the facts themselves
. . . as parts of the one moving life of man and hence common interest." When
the Detroit mainstream press got wind of the scheme, it reacted with mockery and
disdain, compelling Dewey in an interview to distance himself from the project,
while he still earnestly affirmed that "Walt Whitman's poetry . . . the centralizing
tendency in the railroads . . . are all parts of one organic social movement."[11]
Dewey quickly lost interest in the implementation of *Thought News*, which never
published a single issue.

It is puzzling that Dewey would associate himself so closely and so long with
such a flaky character as Ford. But more to the point is Dewey's equally naïve
faith in facts as self-evidential, requiring neither arrangement on the part of their
senders nor interpretation on the part of their receivers. Dewey wanted the sheer
force of *Thought News* to make people think without shaping at all what they
think. But there is no magical, transparent channel of communication that can
bypass mediation. Context matters. Something as simple as how information is
organized and ordered on a newspaper page can alter how "facts" are understood,
as Dewey the pragmatist would come to grasp, if not Dewey the utopian idealist.

Thought News was a valiant practical attempt to address the gaping hole of

Dewey's earlier "The Ethics of Democracy" insofar as it imagined a palpable technology—a newspaper—to bridge the gap between a rarefied organic social whole and a public constituted by citizens. And yet by insisting that this new sort of disinterested national newspaper could somehow convey impartial information without actively shaping readers, that is, guiding their opinions, the philosopher openly exposed the way his prior account of democracy had sidestepped the tangible mechanisms or institutions by which influence and power flow. Before citizens could intelligently process information, Dewey would conclude shortly after the *Thought News* travesty, they would first need to be properly educated. Intelligence does not reside in facts alone. And so Dewey the Progressive turned his attention in the following decade to public education.

Mead seems to have taken away a different lesson from his experience working on the *Thought News* project. His brief essay "The Working Hypothesis in Social Reform" briskly engages the concerns of Wilson and Dewey, but from a striking new perspective.[12] Mead is most interested in America's rapidly merging domains of influence at the turn of the twentieth century: a dynamic of convergence that social reformers had to appreciate before change could be instituted. Concisely describing *social reform* as "the application of intelligence to the control of social conditions" (370), Mead endorses a "working hypothesis" methodology. In this pragmatist approach, reformers would adopt a nimble attitude of perpetual adjustment and readjustment to a world in flux in order to avoid "set[ting] up a detailed statement of the conditions that are to be ultimately attained." For Mead, in sharp contrast to Dewey's utopianism, "every attempt to direct conduct by a fixed idea of the world of the future must be, not only a failure, but also pernicious" (371).

Mead's concrete examples in the first half of his essay are arguably more enlightening than his overall thesis. When a municipality takes over "various common necessities," such as transportation systems considered to be "so-called natural monopolies," for instance, then "the government has become a business concern, which enters into the business world on a basis that is determined by the latter" (367). Although a municipality might initially be motivated "by the public sentiment that finds expression in legislation," once it does so it must act like a business, apart from its other more traditional duties. While Wilson idealistically sought to keep the operations of administration removed from the politics of the state, Mead sees government as a messier process involving multiple intersecting networks of institutional power:

> [T]he functions of government, as an institution, are merging with equal rapidity into the industrial world which it is supposed to control. The whole work of

legislation is not only dependent upon public sentiment, at least in democratic countries, but it is finding constantly fuller expression in other channels of publicity. The newspaper, in its various forms of journal and magazine, is effecting changes that are assumed to be those which follow governmental action. If only it becomes possible to focus public sentiment upon an issue in the delicate organism of the modern civilized community, it is as effective as if the mandate came from legislative halls, and frequently more so. . . . What the court does in reinterpreting laws is being done in increasing extent by simply closer organization of the business world—an organization that depends most immediately upon growing publicity. . . . [G]aining publicity . . . is often done, not by a legislative commission, but by the university as well as the newspaper. (368–369)

In this remarkable passage what ties together a wide array of institutional practices—judicial, academic, legislative, journalistic, commercial—is precisely "growing publicity." Mead contrasts this term with "public sentiment," a more familiar phrase that signifies the kind of organic unity that Dewey posited as the foundation for democracy. "Publicity" functions as an emergent concept, a persuasive and pervasive modern technique deployed instrumentally to influence a myriad of contexts, including the press, the schools, business, and government. In suggesting that a fusion between matters of state and matters of business was causing "publicity" to replace "public opinion," Mead called attention to an increasing blurring between political, social, and economic boundaries.[13] This blurring (in both theory and practice) was especially apparent in the United States, where utopian beliefs in the amorphous ideals of democracy functioned to bridge the various differences between the operations of government, corporations, courts, press, and universities as they sought to harness and organize public support. This vague but powerful embracing of American democracy as somehow exceptional or better than other nations helped sanction the overlapping of domains, which was confirmed by many late nineteenth-century American social scientists in their tendency to dissolve or subsume political theory into a wider theory of society.[14]

More specifically, sociological and social-psychological treatises by Franklin H. Giddings, Charles H. Cooley, and Edward A. Ross, among others, began treating "public opinion" as "no mere aggregate of separate individual judgments, but an organization, a coöperative product of communication and reciprocal influence."[15] Note that in this definition, communication is brought front and center, suggesting that many of these social scientists were growing aware of how the media of influence, such as newspapers, did not convey information transparently or self-evidently, as previously supposed. In this organic model based on mutuality, public opinion leaves the noisy polis, becoming instead one important manifestation or subset of "social control," as Edward Ross called the primary process by which members of a group (community or nation) relate to one another.[16]

While *social control* may sound a bit sinister to our ears, a century ago it carried more benign connotations, as did the term *propaganda*. The modifier "social" denoted a positive alternative to centralized state or tyrannical authority, while the noun "control" implied an effective mode of cohesion in opposition to "chaos" or "drift," which Lippmann used to diagnose the worst and most worrisome tendencies of American politics prior to the First World War. The concept of social control thus sought to mediate between absolutism, on the one hand, and fragmentary individualism, on the other.[17]

These theories of social control emerged from what has been called "a crisis of exceptionalism," which spurred Progressives to articulate how democracy in America was still somehow special—that is, different or at least potentially different from European society—just as such indications of difference were becoming more and more difficult to locate.[18] Responding to contemporaneous European analyses emphasizing the irrational and darker side of group behavior, such as Gustave Le Bon's influential *The Crowd: A Study of the Popular Mind*, these US social scientists took pains to distinguish governable and self-governing collectivities from the unruly mobs, crowds, masses, and herd mentalities that underpinned the social theories of many of their European counterparts.[19]

But this American social science was more than a scholarly enterprise. Progressive thinkers saw themselves and were regarded by others as public intellectuals, in effect "constructing the knowledge base for public policy."[20] What these intellectuals said and thought mattered in practice, especially since many professional social scientists moved back and forth between academia and government. At the heart of their work resided a belief in the pliability of citizens, their openness to shaping by others. Against earlier models of moral character that assumed certain individuals and groups to be inherently flawed, these social scientists emphasized how environment profoundly molded human behavior, which in their view was almost infinitely malleable. This is not inevitably a top-down model of coercion or manipulation as much as a horizontal process of mutual interpenetration among persons assumed to be always already social, members of a larger organic whole that is constantly making and remaking itself.

If a democratic public was a primary goal of Progressive reform, an end in itself, then we need to track propaganda horizontally across various overlapping fields that were undergoing rapid modernization during the early twentieth century. A more vertical approach that concentrates on the development of a single institution (such as the presidency or public relations firms) will risk losing sight of these relations. My first chapter, for instance, takes a fresh look at Theodore Roosevelt's well-known 1906 tirade against men of the press, who according to him perversely enjoyed dredging up the dirt of American society. Roosevelt's disdain for the "muckrakers," as he called them, may have had less to do with their aims, tone, or methods than with their perceived threat to his own executive prerogative as the nation's chief opinion leader. The president's role was being rivaled by these journalists, who were themselves worried about the growing influence of corporations, particularly in relation to the crucial national issue of railroad regulation. Only by illuminating the intersections among the competing public interests of the state, the press, and business does a fuller and clearer picture of Roosevelt's speech come into focus.

This book situates propaganda within particular institutions (economic, political, and social), such as the presidency, journalism, education, public relations, and diplomacy, linking institutional practices to the individual agents most centrally engaged in molding and managing public opinion, including Roosevelt, Wilson, George Creel, Julia Lathrop, Lippmann, Dewey, Ivy Lee, and Edward Bernays. These were some of the most formidable politicians, administrators, intellectuals, and publicists in the early decades of the twentieth century, both exerting a profound influence on American life and self-reflexively analyzing the nature of this influence. My emphasis is on the leaders, makers, and theorizers of public opinion, and thus the other side of the equation—how Progressive propaganda was received, absorbed, or resisted by various groups of citizens—largely remains outside the scope of this book. This is a work primarily of intellectual history, not social history. Scholarly research on propaganda's reception would also fruitfully entail a close look at various technologies of transmission, for instance, the rise of the "yellow press" during the 1890s. The materiality of media is another important matter touched on in these pages, but it deserves more extensive discussion in its own right.

Weapons of Democracy spans a fifty-year period, from 1885, when Wilson published a doctoral dissertation titled *Congressional Government*, to 1934, when public relations counsel Lee was investigated by a House of Representatives special committee (a forerunner of the House Un-American Activities Committee, or HUAC) for helping to spread Nazi propaganda, including consulting directly with the "minister of public enlightenment," Joseph Goebbels. Clearly the path from Wilson to Goebbels will not be a straight and narrow one. But amid the twists and turns, the argument of my book does develop chronologically over the six chapters. The opening chapter examines how various literary, political, commercial, and journalistic sources at the turn of the twentieth century began to entertain new ideas of a public. These discourses and practices included fictional fantasies of absolute social control, both utopian and dystopian; strategies employed by Wilson and other politicians who sought innovative ways to mobilize and direct opinion; publicity outlets in government and in the private sector that were set up to advise business clients such as the railroads and AT&T about how best to promote and protect their interests; and articles by muckrakers who disclosed the methods (such as planted news stories) by which these corporations swayed public opinion, combating one sort of publicity with a counterpublicity of their own.

In the second and third chapters, I discuss how many of these same reform-minded journalists, most notably Creel, took over the task of directing the government's own massive propaganda apparatus during the First World War. The Committee on Public Information (CPI) was established by President Wilson in April 1917, a week after the United States entered the conflict, as a means to drum up support for the war effort. This aptly named agency was administered by the civilian Creel explicitly to advertise the American gospel of democracy, both domestically and abroad. Progressive muckraking and wartime propagandizing were intimately connected not only insofar as they shared certain highly effective techniques of mass persuasion, but also by virtue of their deeply held beliefs embracing the authority of the state to remake its citizens.

Understanding politics as a stark opposition between friend and foe, Creel in his teaching, preaching, and selling of war pioneered a kind of voluntary compulsion whereby proper patriotic attitudes seemed to come from within rather than be imposed on citizens from without. For the first time in US history, the previously competing interests of press, government, and business were fused into a single centralized bureaucracy, disseminating information that penetrated virtually every aspect of American daily life and leading to a "conscription of thought," as Dewey called this saturation, which paralleled the government's large-scale mandatory marshaling of soldiers to fight the war in Europe.

The next three chapters of this book explore the legacies of Progressive propaganda in the disillusioning wake of that war. The fourth chapter is the theoretical centerpiece of the study. Against the threat of engineered and coercive opinion, the public philosophers Lippmann and Dewey sought to reform and revitalize the institutions of the press and education, respectively. In the early 1920s Lippmann published a series of increasingly pessimistic books that examined the unregulated mass manufacturing of consent, a process that rendered "the public" a meaningless construct, he claimed. Later in the decade, Dewey responded to Lippmann's influential arguments by undertaking more optimistically to reaffirm the democratic American public. While it has become common to stage the intellectual encounter between the two thinkers as a debate, their ideas were largely in agreement but rested on two different models of communication: face-to-face conversation for Dewey and a solitary citizen reading printed news for Lippmann. But neither of these models adequately explain how mass-mediated constitutional democracies function.

The fifth chapter turns to another legacy of the war, the institutionalizing of the modern "science" of public relations by a trio of prominent practitioners, Bernays, Carl Byoir, and Lee. Like Lippmann, all three of these PR experts honed their professional skills by performing public service during the war. Well before the war, the innovator Lee had been instrumental in convincing his corporate clients to engage in (controlled) disclosure of their means and methods. Arriving on the scene a decade later, Bernays (like Dewey) was powerfully influenced by Lippmann's work. But instead of trying to contest Lippmann's troubling conclusions, Bernays in his two books from the 1920s, *Crystallizing Public Opinion* (1923) and *Propaganda* (1928), blithely embraced manipulating the perceptions, ideas, tastes, and habits of the masses to bring order to the chaos of democracy. "Invisible government," he called this ruling and schooling, echoing but inverting a key phrase that had originally been invoked by the Progressive Party in 1912 to decry the corrupt power of monopolies and trusts.

Given the ascendancy of big business during the 1920s, it may be something of a stretch to consider Bernays a Progressive, but clearly his reasoning about the need for thoughtful social control by professional experts is in keeping with the logic of Progressivism. Shifting focus from the state to private corporations, PR counsels like Bernays reconfigured the democratic public sphere in two crucial ways: first, these publicity agents served paying clients, thereby substituting a system of commercial patronage for the self-sacrificing nationalism that Progressives had called for before and during the war; and second, public relations campaigns sought to reconstruct citizens primarily as consumers driven by a complex set of emotions and desires—far more than the passive sheep they were often supposed to be. Bernays in particular appreciated how consumers participated in a complex web of social relations that he could activate and arouse by an infectious theatricality.

Up to this point the book concerns itself primarily with domestic matters, but the final chapter takes a transnational turn. President Wilson soon after the war declared that "the men who do the business of the world now shape the destinies

of the world." For PR consultants like Bernays, Byoir, and Lee, this meant drawing on their wartime international experience in order to help shape opinion by
and about other countries around the globe. These nations during the 1920s were
regarded less as allies or adversaries than as potential lucrative markets for American trade. Lee, for instance, traveled to the USSR in 1927 to study the effects of
centralized Communist propaganda. Although in many ways he was curiously
sympathetic to the Bolshevik state, Lee imagined that flooding the USSR with
cheap goods would spell the end of Communism and signal the ultimate triumph
of capitalism. This ambition to develop foreign markets ultimately would give
Lee problems, and he was questioned shortly before his death in 1934 by a congressional committee (which also investigated Byoir) for advising the Nazis on
how best to appeal to US public opinion. On this ominous note, which finds
American publicists linked to Nazi propagandists, my study of Progressivism's
weapons of democracy will draw to a close, followed by a brief concluding rumi-
nation on the legacies of this propaganda.

CHAPTER 1

Giving Direction to Opinion

Invoked throughout the 1800s as a foundation for American democracy, the concept of public opinion began to shift in meaning toward the close of the century, so that traditional beliefs once taken for granted became urgent problems that called for new ways to understand and to manage an increasingly fragmented citizenry. As both a democratic ideal and a basis for information flow, "the public" was beginning to lose coherence. In this chapter I track this crisis in confidence across Progressive Era politics, literature, philosophy, business, administration, and journalism—realms and institutions that sometimes overlapped, and sometimes were in competition with one another. In the first section of this chapter, I offer a series of close readings of utopian fiction, which is followed by a discussion of American and European political theory and the rise of corporate and governmental publicity. The third section concludes the chapter with an account of Progressive muckraking as an emergent mode of mass advocacy.

I

Two bestsellers published in 1888, one a British political treatise, the other a utopian novel, are useful in assessing the customary understanding of public opinion in the United States near the end of the nineteenth century. Following in the footsteps of fellow aristocrat Alexis de Tocqueville earlier in the century, James Bryce offered in his immensely popular *The American Commonwealth* a sweeping multivolume survey of US political, social, religious, and cultural institutions, devoting an entire section (170 pages) to public opinion. That section opens by flatly declaring, "In no country is public opinion so powerful as in the United States,"[1] whose constitutional democracy in effect amounts to "government by public opinion" (14; see also 24, 27). Like other commentators before him, Bryce begins by taking pains to define this Enlightenment ideal, observing that the phrase tends to merge what people believe with the "organs whence people try to gather it," that is, the various means by which opinion is materially made public in venues such as magazines and newspapers and ballot boxes. He then notes a second, related difficulty in that the phrase is sometimes used "to denote everybody's views . . . the aggregate of all that is thought and said on a subject" and other times to refer to "merely the views of the majority" (3).

Right off the bat Bryce introduced two perplexities: where and how to locate or distinguish a "public" apart from the organs of its expression, and whether to understand the concept as a supreme totality akin to a common or general will (Rousseau's *volonté générale* or the Constitution's "we the people") or rather more pragmatically as partial and contingent, as only those shared views that can be said to prevail by number over others at any given moment. Bryce sorted out these difficulties relatively rapidly and easily by invoking an organic model of communication based on the thinking and speaking of an individual: "a sentiment spontaneously rises in the mind and flows from the lips of the average man" (3), and these views then move through various more complex stages by which opinion "grows and spreads" (11). Public opinion thus informs and is reciprocally informed by various modes of publication and democratic expression, such as voting. Bryce admits that "opinion does not merely grow; it is also made" (11). By "made" he was referring to the activity of vigorous and engaged classes of persons, such as statesmen and journalists, who exercise influence over their more passive fellow citizens but are in turn influenced by them "in mutual action and reaction" (13). In this way the forces of large-scale persuasion are naturalized primarily as functions of personality and eloquence that ebb and flow between "leaders" and the "mass" (13).

What followed was a detailed and largely sanguine account of the American public sphere, especially the role of the press. He did note "the fatalism of the multitude," a submissive stance assuming that "individual effort" (127) is futile in the face of "the tyranny of the majority," a phrase echoing Tocqueville. But Bryce depicted this political indifference as a matter of attitude, the internalizing of the majority's dominant views, not as a structural problem stemming from socioeconomic conditions themselves. Although he did allow for social class and regional differences, the big picture he painted emphasized a happy uniformity, so that "what the employer thinks, his workmen think" (32), excluding "questions specifically relating to labour," he conceded in a revealing footnote. In this homogenizing model, people openly express themselves and debate ideas that circulate freely in the press, giving rise to a "public opinion" (reified or even personified as an abstract noun subject) that "secures full discussions of issues of policy and the characters of men. It suffers nothing to be concealed. It listens patiently to all the arguments that are addressed to it" (159). For Bryce, this is what democracy looks like.[2]

It might be going too far to call Bryce's lengthy analysis a wish fulfillment, but certainly it was a largely reassuring account of egalitarian self-governance. The other big bestseller of 1888 offered an even more perfect vision of a smoothly functioning nation, although it had to project its good news one hundred years into the future in order to realize it. After Harriet Beecher Stowe's *Uncle Tom's Cabin*, Edward Bellamy's fantasy *Looking Backward, 2000–1887* was probably the most popular and arguably the most influential American novel of the nineteenth century, triggering a host of other utopian alternatives and imitations and inspiring the formation of dozens of nonpartisan nationalist clubs across the country eager to materialize Bellamy's detailed prophecy.

The American commonwealths of Bryce and Bellamy both take for granted an organic unity. But Bellamy's speculative version is in many ways more honest and accurate than the political treatise, in that the novel is compelled to lay bare the urgent anxieties, ideological fault lines, and social ruptures that prompted his imaginary solution.[3] In giving free rein to fantasy, Bellamy's fiction made explicit the utopian longing for a newly reconstituted polity, which served to spur Progressive reform, as I discussed in the introduction. Positing the widening strife between labor and capital as the central peril to American democracy, Bellamy imagined his middle-class protagonist and first-person narrator, Julian West, falling asleep, like Rip Van Winkle, only to awaken in Boston in the year 2000. Julian discovers that all corporations, including the great trusts and monopolies, have been consolidated and nationalized, and all social relations have been rearranged into an efficient, grand industrial army in which everybody knows his or her place. Selfish, acquisitive impulses have all but vanished, giving way to patriotic feelings of obedience, duty, and respect for the collective authority of the state to govern all equally.

The specifics of Bellamy's utopian blueprint are less pertinent than the means by which his vision of social harmony is generated and maintained. The reader gradually comes to realize that what Bellamy left out of Boston in the year 2000 is more telling than what he retained. When Julian early on asks his host, Dr. Leete, if such a radical transformation in power occasioned great bloodshed, the good doctor explains: "On the contrary . . . there was absolutely no violence. The change had long been foreseen. Public opinion had become fully ripe for it, and the whole mass of the people was behind it. There was no more possibility of opposing it by force than by argument."[4]

The passive voice and the reification of "public opinion" as an abstract noun subject (similar to Bryce's "it" phrasing) work to obscure historical agency, as if public opinion were self-evidently synonymous with the "Nation," a blank placeholder for the "whole mass of the people" (but paradoxically without persons), who are no longer formed or driven by contending forces, contestation, or "argument." This absence of persuasion at the moment of revolution is carried over into Bellamy's rationalized utopia itself, which has virtually abolished—or, rather, made obsolete—lawyers, politicians, lobbyists, salespeople, journalists (other than those subsidized by popular subscription), advertisements (but not commerce of a certain moneyless sort), and anybody and anything else that requires citizens to be actively convinced about what to believe and how to behave. It is as if the unity of the commonwealth so confidently asserted by Bryce can only be preserved for Bellamy by magically vacating the American body politic of all those institutions and interests by which it is constituted, but also which are threatening to tear its fabric apart. So what remains? Without any full expression of "opinion," what could "public" possibly mean here?

Haunting Bellamy's future America are the ghostly residues of a public; we have in effect been left with organs, to borrow Bryce's term, without a body. Boston in the year 2000 is filled with the material trappings of the public sphere, including "large open squares filled with trees" and "public buildings of a colossal size and architectural grandeur" (55), but with no actors onstage to fill the scenes besides the omnipresent Dr. Leete and his ever-hovering wife and daughter. As I have argued at length elsewhere, *Looking Backward*'s utopian vision works by denying us any access to community or communion. There is no vital middle ground—and this is precisely what constitutes a public and its problems—between a claustrophobia-inducing nuclear family and the overarching machinery of the nation: nothing but big squares and empty buildings.[5] As Walter Lippmann would have it some thirty-five years later, the notion of a public serving as any kind of common will has become a sheer phantom.[6]

While the novel is customarily read as presenting a palatable version of Christian socialism, in many ways it more closely resembles and looks forward to the modern post-industrial welfare state. Bryce's organic homogeny has been replaced with media and mechanisms of transmission that operate automatically and invisibly to organize all the citizens of the United States into a single, coherent administrative abstraction. This large-scale totalizing technology includes recessed artificial lighting that casts no dark shadows, soothing music piped into bedrooms from hidden sources, and pneumatic "transmitting tube[s]" (94) that take orders and deliver previously unseen goods on command (an eerie anticipation of Internet shopping). The merits of literary works are unerringly measured by a disembodied "popular voice" (129) in an anticipation of public opinion polling that imagines a seamless feedback loop between successful authors and satisfied readers. And when we inch closer, near the end of the novel, to discover who runs this wonderful show (the wizard behind the curtain), the results are spectacularly unexciting: an apolitical chair presides over a board of regents made up of retired teachers and doctors. No longer driven by power and persuasion, America in the year 2000 has turned into a self-regulating, post-political bureaucracy.

Although it was started before *Looking Backward* was published, it is difficult not to read Mark Twain's comic dystopia *A Connecticut Yankee in King Arthur's Court* (1889) as a direct, complex response to Bellamy's wildly popular utopia.[7] Instead of traveling to the future, Twain's protagonist, Hank Morgan (another first-person narrator), is transplanted to the past, sixth-century England, which he tries to systematically transform into a mirror image of his contemporary America (a warped one, as we shall see). Unlike Bellamy, Twain makes no bones about who is in charge here. Seeing himself surrounded by childlike "white Indians,"[8] as he calls the feudal inhabitants, the pragmatic Morgan (imagined by Twain to be a latter-day conquistador) quickly assumes the mantle of "Boss." This title refers to his former job as a factory foreman as well as to the infamous corrupt ward bosses (such as Tweed) rampant in late nineteenth-century American municipal politics. Just as factories make commodities, Morgan aims to (re)fashion these feudal subjects into democratic citizens via a grand experiment that powerfully and presciently foreshadows the social engineering of Progressives in the two decades to come.[9] There is nothing natural or organic about this manufacture of men, aside perhaps from the humor and personal charisma of Morgan, "a Unique" (87), he immodestly calls himself, clearly a projection and alter ego of author Twain.

To "educate the commonwealth" (61), as he defines his civilizing mission, Morgan must seize control and modify, or more often design from scratch, the administrative and ideological apparatus of the state, the "government machinery" (92), as he puts it. Twain thus gives a textbook analysis of various emerging institutions of indoctrination, from mass media to a "teacher-factory" (101) to advertising—precisely the modes of mass opinion that Bellamy wanted to suppress, even as his utopia registered their effects. Enlisting the knights of the realm to sell stove polish, for instance, even though stoves have not yet been invented, Morgan succinctly articulates the logic of modern marketing practice: "All that the agent needed to do was to deftly and by degrees prepare the public for the great change, and have them established in predilections towards neatness" (175), which indicates how desire in the market precedes necessity and use value. Parts of the novel read like a how-to manual, written in the grammatical second person, for budding publicists, such as when Morgan explains the staged spectacle by which he crafts the restoration of the kingdom's Holy Fountain: "When you are going to do a miracle for an ignorant race, you want to get in every detail that will count; you want to make all the properties impressive to the public eye; you want to make matters comfortable for your head guest; then you can turn loose and play your effects for all they are worth" (210).

As he contemplates starting a newspaper, yet another organ of publicity, the Boss lays out his priorities for his brave new world: "The first thing you want in a new country is a patent office; then work up to your school system; and after that, out with your paper" (93). Hawked by the "Adam-newsboy of the world" (246), this "first newspaper" occasions great wonder in the (mostly illiterate) populace, who call it a "dark work of enchantment" (250) precisely for its capacity to distribute information in identical multiple copies on an immense scale. What ties all of these technologies of mass persuasion together is Morgan's faith in the efficacy of indoctrination, which he deems "everything," elaborating that "training is all there is *to* a person. . . . We have no thoughts of our own, no opinions of our own; they are transmitted to us, trained into us" (161). Returning to his favorite theme later in the narrative, Morgan celebrates the source of his presumed success: "the power of training! of influence! of education! It can bring a body up to believe anything" (181). Here Twain appears to be echoing the industrialist Andrew Carnegie, who proclaimed in *Triumphant Democracy* (1886) that "wherever we peer into the first tiny springs of the national life, how this true panacea for all the ills of the body politic bubbles forth—education, education, education."[10]

But systematic training has its limits, Morgan finally learns. Power is not that simple to manage, nor is consent easy to engineer. Even though he holds sway over both lords and peasants, the Connecticut Yankee cannot contain the Church nor the court's chief miracle maker, Merlin, whose spectacular acts of magic, which exploit the superstitions of the multitude, rival Morgan's own extravagant displays of public showmanship, ostensibly in the name of science and rationality. Competing for the best special effects, both Sir Boss and the wizard are masters in the dark arts of mass persuasion. Beyond the personal enmity between Morgan and his shadowy double, the Catholic Church stands as the supreme institution of indoctrination in the land, a mechanism of propaganda—after all it was a papal bull that gave rise to the very term, as Twain presumably knew—more potent than

Morgan's attempts at training "experts in every sort of handiwork and scientific calling" (101) to help him run the country. Progressive Era efficiency, *avant la lettre*, is doomed to failure. Following a crippling interdiction from the Church, the Boss decides to destroy all that he has wrought, leading to an apocalyptic nightmare of civil war that closes with one of the most disturbing and violent scenes in all of American literature. In a final last stand (akin to Custer's), Morgan blows up his factories, and the invading armies of knights are electrocuted, wave after wave, until they dissolve into a "homogeneous protoplasm" (396). This bubbling melting pot of death is the only way Morgan can achieve the total compliance that he has craved, a macabre mockery of the homogeneity Bryce posited as underlying American public opinion.

Such a conclusion, in which the masses of dead do "not exist as individuals," suggests a deeper reason for Morgan's failure that has little to do with the Church per se. Despite his best efforts to mass manufacture pliable, uniform citizens, the Boss has to acknowledge that the knights each possess a stubborn core of self or an idiosyncratic grain of being, described repeatedly in gendered terms that resist refashioning, so that fundamentally "a man is a man" (279). Although the artifice of his office has turned the feudal monarch, Arthur, into an "automatic doll" (325), when push comes to shove, that is, when he is in a fight while masquerading as a commoner, the king is still a man, and "when a man is a man, you can't knock it out of him" (326). King Arthur never turns against him, but what this means for the Boss's enemies is that while they "can be killed, they cannot be conquered" (397), which Morgan concedes in the final rousing pep talk he gives to his few loyal supporters. "Convincing these people" (363), the Boss understands, perversely requires destroying them. And so Morgan's "dream of a republic" goes up in smoke, "to *be* a dream, and so remain" (382).[11]

It is difficult to know what to make of this homicidal affirmation of individualism, which among other things serves to expose the failure of propaganda. It is significant that it is the domineering (megalomaniac?) first-person protagonist, Morgan, speaking, not the novel's author, although at times in the narrative it is difficult to tell them apart.[12] But whether attributed to Morgan or Twain, this validation of the singular man through violence carries a conservative or even reactionary tinge, especially compared to Bellamy's far more benign, but also more radical, reimagining of the American polis. Both novels (at least in the utopian first half of *Connecticut Yankee*) center on the democratizing potential of education to reform social relations from top to bottom. Yet insofar as Twain's novel conceives of the relation between the individual and the collective to be an adversarial one that threatens to turn men into dolls, autonomous selfhood triumphs only at a fatally high cost. In response to defiance, the Boss transforms the state's authority into a desperate instrument of mass murder. Bellamy's fantasy, by contrast, collapses the familiar binary between public and private, evacuating both terms of any substance, so that indoctrination in the traditional sense is no longer necessary. Bellamy's utopia works by omitting precisely what he fears. Thanks to the invisible self-regulating machinery of the nation, citizens simply are who they are, do what they do, believe what they believe, and belong where they belong. While Bellamy does allow for individual differences (which are cast mainly as differences in taste), none of that really matters in the absence of power, politics, and persuasion.

Even more than prose treatises such as Bryce's, fictional utopias such as Bellamy's and Twain's, which began popping up with increasing frequency in the United States near the end of the nineteenth century, are useful precisely for locating a host of pressing social and economic problems in need of solution, and the greater the author's sense of urgency, it would seem, the more fantastic the means of redress. Tapping America's political unconscious, these fictions in many ways remained ahead of the curve in imagining issues and solutions that only surfaced decades later in mainstream political discourse. In the cases of *Looking Backward* and *A Connecticut Yankee in King Arthur's Court*, the difficulties revolve around representations of the public, publicity, and public opinion—notions that began to slip and slide in meaning and practice in the late 1880s and 1890s, and therefore could no longer be seen as self-evident givens, as Bryce did in his celebration of American unity. A number of subsequent dystopian novels projected conspiratorial visions of fragmentation and chaos akin to Twain's, including Ignatius Donnelly's *Caesar's Column* (1890) and Jack London's *The Iron Heel* (1908).[13] But perhaps the most politically extravagant was a lesser-known fantasy published anonymously in 1912 called *Philip Dru: Administrator, a Story of Tomorrow, 1920–1935*.

Both the name of the book and the year are crucial. As that wonderful title suggests, the novel is a strange mixture of Bellamy and Twain in that it focuses on a charismatic authority figure (like Hank Morgan), even as that individual's leadership takes the mild form of bureaucratic management similar to the kind in Bellamy's novel. This curious idealization of administrative prowess represents one crucial strand of Progressivism, especially when aligned with a peculiar militancy located somewhere between *Looking Backward*'s industrial army of patriotic citizens and *Connecticut Yankee*'s far more aggressive indulgence in apocalyptic violence. It is no coincidence, for instance, that *Philip Dru: Administrator* opens in the near future with a graduation ceremony at West Point, where the eponymous hero is about to commence his life as an officer. When circumstances (a temporary bout of blindness) thwart his plans for a military career, the earnest Dru is thrust into a vocational crisis, and he must search for a means to do justice to his ambition to serve his country, particularly his passionate desire for social reform, "to devote his life to bettering."[14] He quickly switches from working in the tenements of New York (aided by a female love interest, of course) to a job as a muckraking journalist publicizing social ills, because the press offers a way to attain a "broader view" that will allow him to gain "public attention" (51). Extolling in his essays and articles the Progressive virtues of efficiency, organization, and education, the young man counsels his girlfriend in private that to "help the cause" she should interact with the rich, not the poor, since "if we would convince and convert, we must veil our thoughts and curb our enthusiasm, so that those we would influence will think us reasonable" (64).

It would seem that Dru's underlying goal is influence, not reform, and after five years of working as a journalist (a tenure condensed into one sentence), he changes direction once again, concluding that he needs to move into politics. The press is apparently an insufficient means to shape the course of the nation. In one of the many sudden turns in the narrative's convoluted plotting, the novel at this point abruptly drops Dru altogether to focus on the nefarious machinations of Senator Selwyn, who will shortly become Dru's archenemy. Beyond the story line, this is a dramatic shift also in tone, as the narration begins to assume a paranoid style of exposition along the lines of nineteenth-century populists like George Lippard and Ignatius Donnelly, whose political novels are replete with melodrama and conspiracy. As it begins to detail the senator's sinister plans, *Philip Dru: Administrator* picks up in speed, energy, and interest, suggesting that politics, not social work or journalism, is what captures the imagination of the author. We learn, for instance, that Selwyn has cleverly set up a secret cabal of "one thousand multi-millionaires," who each contributed $10,000 to a proto–super political action committee "with which to mislead those that could be misled, and to debauch the weak and uncertain" (67).

This is a far cry from James Bryce, whose thousand pages of genteel political commentary in *The American Commonwealth* do not contain a single instance of the word *debauch*. To make a long and twisted story short, by methodically focusing on a small number of swing states during the election, Selwyn manages to put into power a puppet president (recall Twain's reference to the king as an automatic doll), who answers to the shrewd senator's every beck and call. But the conspiracy is soon discovered, thanks to a hidden dictograph recorder (a technology of surveillance, not persuasion). All hell then breaks loose, a majority of the people demand "a fair and legal expression of opinion" (116), and when Selwyn and his corrupt colleagues refuse to give in, the United States is plunged into a civil war. General Dru (making use of his military training) leads the western states to victory in a decisive, climactic battle, a "holocaust" (137) that ends with 500,000 casualties on both sides, give or take.

And now begins the real interest of the novel. With the preliminaries concluded, the author can concentrate on Dru's most important role—administrator—in effect reversing the direction of Twain's feudal fantasy (which moves from utopia to violent dystopia) by first giving us the bloody revolution, which is followed by Dru's utopian management of the reunited and reconstituted (literally, we shall see) United States of America. Fueling the second half of the novel is a wish fulfillment of complete control and compliance. In order to bypass the lingering corruption of electoral politics and political parties (alternatives hardly worth mentioning), and with "a large and devoted army to do his bidding" (148), Dru simply assumes "the powers of a dictator" (152), proclaiming himself "*Administrator of the Republic*" (153, emphasis in original). He then goes about realizing his ambitious agenda while vowing to retire after his reforms have been completed. Although in response to his altruistic plans "here and there a dissenting voice was heard," a "chorus of approval drown[s]" (157) out these objections when Dru eloquently explains that it would take "a century of public education" (156) to right the "defective" governmental "machinery" he has just overthrown. Training might be everything, but apparently there is no time for it here.

What follows is a host of reforms designed to streamline democratic institutions and encourage greater transparency. The power of the courts is limited "to the extent that they could no longer pass upon the constitutionality of laws" (168); the laws themselves are pruned and revised into plain English; a graduated federal income tax is established, leading to a "more homogeneous population" (179); protectionist tariffs are abolished; new banking regulations are imposed; public utilities are moved more directly under government control; women are given the right to vote; and, most radically, state constitutions and the federal Constitution are rewritten to more closely resemble a parliamentary system of governance.[15] All of these changes require Administrator Dru to set up commissions and boards made up of impartial experts and advisers, including "another board, of even greater ability, to read, digest, and criticize the work of the other two boards and report their findings directly to him" (172). In the name of efficiency, the nation has become a paradise for bureaucrats.

Just as the narrative earlier had veered from Dru as he was about to enter politics in order to focus on the plotting of Senator Selwyn and his fellow plutocrats, in the midst of describing the reforms in the second half of the novel, the story once again shifts back to Selwyn. The defeated senator's "unusual talents for organization and administration" (167) remain useful for Dru, who more and more seeks the advice and help of his former enemy. This is certainly curious, as if Hank Morgan and his nemesis, Merlin, in Twain's novel suddenly became best friends. We discover that Selwyn as a young man learned his dirty tricks from a ward boss, who could only thrive because of the "indifference of our people" (195), which gave the senator "little confidence that the people would take enough interest in public affairs" (166) to wisely govern themselves.

Hence the senator's early turn to autocratic methods of influence, which in the end are not so different from Dru's, beyond the administrator's professed faith in the public to appreciate his reforms. The narrative's rehabilitation of Selwyn culminates in his absurdly bland admission that "we overdid it" (212), quite an understated way to describe the fiendish political corruption that led to the holocaust of civil war and hundreds of thousands of deaths. The novel closes with Dru urging the repentant elderly senator to use his great wealth to spread "propaganda for good" (271), which is followed by the administrator's own retirement after seven effective years on the job, unimpeded by any political opposition. Selwyn may have overdone it, but his counterpart Dru simply gets things done, never wavering in his paternalistic conviction that he knows better than the citizens of his republic what is good for them.

This is strange, indeed. It is hard to know if the senator's life story, so intertwined with the administrator's, should be read as a wake-up call to induce civic activism, or more cynically as a demonstration of the limited capacity of the apathetic masses to think for themselves. And what are we to make of the narrative's fixation on public opinion and public affairs in general? I have dwelled on this novel at length not because of its literary merits (slim to none) or its detailed plans to fix the American democracy, which were not entirely new at the time, but rather for its extravagant celebration of the militant powers of administration. Here is where the author and the year of publication take on special significance. To finally strip away the veil of anonymity that I have preserved up to this point, *Philip Dru: Administrator* was penned early in 1912 by a Texan, Colonel Edward M. House, shortly after House first met Woodrow Wilson, who was beginning his campaign for the presidency. After Wilson's election later that year, House became Wilson's most trusted adviser, along with the president's private secretary, Joseph P. Tumulty, for the next seven years (the exact length of Administrator Dru's tenure). At the time, House was one of the most powerful men in the United States and worked effectively behind the scenes to forward Wilson's agenda, both foreign and domestic.[16] That such an influential operative could write and pub-lish such a paranoid fantasy of violence and omnipotence—what we might call political science fiction—certainly must give us pause.

The energy and detail that the colonel devotes in the first part of the novel to describing Selwyn's installation of his puppet president, for instance, are clearly connected to House's own role in helping his new friend get elected in 1912 and reelected four years later, although of course Wilson was nobody's stooge. Perhaps more to the point is how House represents presidential campaigning in his fic-tion. Although the narrative emphasizes Selwyn's conniving to debauch gullible citizens, beyond such melodramatic conspiracies we see a wily strategist running an effective campaign whose success only requires rational planning, not corrup-tion and deceit per se.

In a chapter titled "The Making of a President," for example, House dwells with some admiration on Selwyn's tactic of targeting swing states, which entails dispensing with the vast majority of the already committed electorate in each of the twelve battleground states to concentrate on the few remaining undecided voters, who have been identified by scientific polling "as to their race, religion, occupation and former political predilection" (89–90); these small numbers of hesitating voters are then subjected to surgical strikes of leafleting and direct per-suasive appeals, with little waste of time or money. Selwyn's careful methods follow the lead of the Republican Party head, Mark Hanna, whose masterful direction of William McKinley's "Front Porch" presidential campaign in 1896 signaled a decided shift in modern American electioneering, particularly in its efficient management of public opinion—a model that the colonel clearly knew very well.[17]

II

These days, House's novel is mainly invoked by conservatives such as George Will and Glenn Beck, who regard it as a revealing example of liberal Progressivism run amok.[18] They tend to assume that Dru simply stands in for Wilson, whose worst tendencies, for these conservatives, have morphed a century later into the big government practices of President Barack Obama, particularly what they see as his contempt for the Constitution's protection of individual liberty and enter-prise. This is not only debatable American history, but also shaky textual analysis, since Dru in the novel actually seems to reverse the relation between House and Wilson by appointing as one of his own advisers a southerner with "intellect and force of character" who is a "trained political economist" and "the masterful head of a university" that "was soon to become one of the foremost in the world"

(167). You cannot get more explicit than that, although Wilson had already left the presidency of Princeton to run for governor of New Jersey in 1910. But even if Dru cannot be equated with Wilson, it is certainly fair for these conservatives to point out (albeit with some degree of paranoia of their own) that House's blueprint for America, published months before Wilson's election, closely resembled the Progressive political agenda of the president.

That agenda was certainly well known by 1912, not simply because of his campaign speeches, but by virtue of the long paper trail Wilson had produced since 1885 as a political scientist, which indicated his preference for parliamentary government, his desire for a strong executive branch, his skepticism about a system of checks and balances, his long-standing criticism of congressional committees (especially for their lack of transparency), and perhaps most fundamentally his rejection of abstract theories of natural rights, going so far as to deem Jefferson's ideas "un-American."[19] Of particular interest in relation to House's novel is Wilson's second book, *The State: Elements of Historical and Practical Politics* (1889). This tome is not only more historical and scholarly than Bryce's more informal *The American Commonwealth* published a year prior, but diverges from Bryce's Anglo-American pragmatic emphasis on democratic homogeneity to offer an account of a different sort of unity inflected by Hegelian idealism, thanks in part to Wilson's academic training at Johns Hopkins, which was the most European-oriented graduate institution in the United States at the time.[20]

As one historian puts it, near the end of the nineteenth century, "as rights dropped out of political science, the term which swelled to fill their place was the State,"[21] which was conceived not as divine or bound together by contracts, but as a single omnipotent entity forged by history and custom. Wilson's *The State* shares some elements of Bryce's brand of organic give-and-take among citizens via organs of public opinion, such as the press. Yet, crucially, shifting the location of supreme sovereignty from "the people" to the state (a shift suggested by Bellamy's nation) means that public opinion can no longer be understood to simply "grow," as Bryce confidently asserted, but must be actively managed. Beginning in the late eighteenth century, especially in reaction to the excesses of the French Revolution, European intellectuals cast this relation between the state and the masses in decidedly darker terms than did their American counterparts. In a (mis) reading of Kant, for instance, Friedrich Schiller in *Aesthetic Education* (1794) suggestively compared the work of artisans, sculptors, teachers, and statesmen, who are all concerned with molding the "formless mass" (whether inert material or humans) to particular ends, a process that inevitably requires some violence. Although conceding this violence, Schiller makes a key moral distinction between shaping a block of stone and shaping people, because humans are not just the medium through which the "pedagogic or political artist" works but the very object or goal of the process: to turn the undifferentiated mass into productive citizens of the state.[22]

As *Connecticut Yankee* so graphically depicts (although it is doubtful that Twain read Schiller, while Wilson presumably did), the endeavor to manufacture men—both the means and the ends of the Boss—ultimately results only in bloody failure. Looking forward rather than backward, Twain's apocalyptic novel also anticipated by a few years the theories of Gustave Le Bon, a French social psychologist haunted by the traumas of the Paris Commune and the French Revolution a full century after the events. In *The Crowd: A Study of the Popular Mind* (1895), Le Bon insisted that the crowd (more akin to a mob) is greater than the sum total of its parts, possessing an irrational energy and a potential for violence, but also a potential for being manipulated, even to the point of falling into a mass hypnosis or hysteria. These twin capacities for destruction and subjugation, Le Bon argued, can be cleverly exploited and controlled by charismatic leaders, especially those who understand how to deploy spectacle: consider the magical visual effects of Morgan and Merlin.[23]

A contemporary of Le Bon, Gabriel Tarde, offered a fuller and more nuanced analysis of the psychology of mass behavior. In his sociological masterpiece *The Laws of Imitation* (1890; English translation, 1903), Tarde posited a self already always social (an assumption more along the lines of Bellamy than Twain) and paradoxically suggested that personal identity is forged by imitating others. In subsequent works, Tarde explicitly took up the question of influence, carefully distinguishing between "the public" and "the crowd" (in response to Le Bon) and between "opinion" as an aggregate of judgments and the "general will" as a totality of desires—a distinction that Wilson and other politicians tended to blur.[24] Of particular interest for Tarde is how opinion "is reproduced many times over in people of the same country, at the same time, in the same society" (300). His mechanism for such social reproduction (which is necessary for opinion to become public) is conversation, materialized and made manifest in modern society most directly by newspapers. Like Bryce and in advance of the influential arguments of Benedict Anderson, Tarde saw the press as the key to building and unifying a national culture. But unlike Bryce, his emphasis was not on these organs of public opinion fostering open debate and free expression, or even reflecting what people believe. Tarde instead stressed the leveling effects of journalism, how "the papers give their publics the conversations of the day" (312), so that even those who do not read newspapers "are forced to follow the groove of their borrowed thoughts. One pen suffices to set off a million tongues" (304). For Tarde public opinion is clearly made, not grown.[25]

The populace as a formless block, as witless dupes manipulated by demagogic leaders, as directed by the opinions of others—all of these powerful views of the politics of the modern state weighed heavily at the turn of the nineteenth century on American intellectuals schooled in European thought, including Wilson himself.[26] Insisting on the distinctly democratic potential of the United States, Herbert Croly in his 1909 book, *The Promise of American Life*, and educators, philosophers, and social psychologists, such as John Dewey, William James, and George Herbert Mead, struggled to remind themselves that the American Revolution and the French Revolution were dramatically different affairs. But this long-standing faith in the exceptional dimensions of American democracy was beginning to show signs of wear toward the end of the nineteenth century.

Resisting the ponderous pressures of German idealism, pragmatists like James sought to develop more nimble models for understanding self and society, endorsing ideas based not on rigid abstractions, but on whether they could be tested and whether they worked. Arguing that beliefs are inflected by values and uses, not fixed or eternal, may have been an effective way to counter idealism, but it turned the formation of public opinion into an even more uncertain proposition. It was a central tenet of liberal pragmatism that once properly informed, citizens in a democracy would be capable of making the right decisions. Such education in civics, Croly argued in *The Promise of American Life*, was a duty of "the modern nation," which was "the best machinery as yet developed for raising the level of human association. It really teaches men how they must feel, what they must think, and what they must do, in order that they live together amicably and profitably."[27]

Croly's faith in the machinery of the federal government grew out of his abiding admiration for the recently completed presidency of Theodore Roosevelt, who in turn greatly admired Croly's ideas, suggesting once again the close ties between Progressive politics and prescriptive theorizing. A similar connection between practice and theory holds for Wilson. As a thinker and social scientist, Wilson was certainly not in the category of a Dewey or Mead, but it is worth briefly considering what he said about public opinion in his voluminous writings, especially since as an adroit politician, he was in a better position than the other intellectuals to put many of his ideas into practice, particularly once he became president. To simplify, in practice Wilson's idealist inclinations were leavened by pragmatism (at once political and philosophical), which was in turn inflated by occasional grandiose religiosity, evangelical intensity, and messianic certitude, mixed with a strong emphasis on self-discipline, which was not always shared by his (somewhat) more secular contemporaries and made his speeches resemble sermons at times.[28]

His earliest academic works tended to treat the question of public opinion along conventional lines, similar to Bryce's work. In *Congressional Government* (1885), for instance, he expressed disdain for the private backroom dealings of congressional committees because "the most essential object of all discussion of public business is the enlightenment of public opinion; and of course since it cannot hear the debates of the Committees, the nation is not apt to be much instructed by them."[29] *The State* (1889) similarly assumed the importance of the "free consent of the governed," but because it is a historical and anthropological survey, Wilson made a distinction between ancient political societies, in which the standards of public opinion remained "changeless" by force of tradition, and more modern ones, which allowed for change: "[W]e are like primitive men in the public opinion which preserves, though unlike them in the public opinion which alters our institutions."[30]

That public opinion simply does not reflect preexisting belief, but can actively transform institutions, argues for its significant role in democracy, yet this still does not address the question of how opinion itself is shaped. In one of his last academic studies, *Constitutional Government* (1908), Wilson offered a kind of answer by distinguishing between the "unorganized opinion" that he found circulating in despotic regimes and the "organized" opinion located in constitutional systems. The question, of course, is, how exactly does this organizing of opinion get done? Wilson's position is unambiguous: Only the president can so "dominate his party" to become the "spokesman for the real sentiment and purpose of the country, by giving direction to opinion, by giving the country at once the information and statements of policy which will enable it to form its judgments alike of parties and men."[31] In his 1914 study, *Progressive Democracy*, Croly would give (now President) Wilson's ideas a doctrinaire elaboration and endorsement: "Public opinion requires to be aroused, elicited, informed, developed, concentrated and brought to an understanding of its own dominant purposes. The value of executive leadership consists in its peculiar serviceability not merely as the agent of a prevailing public opinion, but also as the invigorator and concentrator of such opinion."[32]

Public opinion must be organized and directed by "information" that originates from the top, with the press assuming a secondary role in "partnership" with the president, as he told reporters at his first press conference on March 15, 1913. These biweekly conferences were among a number of innovative measures Wilson put into practice to mobilize public opinion, including delivering messages to Congress in person (short and sweet, so they would be quoted by newspapers in full) and installing as his personal secretary Joseph P. Tumulty, who would deal exclusively with the press. Tumulty was not a mere spokesperson, but a trusted confidant and experienced speech writer with impressive rhetorical skills of his own. As politically savvy as Colonel House, Tumulty scheduled daily briefings with White House correspondents and ran his office as an executive public relations outfit. Wilson also each day got reports from Tumulty and his staff drawn from news clippings compiled from papers across the country. While his predecessor, Teddy Roosevelt, had sought to court and cultivate (selected) journalists and to grab headlines by way of his magnetic personality, it was the less flamboyant Wilson who introduced an array of structural transformations that effectively rationalized and regulated relations between the executive office and mass media for decades to follow.[33]

Despite the new measures that granted fuller access in both directions between president and press, some reporters were bothered by Wilson's "cool reserve," as one publisher put it. The impression the president gave during press conferences was "that he was the best judge of what was good for the newspapers to have."[34] By July 1915, soon after a German submarine sunk the ocean liner *Lusitania*, the president canceled these conferences, and by his second term, with war looming, Wilson sought to circumvent the press altogether in order to manage national sentiment more directly. The president's lukewarm attitude toward reporters is not surprising given his explicit statement in *Constitutional Government* that "even if the chief newspapers were not owned by special interests; even if their utterances really spoke to the general opinion of the communities in which they are printed, as very few of them now do, their discussion of affairs would not be of the kind necessary for the maintenance of constitutional government" (102–103). For years Wilson had advocated for a national newspaper, but in its absence the hundreds of dailies scattered across the country remained too partial and too provincial in outlook and scope to serve the nation.[35]

Wilson's phrase "special interests" is especially telling—Progressive shorthand for the enemy that showed up in political discourse with increasing frequency and urgency in the first decade of the twentieth century. What drove Selwyn's devious machinations in the first half of *Philip Dru: Administrator*, for instance, were "the interests," a stock phrase that Colonel House repeated without any further explanation: a self-evident given, like "public opinion" for Bryce and "the state" for Wilson. As the novel suggested, the term was mostly deployed by muckraking journalists seeking to expose the excesses and corruption of big business and ward bosses, making Wilson's reference to newspapers as owned by special interests all the more intriguing, although, to be clear, most of the reform-minded journalists were magazine writers, not newspaper reporters. In his engaging study of a succession of keywords in American politics since independence, the historian Daniel T. Rodgers concluded a chapter-by-chapter analysis of the terms "the People," "Government," and "the State," with "Interests," a concept that clearly threatened to fragment and destroy the state's cohesive unity.[36] It is as if Schiller's "political artist" came to give shape to his block, only to find the stone already in pieces.

What does this mean for the very notion of public opinion, or even of a public? Acknowledging the power and presence of special interests, Wilson in effect tried to have it both ways, pitting these multiple threats against a unitary "general opinion" still assumed to carry some force. During a campaign speech in early 1912, for example, he noted: "Men who are behind any interest always unite in organization, and the danger in every country is that these special interests will be the only things organized, and that the common interest will be unorganized against them. The business of government is to organize the common interest against the special interests."[37] But this might be an instance of Wilson's idealism taking hold or, more conveniently, the opportunistic rhetoric of a candidate running for national office, since a "common interest" sounds like an oxymoron. Or to put it more harshly, as a conservative like George Will might argue, what President Wilson (aka Philip Dru) really tried to do was to organize government into its own special interest, the biggest one ("a business") among many. Public opinion in this cynical interpretation simply becomes what the administrator/president wants it to be, invoked strictly to pursue and legitimize his self-aggrandizing, statist agenda with support from his followers. What the Oval Office deems neutral "information" from other perspectives looks and functions more like propaganda. But without the belief in the idea of a single interest uniting citizens, what alternative is there?

Little or none, suggested another political scientist in 1908, the same year Wilson published *Constitutional Government*. More explicitly and extensively than Wilson, Arthur Bentley in *Process of Government* took up the problem of public opinion specifically in relation to leadership. He saw the two as interlinked aspects of government, both defined pragmatically by group dynamics. Calling the "unanimity of opinion" a "myth," Bentley stripped the concept of its abstract, organic idealism to show how opinions in the absence of any "social whole" are simply made by specific groups whose work is always "directed against the activity of some other group," even as these competing interests or pressure groups try to gain advantage by falsely claiming that their own positions and policies reflect "public opinion."[38] In this view, which understands politics to be primarily constituted by power relations, to be in favor of something inevitably means to be against (a collective) somebody. On any given issue or set of issues there are majorities and minorities, and people can certainly be swayed to believe one thing or another, but there is simply no such thing as disinterested interest. All interests are special and plural.[39] In his seminal *An Economic Interpretation of the Constitution of the United States* (1913), the Progressive historian Charles Beard (who was heavily influenced by Bentley) made basically the same point about the founding framers: "[O]ur fundamental law was not the product of an abstraction known as 'the whole people,' but of a group of economic interests which must have experienced beneficial results from its adoption."[40]

No wonder that by the time Wilson became president his repeated invocation of a common interest, mind, or will might already have begun to ring hollow to some. Saying something does not automatically make it so. Although dubious in both theory and practice, this populist insistence on general opinion could be effective as a necessary fiction, a tactical essentialism designed to combat the clearly "special" interests of some powerful groups. Semantically little more than an empty signifier, "the common will" still could carry symbolic force in particular contexts, less as an empirical description than as a yet unrealized proposition awaiting fulfillment. In this regard, Wilson's pointed emphasis during his 1912 campaign on "the business of government" is revealing. The government's "business" was set against the money trusts and the large-scale corporate interests of capitalists who by the turn of the twentieth century had started to learn how to organize and direct opinion on their own behalf.

This was not a matter of advertising or marketing as conventionally understood, but rather the emergence of public relations as a new way to promote entire companies and industries, not simply to sell specific products. The aim was not to make people buy, but to make them believe. Most corporations did not own organs of public opinion in the way that Wilson referred to newspapers being owned by special interests or the way we might today understand media conglomerates. But how could a company or institution make itself heard or brand itself amid the clamor of competing stakeholders? Coinciding with a growing awareness of the power of interests to shape public affairs, firms starting around 1900 began to set themselves up to serve as conduits between corporations and the press. Among the first was Boston's Publicity Bureau, a name that perfectly captures this nascent institutionalization and rationalization of the very concept and practice of publicity.[41] Corporations such as railroads in the nineteenth century had established publicity departments to help promote their agendas, but the

Boston bureau was an autonomous business for hire. For a fixed fee plus charges for expenses, the Publicity Bureau would organize and furnish information to newspapers in order to paint the activities of its clients in a favorable light.

More important than being first is the fact that the bureau's founders explicitly grasped that they were doing something quite new, as a May 1901 letter from co-founder Herbert Small to Charles W. Eliot, the influential head of Harvard, explained: "The idea of publicity as we have learned to hold it . . . is entirely distinct from the idea either of advertising or of a press agency. . . . its work [is] very different from anything which has ever been attempted before."[42] Leaving aside the hyperbole of these claims, a habit of public relations counsels ever since, we can still appreciate Small's important insight. Abstracted, reified, and bureaucratized, "publicity" (or rather its "idea") was now an instrument to be expertly held and directed, much as surgeons use scalpels, for and against presumed interests. The bureau's professionals were not simply functioning like theater press agents of the nineteenth century, who called on newspapers to promote specific actors and plays, but instead were offering the press ongoing information of value and concern for a much broader readership.

Interestingly, as Small's letter indicated, the bureau's initial clients were not businesses, but rather universities like Harvard and MIT, which were intent on furthering the prominence of higher education in the United States. (Training is everything, as Hank Morgan put it.) But quickly the vast majority of the bureau's accounts became large corporations, especially transportation companies such as Boston Elevated (a railway) and burgeoning communications giants like AT&T, whose private enterprise was threatened by Progressive demands for the nationalization or at least municipal ownership and strict regulation of utilities for the common good. Precisely because Progressives could reasonably invoke that overarching commonality, since networks of transportation and communication affected all citizens, although not precisely in the same ways, these companies were the first to push back via large-scale publicity operations for hire and insist on their own rights (mainly to make a profit) and their own great worth for the commonwealth (puns intended). Capitalists in the past had tended toward secrecy, sometimes to the point of contempt (exemplified in Cornelius Vanderbilt's infamous 1880 remark, "the public be damned"), preferring to gain influence by more private methods, such as the lobbying of politicians. But corporations in the new century were beginning to recognize the need to aggressively defend themselves and to more openly account for their activities and motives with an explicitness of a certain (propagandistic) sort.

A new field requires new professionals, so we should consider what training and skills Small and his co-founders brought to the bureau. Not surprisingly, from the start they were all press men, including a young journalist "full of new ideas and . . . a rapid talker"[43] who had worked for the *Boston Globe* and *Boston Journal* in a variety of capacities; an editor and co-owner of a Boston book publishing house; a reporter who had started his career in Colorado; and an editorial writer for the *Journal* who in the 1890s had been a minister in a New England church. Later in the bureau's short history (it lasted only until 1912), the firm also employed former government officials, suggesting the close ties among business, the press, and federal vocations at the turn of the twentieth century, even if these interests frequently came into conflict, as can be seen most clearly in the case of Progressive debates about the future of transportation and communications industries.

If we are looking for public relations firsts, it might make sense to shift from the Boston bureau to the government itself, specifically the work of Gifford Pinchot, who ran the US Forest Service (in the Department of Agriculture) from 1898 to 1910. Appreciating the importance of enlisting wide support for federal policy, Pinchot from the beginning of his tenure relied on the Government Printing Office to help promote the conservation work of his agency, expanding its mailing list from 1,200 to 6,000, including 2,000 newspapers, and increasing the press run of agency pamphlets from 58,000 to 92,500. By 1910 the agency had published over 10 million copies of various bulletins, reports, and pamphlets. After his prime backer, Roosevelt, left office, Pinchot's doctrinaire zeal got him into hot water with President William H. Taft, who fired him in early 1910 for helping a muckraking magazine accuse the newly appointed secretary of the interior, Richard Ballinger, of allowing corruption to go untouched during his oversight of public lands in Alaska.[44]

Despite this fall from grace, Pinchot's model for mass persuasion began to be copied by other federal agencies, which set up their own press bureaus, until Congress in 1913 felt compelled to outlaw the hiring of "publicity experts" within the civil service. Of course public relations (even if not named such) continued to live on in these agencies even after its official prohibition. Congressional representatives were angered that Pinchot and other bureaucrats had sought to bypass their own legislative authority by addressing the public and press directly on matters of policy, raising key questions about the role of government administration in shaping public opinion. In this particular case, because of Pinchot's relentless efforts at "propaganda" (a term that he embraced), backed by the full force of Forest Service publications, his utilitarian brand of conservation would win out over John Muir's environmentalist pleas for the preservation of public lands. This seems to confirm the point that Bentley made in 1908: even when it came to the country's natural resources, there could be no unitary interest shared by all citizens, only interests, plural.[45]

But was there a chance that Progressive government could successfully conceive and promote some sort of unifying common good beyond partisan politics? The federal agency that came closest to this ideal was the Children's Bureau (CB), which was signed into law by President Taft in April 1912 and run by former Hull House resident Julia Lathrop until 1921.[46] The congressional mandate for the CB was remarkably broad: to investigate and report "upon all matters pertaining to the welfare of children and child life among all classes of our people."[47] That loose description therefore could include such issues as orphans, juvenile courts, desertion, adoption, accidents, illness, and dangerous occupations. But the initial idea for such a national bureau had been closely allied a decade earlier specifically to agitation for child labor regulation. For both ideological and practical reasons, this was a risky connection. Conservatives deemed child labor laws unconstitutional, a violation of states' rights, while many poor families relied on their children to supplement their income and resented the government intruding on their decisions.

But the pragmatic shrewdness of Lathrop, the first woman to administer a federal agency, shifted the agenda away from such potentially divisive political concerns to concentrate initially on the health problem of infant mortality—an issue largely immune to the charge of special interests. Who would not be in favor of preventing innocent babies from dying? While some opposed to the bureau argued that the government had no business meddling in the private lives of families, the agency's early focus on infant mortality helped to blunt this criticism. The CB's efforts to save lives was paralleled by a national birth drive (which Lathrop took pains to distinguish from military conscription) run primarily by community volunteers from local women's clubs and civic groups, which sought to register and inventory infants in a more comprehensive way than the Census Bureau was able to do. Praising the Children's Bureau and Lathrop's leadership, the journalist George Creel in 1914 compared what the CB was "do[ing] for babies" to "what the Bureau of Fisheries and the Department of Agriculture have been doing for trout, seeds and soils for lo, these many years."[48] By this popular analogy, children were construed as part of the natural resources of the nation and in need of stewardship and conservation, but in many ways they were a less controversial resource to manage in comparison to Pinchot's aggressive efforts to direct the Forest Service.[49]

Once she settled on a program that spoke powerfully to a common good, Lathrop was able to effectively mobilize public opinion. Having "aroused and organized the public interest" by way of a "publicity campaign," as Lathrop explained in an address laying out the new bureau's agenda, women grassroots reformers such as herself were now in a position "through some governmental agency to make articulate and intelligible" "certain aspects of dumb misery" that demanded the entire nation's attention.[50] With the phrase "to make articulate" Lathrop cast the primary function of the CB as a clearinghouse of information and investigation, but "to make . . . intelligible" implied that this information needed to be actively interpreted and shaped. To fulfill its mission, the CB created and widely disseminated instructional pamphlets, such as *Prenatal Care* (1913) and *Infant Care* (1914), which rapidly became in high demand by members of Congress and their constituents.[51] It is eye-opening that the most popular and bestselling government publications up to the First World War were issued by this small bureau with a relatively paltry budget. Lathrop also oversaw original research studies that unequivocally correlated infant mortality with poverty, which therefore carried broader economic and political implications. Because these studies did not weigh in directly on policy and legislative matters (as Pinchot had attempted to do), Lathrop was able to maintain a clear separation between administration and politics, as Professor Woodrow Wilson had urged in 1887 (see the introduction), while at the same time underscoring the need to vigorously alleviate poverty. To dramatize the urgency for reform, the CB came up with an "infant thermometer" that depicted the inverse ratio between a father's income and infant mortality. Beyond these enlightening graphic displays and bulletins, the CB also pioneered other unusual and innovative modes of mass publicity, including conducting Baby Saving campaigns and organizing a National Baby Week.[52] It also participated in the National Conservation Exposition at Knoxville (co-organized by Pinchot in the fall of 1913), where the CB presented a series of exhibits and demonstrations, using a score card, for instance, to assess the development of infants, presumably in an effort to capitalize on the increasing popularity of baby contests, which had started to pop up in state agricultural fairs across the country.[53]

What made the CB under Lathrop's direction so remarkable was the degree to which, even with a relatively modest budget, this federal agency was able to reach directly so many of its constituents. Each year thousands of women from all walks of life and from every region of the nation sent the bureau letters (90,000 in 1919), grateful, anxious, inquiring. Lathrop and her staff sought to respond to each and every letter with individualized advice.[54] Thanks to the large network of professional contacts that Lathrop had amassed since her days at Hull House —

clubwomen, college women, social workers, philanthropists, doctors, academics, lawyers, and politicians, not to mention the extensive network of grassroots volunteers working on the CB's behalf—the bureau did not need to depend heavily on conventional outlets of publicity, such as newspapers, to make its impact felt, unlike the way that other bureaus and politicians relied on the press to broadcast their positions and concerns. It was this web of association via local, intimate contact combined with an eye always toward what could reasonably be deemed a single, common national good that made the CB such an extraordinary government agency and so different from most of its male-dominated counterparts.

III

By targeting the press for the purposes of mass persuasion, by sending countless releases and statements to newspapers, federal officials like Pinchot and firms like the Boston Publicity Bureau seem to have assumed newspapers to be a relatively transparent medium for passing along the judgments of others, akin to Bryce's nineteenth-century notion of "organs" that reflect and disseminate public opinion. But as Wilson suggested in his reference to newspapers being owned by partisan special interests, the press itself clearly could serve as a powerful instrument of propaganda when wielded in particular ways for specific reasons. It is no coincidence that muckraking practices emerged at the turn of the twentieth century (well before Theodore Roosevelt coined the pejorative term in remarks made in the spring of 1906), closely paralleling the rise of corporate public relations outfits such as the Publicity Bureau.

The two modes of publicity precisely shadowed one another, both national in scope, both intimately engaged in shaping political affairs, and both clearly distinct from the administrative activity of the state. As one historian explained, "The advent of inexpensive, well-produced, mass-circulation magazines proved decisive to muckraking. For the first time Americans of diverse social classes had a consistently produced and nationally distributed source of information, entertainment, and news."[55] It is customary for scholars to see journalists like Lincoln Steffens and Ida Tarbell as both reflecting and agitating for Progressive reformist ideology on a number of fronts, including redistributing wealth, wiping out corrupt municipal politics, restricting big business, regulating public utilities, reforming banking, standardizing food and drug manufacture, prohibiting child labor, and cleaning up tenements. Many of the same issues occupied Administrator Dru in House's novel. American muckrakers in this view acted as pedagogues shedding light on a variety of domestic social problems and offering solutions.

But subsuming all these battles for reform was the overarching struggle to control public opinion itself. In other words, propaganda was not simply the means by which Progressives furthered their agendas, but the very ground of the battle.

How else to explain Roosevelt's disdain for the activist journalists? The president made two related points in a rousing impromptu speech he delivered first on March 17, 1906, at the Gridiron Club (an organization of Washington correspondents) and then more formally in public in mid-April. He said that the men with "the Muck-Rake" (a reference to John Bunyan's *Pilgrim's Progress*) go too far in their "indiscriminate assault upon men in business or men in public life," and second, that this strictly negative mudslinging, without offering any positive hope for improvement, will boomerang and only breed cynicism and indifference among citizens. Roosevelt did not directly challenge the right of these journalists to advocate for partisan positions or hold biases, but rather expressed his familiar preference for temperate policies that would foster gradual change by evolution, not revolution. Yet it is difficult to fully buy his argument for moderation, given what we know about the president's own tendencies toward "violent emotionalism," as he characterized the publications of these journalists, whose styles and aims were far more varied than his sweeping generalizations allowed.[56]

In this speech, moreover, as he worked himself into a fever pitch over "hysterical sensationalism," against those "wild preachers of unrest and discontent, the wild agitators against the entire existing order," Roosevelt became guilty of the very rhetorical excesses he castigated in the writers, who were not radical anarchists, after all. Increasingly popular, if not exactly mainstream, the exposés they wrote "in the public press, or in magazines, or in books," which reached millions of readers, could not simply be dismissed as "mere spasm[s] of reform," as Roosevelt would have it.[57] Although the term *muckraker* stuck, many of these journalists were quick to take umbrage at the president's aspersions, which they felt constituted something of an ambush and a betrayal in that Roosevelt in his first term had frequently sought the advice and support of the press to promote his policies.

One clue to the source of Roosevelt's anger beyond any president's occasional peevishness with journalists can be found toward the end of the speech when he refers to "public servants" whose first prerequisite, either as "legislators or as executives," is "honesty." What Roosevelt pointedly omitted in his description of the ethical responsibilities of the "public servant" or the "public man" (phrases he repeated four times in a short space) is the role of the press, which had become something of a usurping rival for the president because of its capacity to stir up a "popular clamor" of its own. Understood as intimidation, Boss Teddy's speech served notice about who was in charge of managing public opinion, implicitly insisting on his executive privilege as commander in chief to galvanize (if not monopolize) the nation's righteous indignation. To quote another of his memorable phrases, the president's "bully pulpit" (coined in 1909) was to be his and his alone. A second clue explaining Roosevelt's annoyance can be found in his fleeting reference to "railway rate legislation," one of the few specific reforms mentioned in the whole speech. Although the president never singled out any particular writers in his rant against the muckrakers, his invocation of railway reform was clearly meant as a rebuke to Ray Stannard Baker, who in the spring of 1906 had nearly completed a detailed six-part series of articles published in *McClure's Magazine* under the collective title "The Railroads on Trial."

Largely forgotten today, Baker was a crucial figure in Progressive politics, although he never held office. Thanks to Doris Kearns Goodwin's popular history of muckraking, *The Bully Pulpit*, Baker is now beginning to garner the attention he deserves.[58] After attending law school, he worked on newspapers covering national politics, including the labor strife of 1894 (the Pullman Strike and Coxey's Army). He then turned to magazine journalism in 1898, writing alongside the better known muckrakers Steffens and Tarbell for *McClure's Magazine*, including a piece on Roosevelt's Rough Riders. Baker left *McClure's* in 1906 and shifted his attention to America's racial divide, publishing *Following the Color Line* (1908), a study that focused on the wretched conditions of poor blacks living in the South.[59] After he met Woodrow Wilson in 1910, Baker actively began to drum up popular support for the presidential candidate, and they established a close friendship that would continue throughout Wilson's tenure in office. Wilson so trusted Baker that he sent him to Europe in 1918 to help oversee the preparations for the end of World War I. Baker served as the president's press secretary during the peace negotiations at Versailles, and after Wilson's death in 1924, he published an eight-volume, Pulitzer Prize–winning biography of the president. With the exception of Walter Lippmann, perhaps no other American journalist in the first two decades of the twentieth century had a more intimate and influential connection with presidential power.

Baker's relationship with Theodore Roosevelt is especially fascinating. Responding favorably to an article on lynching Baker had published in *McClure's*, Roosevelt wrote Baker a letter in January 1905 inviting him to the White House to discuss labor matters, the journalist's specialty. Later that year, as he began an investigation of the railroads, Baker wrote to Roosevelt to ask if the president wanted to see advance proofs of the first article in the series, which was slated for November publication. Roosevelt accepted, "not because of any good I can do you, but because I have learned to look at your articles for real help" (September 8, 1905). It is striking that a sitting president would seriously consider a reporter's suggestions for reform on a complex policy issue of such national significance. In keeping with his initial high esteem, Roosevelt's reaction to this first article was positive, and he praised Baker's balanced assessment of "railroad men" as "ordinary Americans," not "exceptional villains"—praise clearly intended to influence the future course of the series. As Roosevelt during the autumn sought to work with Congress to empower the Interstate Commerce Commission (ICC) to regulate rates (legislation that would become the Hepburn Act), he in turn sent Baker galley proofs of his proposed address to Congress, soliciting the journalist's comments while cautioning him to keep the October draft "strictly confidential."[60]

Disappointed by the draft's vague references to good corporations and bad corporations, Baker responded on November 11 with a detailed analysis of how the beef trust (J. Ogden Armour, most notably) unfairly profited from rigging, which would become the third article in his series. Based on his investigation, Baker strongly urged fixing these rates, rather than simply establishing a rate ceiling, as Roosevelt was proposing. The president was not happy to receive Baker's recommendation, which he claimed might be unconstitutional. Their ongoing epistolary exchange about policy quickly became less polite and more heated, with Roosevelt beginning a four-page typewritten response by bluntly asserting, "I think you are entirely mistaken."

By March 1906, when the railroads had begun to push back against Baker's articles, pulling ads from McClure's and initiating a libel lawsuit against the magazine, Roosevelt felt emboldened to turn against the muckrakers, including the journalist with whom he had been exchanging views for well over a year and who would unsuccessfully caution the president after his Gridiron remarks against going public with his attack denouncing muckrakers the following month. While Roosevelt's professed reason was to chide their intemperance, a letter to William Howard Taft penned two days before the March speech offered another explanation: "the outpouring of the Cosmopolitan, of McClure's, of Collier's" might be the work of "merely lurid sensationalists, but they are all building up a revolutionary feeling that will most probably take the form of a political campaign."[61] Even as he solicited advice from journalists and in turn sought to influence what they published, the president had grown worried over the potential of the fourth estate to publicly "build feeling" that could directly translate into a group interest challenging the power of his office. Helping to craft legislation is one thing, forming a political party, another. This was not a battle over reform policies per se, but over the very grounds of mass persuasion.[62] In a letter penned July 18, 1906, to his friend Lyman Abbott, who edited the *Outlook* (a journal that viewed Roosevelt and his policies very favorably), the president complained that most periodicals stirring up public opinion were slanted too far in one direction (capital) or the other (labor), and that therefore "what is necessary and at the same time what is exceedingly difficult, is to steer the straight course, the only proper course, and to hold down each set of would-be wrongdoers with a steady hand."[63] Whose single "steady hand" could that be, other than the president's own?

What are we to take away from this falling out between Roosevelt and Baker? First, at the beginning of the twentieth century there was a remarkable intimacy between the American press (Baker, at least) and the president, evidenced in their willingness to confidentially trade preliminary drafts. This closeness bespeaks a certain mutual trust when it came to the shaping of public opinion. It is difficult to imagine that either would have wanted their views on such a touchy issue as railroad regulation leaked in advance of publication, although that was a possibility, since Roosevelt on other topics sometimes launched trial balloons to gauge potential reactions. Second, as Baker's subsequent career demonstrated, and even more so the fictional career of Philip Dru, who moved from military officer to social worker to journalist to politician to Administrator (with a capital A), vocations centered on influence were (and still are) quite porous and fluid; publicity experts easily move back and forth between the private and public sectors. It was difficult to keep track, let alone keep score, when the specialists could switch roles so effortlessly, shifting allegiances among government, corporations, and press. Publicity had become an end in itself, a set of techniques and methods that could be deployed by all sides of an issue to mold opinion. Third, given this mobility, friends could quickly turn into foes, as Roosevelt clearly felt Baker had done. Fourth, and perhaps most interesting, the press in some ways seemed the group best positioned to offer propaganda against the other interests, because its roles were less constrained than even the president's.

Here Roosevelt's concern about the legitimacy of Baker's policy advice is revealing. Whether he actually believed it or not, the president felt compelled to acknowledge that he remained beholden to a system of checks and balances (which Wilson disliked), specifically the power of the Supreme Court to overturn legislation. As he explained to Baker, he did not want to "have a law passed and then declared unconstitutional."[64] But the journalist was under no such restraint; as the announcement and title of his *McClure's* series made clear, the investigation into railroad operators was to take the form of a trial, "not merely because President [Roosevelt] has called a special session of Congress to decide whether these men have properly conducted the large interests intrusted [*sic*] to their care, but they are on trial before the higher court of public opinion."[65] By appealing to this higher court, Baker did not have to worry about the Supreme Court, because he was conducting a trial of another sort (although one that found *McClure's* eventually convicted of libel).

As he pursued his case before the public, Baker's attention began to shift from how the railroads operated (issues like the management of rates, rebates, beef trusts, and produce shipments) to a more direct consideration of how the railroads sought to control what people thought about them. In March 1906, the same month that Roosevelt would initiate his attack on crusading journalists, Baker published the fifth article in the series, one of the most important muckraking essays of the decade, simply titled "How Railroads Make Public Opinion." In anticipation of this essay, *McClure's* a month prior had included a brief piece chiding newspapers for publishing veiled corporate advocacy, asserting that "to print an article as news, as reading matter, or as editorial comment and receive pay for it—is to deceive the reader."[66] Baker in his longer article expanded the scope of the inquiry and shifted the emphasis from newspaper ethics to the surreptitious methods of corporate public relations.

It was a devastating analysis centered on a familiar player, the Boston Publicity Bureau. Hired by the railroad corporations to represent their interests, the Publicity Bureau had recently embarked on what Baker called "the most sweeping campaign for reaching and changing public thought ever undertaken in this country."[67] Baker backed up his strong claim (which Roosevelt might have dismissed as hysterical sensationalism) with a close examination of this "campaign," a resonant word suggesting military, political, and marketing strategies all at once. Adopting an approach as systematic as his subject, Baker proceeded step-by-step to deconstruct the "machine" (537) or "engine of publicity" (541) that the bureau had built "for shaping public opinion" (543) on the crucial national issue of railroad reform. All of Baker's metaphors describing how the country's "public opinion is manufactured" (545) and "constructed" (547) were mechanical, not organic, suggesting that opinion could no longer be assumed (along the lines of Bryce) to be a natural outgrowth of democratic governance. The engineering metaphors matched his detailed descriptions of the bureau's deliberate methods of information gathering and dispersal; their carefully chosen venues for "broadcast" (544, 549),[68] including ICC hearings and conventions; and their calculated splintering of their overmatched opponents, whom Baker regarded as "undisciplined and unorganized" (535) from the start.

Baker was most compelling on methods. Asserting a clear distinction between arguments made openly and freely and those "paid by some one else" (535), Baker offered a blow-by-blow account of how the "experienced newspaper men" (537) in the bureau's Chicago office went about their business. The first step was to collect data, clipping every article about railroads published in "every little village paper" in the region, much as Wilson's secretary, Tumulty, provided a daily report of the news to the president. The second step was to employ "traveling agents" to visit the newspapers' editors, recording in "an extensive card-catalogue" facts about circulation, the character of the paper, its finances, and the editor's views on a variety of issues (trusts, religion, politics). In reading these detailed records, Baker remarked, "I could almost . . . see the country editor in his small office, and understand all his hopes, fears, ambitions" (ibid.). The publicity experts even gave this master catalog or data bank its own name, "The Barometer."

Once such information was compiled and organized, the next step (along the lines of Senator Selwyn's campaign tactics in House's novel) was to precisely target these newspapers one by one, keeping track of the number of "volleys" mailed out, with each shot "carefully aimed." In this way, tailoring its messages for each specific town, the bureau commanded its own centralized organ of publication, a mega- or meta-newspaper overseeing the local ones, national (or at least regional) in scope and yet carefully attuned to provincial concerns. As Baker characterized the content provided, "It is really interesting material often mingled with valuable matter on other subjects, and the country editor, like every editor, is eager for the good things" (537). Because the editor sometimes "has no idea where this material comes from," this "masked material" favoring the railroad corporations ends up in the local newspapers, but unidentified as such, since "these publicity agents are careful not to advertise the fact that they are in any way connected with the railroads" (ibid.).

What these papers actually published from the planted news features then was duly registered in "The Barometer," completing the cycle of reading (what the newspapers published), writing (what the bureau wanted them to say), and reading (what they reprinted from what the bureau sent them). Distressed by this operation's "hopeless perfection" (537), as he glumly called it, Baker offered a striking example of its success, noting that Nebraska newspapers went from publishing a ratio of 212–2 columns against railroad corporations to 202–4 in favor after only eleven weeks of the bureau's campaigning.

The rest of Baker's article continued in this vein, focusing on the Publicity Bureau's secret efficiency, lack of transparency, and recourse to "unlimited money" while representing "a private interest which wishes to defeat the public will" (538). This last phrase suggests a cognitive shift on Baker's part, an asymmetry in his argument. Even though he saw the work of the bureau's "publicity machine" as "manufacturing opinion," Baker in depicting the opposition to the railroads fell back (like Wilson) on metaphysical evocations of "the great unorganized public" (538); it was not that citizens did not have views (such as the ones that he himself was trying to give the readers of *McClure's*), only that the opinion (singular) that they already held was insufficiently "organized" to combat the railroads. In this older model, which resonated with Bryce, once the false opinions constructed by the deceptive practices of publicity experts are stripped away, then the self-evident, unmediated, preexisting truth of the "real public interest" (542) possessed by "the people" will triumphantly emerge, come out of hiding as it were. There is propaganda to be made and unmade in Baker's account, but nothing that amounts to counter- or alternative propaganda.

When it came to acknowledging his own engagement in publicity, in other words, Baker expressed no awareness of his persuasive role as a muckraking journalist. Baker's inability to grasp the implications of his own analysis stemmed partly from the very way the case against the railroads had been prosecuted in *McClure's* "before the higher court of public opinion." Appealing to this supreme (mythic) authority, the editors in their preface to the series proclaimed that this court was constituted by "citizens of the United States, who are greater than Congress, or the legislature, or the desires of any class or party in the nation."[69] Their announcement continued by listing a familiar set of charges against the railroads—they had violated laws, engaged in unjust practices such as bribery, and smothered competition—that were all predicated on a broader assumption: that by granting "peculiar and extraordinary charter rights . . . the states have created the railroad corporation for public purposes. It performs a function of the state" (672). Railroads thus represented a special case; although they were privately owned, they were sanctioned by the state for the public welfare. This was a key argument that many Progressive reformers made about transportation companies and utilities in general.[70] But such a position suggested that in order to speak out against the railroads on behalf of a unitary public, the muckrakers needed to presume that they too were functionaries of the state. No wonder Roosevelt seemed to regard them as usurpers.

Less than a decade after Baker's exposé, the practice of muckraking, but certainly not Progressivism itself, had already begun to fade from the American scene, thanks in part to Roosevelt's influential disparagement. As early as 1914, the same year the promising young journalist Walter Lippmann and Croly cofounded the magazine the *New Republic* as an intellectually substantive alternative to dime magazines like *McClure's*, Lippmann (a former protégé of Lincoln Steffens) could confidently offer something of a postmortem examination in the opening chapter of *Drift and Mastery*. As his book's subtitle announced, this was an "attempt to diagnose the current unrest" plaguing the nation. Referring to muckraking alternately in the past tense and the present, Lippmann hardly dwelled on the content of that writing. Instead, he brilliantly turned his attention to the question of audience: how and why in "the land notorious for its worship of success" would readers suddenly turn "so savagely upon those who had achieved it"?[71] Not because "Americans fell in love with honesty," he argued, but rather because "the world has been altered radically" (9), and it is these "new necessities and new expectations" that have spurred on muckrakers and their followers. As he noted, "There has always been corruption in American politics, but it didn't worry people very much, so long as the sphere of government was narrowly limited. Corruption became a real problem when reform through state action began to take hold of men's thought" (19).

This was an intriguing if ambiguously worded observation, since he seemed to be crediting state action (meaning the widening activity of the state) not only with the spreading of reform, but also with the very means of taking hold of "men's thought." In anticipation of his later work, Lippmann's insight suggested that state expansion developed dialectically in relation to managing opinion, understood and practiced as a thing unto itself. Certainly that is the pattern traced in this chapter from Twain's novel (1889) to Woodrow Wilson's presidency (1913), although in resistance to teleological schemes, it should be noted that *Connecticut Yankee* in its rendering of schools, advertising, newspapers, and "man-factories" already pointed to the problems inherent in training modern democratic citizens.[72] With an awareness of growing statism framing his assessment, Lippmann went on to chart a series of stages for muckraking, from applying "the standards of public life to certain parts of the business world" (19–20) and hence the popular preoccupation with corruption, to criticizing "the inefficiency of business" (24) or "the waste in management" (12).

This shift to management pushed muckraking closer to taking on the role of the state itself, a direction also indicated in Baker's essay on opinion making, as we have seen. But for Lippmann, such a direction spelled the end of the practice, which he concluded was "considerably more of an effect than a sign of leadership" (25). Yet however acute, Lippmann's analysis failed to consider one big thing (*the* big thing) looming on the horizon: the Great War that would break out only one month after his book was published. He had not counted on how the energies of the muckrakers, with President Wilson's support, would within a few years find a new outlet: promoting America's military intervention. While the Boss's failed technologies of indoctrination led to nightmarish domestic conflict in Twain's novel, for Wilson's administration global conflagration would become the occasion to perfect such indoctrination. To Lippmann's increasing dismay, the result of America joining the Allies would be the rapid emergence of a national propaganda apparatus unprecedented in its size, scope, and astonishing efficiency. The United States now had its own publicity bureau, and quite an effective one at that.

CHAPTER 2

Friend or Foe

George Creel, from Agitation to Administration

On April 14, 1917, exactly eleven years to the day after President Theodore Roosevelt publicly denounced the extremism of men wielding the muckrake and a week after the United States formally entered World War I, President Woodrow Wilson issued an executive order establishing the Committee on Public Information (CPI).[1] He appointed as its civilian head George Creel, who had been one of the most vocal and visible of the crusading journalists. I will look carefully at Creel's journalism before the war (this chapter) and his administering of the CPI (the next chapter) in order to examine the close relationship between Progressive muckraking and war propagandizing. There are four kinds of connection: formal (techniques of mass persuasion developed by professional publicists); ideological (an evangelical belief in American democracy as a model for the world, coupled with an abiding faith in the exercise of executive power); structural (an expanding regulatory or reformist state); and, tying these three together, affective (a strain of utopian militancy running throughout Progressivism, as previously discussed).

For over two and a half years, since war broke out in Europe in August 1914, American citizens had deliberated and debated the ins and outs of preparedness, conscription, neutrality, and intervention. These were urgent matters of policy that Wilson and his advisers confronted with some degree of indecision, both before and after the sinking of the *Lusitania* in May 1915, which was also the month that the Bryce Report—an incendiary publication from Great Britain that detailed German military atrocities against Belgian civilians—came out. As the name indicates, this piece of propaganda was overseen by the same distinguished political commentator who more than twenty-five years earlier had celebrated rule by public opinion in *The American Commonwealth*. My aim here is not to rehearse these policy debates, which have been treated extensively by historians, nor to examine the German and British propaganda efforts to sway American opinion leading up to the April 1917 declaration, nor even to trace how various important Progressive writers, such as Ray Stannard Baker, Herbert Croly, Walter Lippmann, Walter Weyl, Amos Pinchot, William Allen White, and Lincoln Steffens, responded to these complex issues in hundreds of magazine and newspaper articles published between 1914 and 1918.[2] Instead, I will explore how as soon as America went to war, the CPI quickly began to "weld the people of the United States" and an array of competing interests—corporate, governmental, labor, ethnic, racial, and regional, not to mention the press—into what Creel called "one white-hot mass" solidified by "fraternity, devotion, courage, and deathless determination." A bit less breathlessly, I examine here how citizens were persuaded to make "every task a common task for a single purpose."[3]

Unlike Bryce's notion of government by public opinion, which conceived of an open process of democratic give-and-take underlying American politics, in this case the decision to enter the Great War had already been made: forcefully argued by President Wilson, ratified by the Senate by a vote of 82–6, and by the House 373–50. The deliberative discourse so vital for the formation of publics and counterpublics no longer centered on what to do, but rather on explanations, after the fact, for what had already been done—a momentous action requiring money, manpower, and "the *war-will*" (to again quote Creel). Congress clearly approved, but what about the public at large?

Wilson's creation of the Committee on Public Information only a week after the United States formally entered the war indicated the severity and urgency of his public relations problem, since just six months earlier he had been reelected largely by virtue of his firm pledge of neutrality. Creel had vigorously articulated and defended the president's neutrality stance in his polemical campaign book, *Woodrow Wilson and the Issues*, published in September 1916. But by early 1917, despite Wilson's January plea for "peace without victory" and especially after Germany resumed unrestricted submarine warfare on February 1, circumstances had significantly changed. Neutrality suddenly gave way to the nation's participating in "the war to end all wars." Or to perversely merge two of the conflicting slogans associated with Wilson's presidency: "he kept us out of war / the war to make the world safe for democracy." No wonder many people felt some cognitive dissonance, especially those already holding serious doubts or misgivings.[4] Citizens clearly were in need of some compelling reasons showing that war was necessary: why, for instance, the "Hun" suddenly constituted such a dire threat. Americans with ancestral ties to the Central Powers (mainly Germany and Austria-Hungary), over 10 million of them, must have been especially prone to these doubts.[5]

While the previous chapter ranged over more than a dozen authors and texts, this one will focus on the crucial figure of Creel. No other minister of propaganda in the twentieth century, with the possible exception of Joseph Goebbels, put his personal stamp on the machinery of state publicity, so much so that the CPI quickly became known simply as the Creel Committee. Scholars have closely studied the ideological content of the millions and millions of CPI pamphlets, leaflets, news bulletins, speeches, films, and posters that saturated the American public and nations abroad from April 1917 to the end of the war in November 1918, which included on the domestic side a combination of practical exhortation (buy Liberty Bonds, enlist), persuasive justification (including the omission or suppression of alternative viewpoints), and patriotic boosterism.[6]

Less analyzed is how the CPI quickly grew as a bureaucracy, shaped by Creel's skills as a manager and by his grander Progressive aspirations for the country as a whole, which predated his tenure as state propagandist. Informing his work at the CPI, these ambitions deserve careful attention, especially in light of the transformations in publicity and in understandings of public opinion sketched in the previous chapter. In a career that uncannily resembled the trajectory of Colonel House's fictional hero, Philip Dru, from a young do-gooder yearning to gain influence to a combative journalist to a federal administrator controlling a big budget with little oversight, Creel up to his 1917 appointment fought for what amounted to a "greatest hits" of Progressive reform initiatives, writing passionately on child labor, immigrants, women's suffrage, prostitution, military training, foreign affairs, municipal corruption, and quack medicine, among other things, in a variety of popular publications. Little studied or noted by scholars, these publications offer crucial insights into Creel's work as a state propagandist. Although not quite a socialist, the muckraker tended to adopt relatively radical positions compared to other Progressives, a fact that at first glance might make his zealous embrace of Wilson's war difficult to fathom.

There is as yet no critical biography of Creel, compelling those interested in his career to rely primarily on the self-serving autobiography he wrote in 1947, *Rebel at Large*. That the former head of the most powerful propaganda agency in the world would consider himself "a rebel" ("at large," no less) suggests that Creel's retrospective account is more valuable to read as an exercise in impression management than for shedding much light on the facts of his life. In an early passage meditating on his turn-of-the-century apprentice newspaper work, for example, Creel remarked, "out of a naïve respect for the printed word, I believed that every editor, even the humblest, had it in his power to be a Molder of Public Opinion, a Light for the Feet of the People. Sophomoric, to be sure, but I was only twenty-three. Like every youth with any generosity of spirit, I knew that I wanted to fight for the underdogs of life, but had no very clear idea how to go about it. What was the right gospel for me to preach in order to be a True Guide?"[7]

This sense of himself as a feisty champion of the underdog remained the most consistent leitmotif in his life story: he saw himself as a secular preacher dedicated to moving the masses by the power of his words. As he described, he bounced back and forth between Kansas City and New York, working for various newspapers, until he became an editorial writer for the *Denver Post* in 1908. That same year, persuaded that "journalism—meaning the intellectual comprehension of passing events—was bound to be the dominant force in our national life, if not the sovereign power" (74–75), he helped launch *Newsbook*, an abortive effort to link weekly newspapers with "a university of the people" that would constitute "the National Fellowship of the University Militant," a utopian project curiously resembling John Dewey's 1890s *Thought News* experiment (see the introduction). As Creel's friend Frank P. Walsh at the time explained the venture to a reporter, "the municipal university is intended to take the place of the old town meeting, to which all citizens rallied when their interests were at stake, before the complex industrial and business systems claimed the attention of individuals before everything else."[8]

A few years after this "monumental flop," as Creel called it, he directly tried his hand at politics, serving a short stint as the commissioner of police in Denver, where he did his best imitation of Teddy Roosevelt (who had been the New York City police commissioner), cleaning up vice and corruption. But he alienated his fellow reformers, who quickly took offense at his belligerent tactics. Creel soon began to secure and consolidate a modest national profile as a magazine writer, enthusiastically backing Wilson in 1912 for president, a "devotion" he dated to his Kansas City high school days when he first heard Wilson address his class "on the meaning of democracy" (101), and publishing a slew of articles that agitated for Progressive reform in middlebrow venues such as *Century*, *Everybody's*, and *Pearson's*. Creel was not an especially nuanced thinker on these issues, far more superficial and crude than a Baker or a Lippmann, but he made up in range for what he lacked in depth. Moreover, it was this very lack of intellectual subtlety, coupled with a brilliant, intense feeling for feeling, that made him so effective as a propaganda minister, enabling him to create through the CPI the powerful semblance (yet only a semblance) of a unified national culture—that dream so devoutly cherished by virtually all Progressives since the turn of the twentieth century.

Such a utopian hope, state-centered but not necessarily state-run, was intimately linked to war, as the pragmatist philosopher William James had cogently articulated a decade earlier in a 1906 speech at Stanford only a few weeks before his former Harvard student Theodore Roosevelt launched his tirade against muckrakers. In vigorous tones reminiscent of Roosevelt's rousing speaking style, the elderly pacifist in "The Moral Equivalent of War" offered a surprisingly sympathetic analysis of how combat can galvanize the public. War allowed citizens to rise above the petty habits of individualism and materialism that so many Progressives regarded as the debilitating legacy of nineteenth-century laissez-faire liberalism. James tried to displace onto the moral/social domain what might be considered a decisively political matter: the authority of the modern state to require its citizens to give up their lives to fight an actual adversary. Invoking the Civil War, as Edward Bellamy did in his embrace of an altruistic collective industrial army in *Looking Backward*, James concentrated on mobilization, the preparation leading up to war, not on the battle itself, as the "essence of nationality," the "supreme measure of the health of nations." Since he was more preoccupied with means rather than ends, his specific proposals were relatively brief and modest; for example, he endorsed a system of mandatory service for youths ("road-building and tunnel-making" and so on) to replace military conscription. But if "so far, war has been the only force that can discipline a whole community," what would be that "spark" that would enable "the whole population" to grow "incandescent," until "on the ruins of the old morals of military honor, a stable system of morals of civic honor builds itself up?" For James, it was "but a question of time, of skillful propagandism, and of opinion-making men seizing historic opportunities."[9]

Ten years later, with the Great War engulfing Europe, if not the United States quite yet, the cultural critic Randolph Bourne in July 1916 explicitly echoed James's call but tried to give it a more practical bite, knowing that a compulsory draft for American men might be just around the corner. Dismissing military service as merely a "sham universality" because "it omits the feminine half of the nation's youth," Bourne eloquently argued for a national labor service that "would aim at stimulation, not obedience": a distinction clearly inspired by the pedagogical theories of his former mentor John Dewey.[10] And in scope and mission, Bourne's specifics for this work sounded a lot like James's Progressive plans: "food inspection, factory inspection, organized relief, the care of dependents, playground service, nursing in hospitals" (145–146).

Yet as with James's proposal, Bourne's essay "A Moral Equivalent for Universal Military Service" tended to settle on ideal ends rather than tangible means, because what tied all this obligatory service together for him was its singular pedagogical function. The faith that James put in propaganda and in "opinion-making men" to spark civic passion Bourne located—not such a big shift, really—in public education, which he called "the only form of 'conscription' to which Americans have ever given consent" (144). Of course he would be proven wrong when the government's Selective Service System (note the appropriation of the word *service*) was launched less than a year later, leading to the successful "volunteer[ing] in mass" (registration followed by mandatory enlistment via lottery selection) that President Wilson had confidently predicted.[11] On this and all matters pertaining to the war, the diehard anti-interventionist Bourne remained a distinct outlier: to him, war could have no equivalent, moral or otherwise, but itself. In a posthumously published essay again riffing on James, Bourne mournfully concluded, "War is the health of the State. It automatically sets in motion throughout society those irresistible forces for uniformity, for passionate cooperation with the Government in coercing into obedience the minority groups and individuals which lack the larger herd sense."[12]

In establishing the Committee on Public Information, Wilson realized that the engines of mobilization would not entirely run themselves, especially on the cultural front, and Creel's organization naturally was instrumental from the start in getting Americans to consent to conscription. Like Bourne and just about everybody else, Creel had weighed in on the subject when the United States was still officially neutral, publishing two articles in May and July 1916. In the first of these essays, Creel deemed the volunteer system "on trial in the court of public opinion," and he found it wanting. He endorsed instead a compulsory "federalization," with the distinction (his one nuance in the argument) that this obligatory "training" was not the same as "service" but more akin (pace Bourne) to compulsory education. Such training, Creel concluded after some extensive number crunching, would actually reduce the national "brag and bluster and hysteria" by making it "more difficult for a yellow press and yellower politicians to work up emotional debauches by preaching a religion of valor," although he did not explain why this preparedness would need to be mandatory.[13] In the second article he took direct aim against those who regarded compulsion as an evil, arguing instead that it functioned positively "as an active, driving force" in American life. To apply these "compulsions of a democracy" to military defense, according to Creel, is "no more than a further expression of the majority agreement that decides upon the action best fitted to advance and protect the nation, the state, the city and individual"—as if this quartet of interlocking interests never conflicted, and as if sheer numbers dictated the best course of action in a democracy.[14]

What is striking about these articles is their forceful, browbeating, sometimes derisive tone rather than their content—which is conventional enough, if hazy in logic and rhapsodic about compulsion. Like all of his prose, Creel's arguments did not proceed by sustained lines of reasoning as much as via a polarizing rhetoric of celebration and accusation, with scattered specifics thrown in for good measure. While Bourne and James in their essays philosophized on the subject of collective service, Creel at key moments seemed to be directly offering policy recommendations, however couched in high-minded moralistic platitudes about democracy versus "undemocracy," a strange noun he used to dismiss the "stupidity" of those who disagreed with him on the need for universal military training.[15] This is the key to understanding Creel and the effectiveness of his propaganda: he was much more adept at what Lippmann identified as the second stage of muckraking—making grandiose, emotional declamations linked to solutions that were concrete but glib (for Lippmann, at least)—rather than investigating and exposing corruption, which Lippmann had described as the first stage of this brand of journalism.

Four related points tend to follow. First, as these two articles on conscription indicate, Creel self-consciously and overtly regarded public opinion as contested terrain to hold or be taken by others. Treating the public as the spoils of battle (an apt trope for a nation at war) gave Creel a source of discursive authority that he confidently invoked over and over again, even as he was guilty of the highly charged rhetoric ("brag and bluster and hysteria") that he detected in others, much the same way that Teddy Roosevelt duplicated the mode of the muckrakers in the very midst of his accusations against them. There is no better way to appreciate how Creel operated than to listen carefully to his characterizations of his opponents and detractors. Second, beyond vague references to "the voice of a people," public opinion for Creel would become more and more positively associated with strong individuals in power, especially Woodrow Wilson once he was elected in 1912, with Creel's passionate support. Third, his total allegiance to President Wilson signaled his equally loyal investment in the state. And fourth, starting in the campaign year 1916, Creel's publications served in effect as auditions (directed at Wilson and his inner circle) for the job of CPI chair.

By 1916, it did not take a weatherman to know which way the wind blew, even though Wilson struggled to keep the United States out of the war. As co-director of publicity for the Democratic National Party, Creel vigorously worked for

Wilson's reelection by defending the incumbent's "moral courage of neutrality" against all criticism, both pacifist and interventionist. He even went so far in his campaign book to question the country's fixation on preparedness, which was stoked by "the bonfires of jingoism," as he colorfully put it: a method of "manufacturing hysteria" (there is that resonant verb again), whose intent was "to keep people so busy feeling that they will have no time for thinking."[16] Not only was this a perfect description of his own most hyperbolic tendencies as a writer, but at the level of policy it flew in the face of his recently published essays extolling mandatory conscription—a contradiction (or at least an inconsistency) that neither he nor Wilson appeared to register.

If anything, Creel's essays seem more honest than his campaign polemics in that everybody could see what was coming. If not inevitable, intervention was growing increasingly likely by late 1916, spurring many commentators to offer specific suggestions for mobilization, including the formation of a national publicity bureau. In a book published the same month the United States entered the fray, for instance, journalist Arthur Bullard referred to democracies as "fighting machines," arguing that the United States was in effect already at war with Germany. In addition to proposing the founding of a nonpartisan "National Emergency Party" (echoing Bellamy's utopian nationalist clubs) and offering details about how to raise money and field an army, he advised that the first step in the conduct of the war must be a "Call to Arms, which will electrify Public Opinion."[17]

A full year before America intervened, Bullard had been writing letters to Colonel House with advice along these lines. He was among a number of publicists whom Wilson apparently considered to head the CPI, even though later Creel asserted, with some confirmation by Josephus Daniels (the secretary of the navy), that as far as he knew, he was the only one in the running. Three weeks before the United States entered the war, Creel wrote to Daniels that he was looking for a job: "If [a] censor is to be appointed, I want to be it." A week later he followed up, suggesting to Daniels that a "Bureau of Publicity" would be needed to "issue the big, ringing statements that will arouse the patriotism of the nation." He urged Daniels, whom he had vigorously defended in *Woodrow Wilson and the Issues*, to speak to the president, insisting, "I know the newspaper game, I can write, I have executive ability, and I think I have the vision."[18]

But other contenders were considered. On April 9 Lippmann wrote to House, offering to help with "government publicity work, especially toward any organization designed to wake up the country to its international responsibilities."[19] He discussed with House various candidates who might head the organization, including a Yale professor of literature. On April 12, right before Wilson issued his executive order, Lippmann sent House a long letter suggesting other names and spelling out a list of seven functions that this "clearing house of information" would fulfill, most notably "to invent a form of publicity which will enlist attention in the comparatively prosaic tasks of industrial warfare" and to "keep a close watch on the movement of public opinion in this country in order to supply the government with ideas and criticisms and to be able to advise and warn and suggest to editors."[20]

In both policy and rhetoric, you could not find a starker contrast between Creel's conception of war propaganda and Lippmann's. In measured tones Lippmann referred to "responsibilities," "prosaic tasks," "public opinion," and supplying the government with "ideas and criticisms," while Creel eagerly promoted himself as a "censor" with "vision" intent on arousing "big, ringing . . . patriotism." Lippmann's notion of the role of government publicity, a form to be newly invented, was essentially educational: informing the public and in turn being attentive to public criticism, with the publicity agency's advice to the press serving to mediate between state and citizens. Creel's notion was at once exhortatory and unilateral, driven by an all-consuming (suffocating) fervor—a suppression that worked less by conniving deceit than by loudly drowning out or by simply stifling any opposition. Soon after the war ended, Creel published a detailed account of the CPI, a mixture of glorification and justification that he wonderfully titled *How We Advertised America: The First Telling of the Amazing Story of the Committee on Public Information That Carried the Gospel of Americanism to Every Corner of the Globe.* Creel was nothing if not explicit, and his invocation of the terms *advertised* and *gospel* speak volumes about his understanding of his role as the country's chief propagandist.

But his initial, private self-identification to Secretary of the Navy Daniels as a censor pointed in another direction. Censorship is inevitably the flip side of propaganda, for to stir the mass public with certain facts, ideas, values, and feelings means to actively exclude other information and alternative points of view that might work against such persuasion. In early February 1917, a full two months before war was declared, Lippmann directly wrote Wilson to offer a related pair of warnings. Military recruitment could only succeed by a "newspaper campaign of manufactured hatred," and, conversely, the "military censorship" of journalists would be a mistake: "In case of war the protection of a healthy public opinion in this country will be of the first importance." To manage matters of censorship—a clear necessity during wartime for national security—Lippmann recommended that Wilson appoint his secretary of the interior, Franklin K. Lane, who was neither military nor press.[21]

From this point until the end of the war, Congress introduced one bill after another that severely curtailed civil liberties, most notably, with Wilson's backing, the Espionage and Sedition Acts of 1917 and 1918, which sanctioned US postmaster general Albert S. Burleson's banning of antiwar publications sent through the mail, such as the socialist magazine the *Masses*. Fearing precisely such "an intellectual reign of terror," Lippmann and his fellow editor Herbert Croly at the *New Republic* repeatedly urged "freedom of discussion" during the crisis. As they made clear, this was not an abstract defense of the First Amendment, but rather a practical consideration to ensure sound policymaking: "[T]he real reason for preserving minority criticism is the need for it on the part of the community, of the majority" in order to avoid "defective judgment."[22] Such a stance assumed, perhaps idealistically, that public opinion could continue collectively to exert some control over the conduct of war policy. Yet even if citizens were free to say what they thought, how would it matter?[23]

Creel for his part took pains to counter the accusations of heavy-handed censorship that dogged him during his tenure as CPI chair. Pointing out (correctly) that the CPI, unlike the Department of Justice, had no powers of prosecution and only a weak formal authority of any sort, Creel insisted that the press's relation to his agency was one of "voluntary censorship": a seeming oxymoron perfectly in keeping with the inner discipline by which a democracy compels its citizens. In his initial statement to journalists as CPI chair, he described the committee's primary aim as "creating loyalty through enlightenment," a process that made "co-operation" the "vital need, not grudging obedience to resented orders."[24] We stand "for the freest discussion," he assured the public a year later, "aside from the disclosure of military secrets of importance, aside [from] any protest that is liable to weaken the country to continue this war."[25]

Naturally this sort of dubious logic, merging treason and protest, a line blurred by the Espionage and Sedition Acts, did not stop critics from accusing the CPI of clamping down on dissent. In an article simply titled "Creel—Censor," for example, fellow journalist Mark Sullivan called Creel "a man of primitive violence," a bull in a china shop whose fiery temperament made him ill suited to deal with and monitor the press.[26] Near the beginning of *How We Advertised America*, Creel offered something of a paranoid caricature of members of this opposition, whom he said believed falsely that "the Committee was a machinery of secrecy and repression organized solely to crush free speech and a free press." Not so, responded Creel: "[W]ith the nation in arms, the need was not so much to keep the press from doing hurtful things as to get it to do the helpful things. It was not servants we wanted, but associates. Better far to have the desired compulsions proceed from within than to apply them from without" (*HWAA*, 16–17).

This is a fundamental insight about Progressive propaganda. For all his hyperbole and oversimplification, Creel was quite shrewd, arriving at a profound appreciation of how "desired compulsions" could be made to feel as if "proceed[ing] from within." Lippmann and public relations experts like Edward Bernays (see chapters 5 and 6) would only in the 1920s gradually come around to this view of public opinion as elicited by consent, rather than being coerced, imposed, or corrupted. Of course, Creel's acknowledgment that the CPI needed to "get" the press "to do the helpful things" that the agency wanted explains the "as if" nature of this internalized persuasion process. The convictions of a mass public do not and cannot spontaneously arise from within individuals, but must be cultivated and managed to maintain those "compulsions of democracy" that Creel praised in his appeal for military conscription. It is important to emphasize that in his self-defense Creel was not being cynical or hypocritical or underhanded, but he was expressing a pragmatic truth not so different from Edward Ross's notion of "social control" (as I discuss in the introduction) about how people come to accept certain prepackaged beliefs and values.

We therefore need to take Creel seriously. In his slightly bemused and somewhat exasperated character analysis of the CPI chair, which is still the best one we have, Sullivan perceptively noted: "To Creel there are only two classes of men. There are skunks, and the greatest man that ever lived. The greatest man that ever lived is plural, and includes everyone who is on Creel's side in whatever public issue he happens at the moment to be concerned with"—a comment that Creel, who might have appreciated the depiction of himself as morally uncompromising and uncompromisingly loyal, reproduced in his 1947 autobiography with some degree of pride.[27] But Sullivan's remarks are quite suggestive for another reason: they reveal a prime value driving Creel's politics, and so the politics of the Committee on Public Information. Creel was a man of principles, but principles of a peculiar sort. The muckraker divided the world into friend and foe not simply for the sake of expediency, as Sullivan assumed. The effect, rather, was the short-circuiting of deliberative debate, thereby enabling power to decisively accrue to the state thanks to the propagandist's command of publicity.

Writing in the aftermath of Germany's defeat in World War I, the Treaty of Versailles, and the growing crisis of authority facing the Weimar Republic during the 1920s, the jurist and theorist Carl Schmitt would install this sort of friend-foe binary as the foundational concept of the political. Deriding the depoliticizing

tendencies of nineteenth-century liberalism in its fixation on protecting individual freedom and private property, Schmitt construed the sovereignty of the modern democratic "total state" as derived from a core distinction between friend and
foe. This is not a "private adversary" but a "public enemy" whose identification
serves to organize collective modes of behavior: "[E]very religious, moral, economic, ethical, or other antithesis transforms into a political one if it is sufficiently
strong to group human beings according to friend and enemy." Such conflict is
not symbolic or abstract, but concrete, depending on "the extreme case taking
place, the real war," which Schmitt called "an exception" that "does not negate
its decisive character but confirms it all the more."[28] War (and the constant threat
of war) is not simply the health of the state, as Bourne would have it, but its very
being.

Against pluralistic accounts that regarded government as "a mere servant of
the essentially economically determined society" or grandiose idealist views that
grounded the omnipotence of the state in "the omnipotence of God,"[29] Schmitt
saw the secular, modern state as defined, authorized, and unified by antagonism
against enemies. This severe line of argument goes well beyond Arthur Bentley's
notion (discussed in chapter 1) of democratic politics as organized by contending
interest groups. It is not hard to see how Schmitt's position would lend itself to
totalitarian ideology, and in fact he turned to Nazism in the 1930s. But his theorizing also helps illuminate Creel's friend-foe public polemics both before and
during the war, which was driven more by militant emotional animus than by
attempts to persuade via rational argument. This is not to say that Creel was a fascist, only that his understanding and pursuit of politics carried certain absolutist
tendencies even as he held an intense belief in democracy, however disconcerting that (in)congruence might seem to some.

It is difficult to say whether Creel during his tenure at the CPI projected his
long-standing friend-foe mentality onto the state, or whether he had from early
on simply internalized the twentieth-century emergence of government by exception. In all fairness to President Wilson, his wartime administration as a whole did
not depend on this political logic of continuous emergency, fighting perpetual
war for perpetual security. But on the home front dissenters did experience harsh
suppression, as various scholars have noted.[30] Pushing for the Espionage Act of
1917, Wilson insisted that disloyal Americans "had sacrificed their right to civil
liberties."[31] Despite vigorous debate in Congress and numerous modifications of
the proposed wording of the act, these nuanced qualifications tended to fall by
the wayside as the Justice Department broadly interpreted and enforced the law to
crack down and imprison socialists like Eugene V. Debs. Even that stalwart

champion of liberal causes Supreme Court justice Oliver Wendell Holmes Jr. fell in line with this pattern of suppression, positing in a unanimous decision the test of a "clear and present danger" to uphold the Espionage Act in *Schenck v. United States* (1919).[32]

Conscientious objectors who opposed the war on religious grounds were also harshly treated, with mainstream Protestant organizations such as the National Council of the Churches of Christ encouraging their ministers to preach against the objectors. As historian Christopher Capozzola explained, such suppression "enforced a political culture that connected citizenship to the voluntary fulfillment of obligations," including unequivocally supporting the US war effort.[33] What Capozzola calls a climate of "coercive voluntarism" matches perfectly the ethos of Creel and the CPI, which did not directly police dissent or drum up war hysteria (a bombastic term in itself), but more subtly created an atmosphere short on any tolerance for alternative points of view. Obligation to the nation was made to seem natural and inevitable, a matter of patriotic duty—and the compulsions seemed to come from within, to borrow the ex-muckraker's phrase. Creel was a publicist, not an elected politician or officer of the law. If war could be considered diplomacy continued by other means (to paraphrase Clausewitz), then propaganda might be regarded as a mode of politics managed by other means. Before I examine how Creel ran the CPI, I therefore consider an interlocking pair of episodes that figured prominently in his muckraking career, both centered on charges of undue influence, to see how this friend-foe binary worked in practice.

In March 1915 Creel published an article in *Pearson's Magazine* titled "How 'Tainted' Money Taints," which accused fellow Progressive journalist Paul U. Kellogg of pandering to the special interests of big business. Kellogg was the editor of the well-respected weekly journal the *Survey*, whose name derived from the Pittsburgh Survey, an innovative piece of social analysis that combined research and advocacy.[34] Published under the aegis of the Charity Organization Society, the magazine was closely associated with various philanthropic institutions, which Creel in his article mocked as its "Monopolized Altruism." Fueling Creel's ire was a cautious editorial Kellogg had written commending the plans of the Rockefeller Foundation to investigate the protracted mining strike in Colorado, which had led in April 1914 to the infamous Ludlow Massacre. In his editorial Kellogg criticized a good friend of Creel's, Frank P. Walsh, who had been conducting hearings on the strike as chair of the federal Commission on Industrial Relations. Just as the CPI quickly became known as the Creel Committee, this one was dubbed the Walsh Commission, suggesting that Walsh, like Creel, was a commanding, charismatic figure. Deeming certain aspects of Walsh's inquiry to be ineffectual and poorly run, Kellogg endorsed the Rockefeller Foundation as an additional forum for investigation. What ensued was an acrimonious published dispute between Walsh and Kellogg, which Creel selectively excerpted in big chunks in his own essay, framed by a pair of questions at the beginning and an insinuation toward the end about Kellogg's intellectual and moral integrity.

Creel began by asking, "Is Organized Charity no more than a carefully premeditated fraud, designed by unscrupulous millionaires to chloroform public opinion?" This was followed by "Is the Rockefeller Foundation's million dollar investigation into 'the causes of industrial unrest' only a scheme to muddy the waters?" The effect of these two leading questions was to "chloroform" (to borrow Creel's lurid metaphor) the reader's ability to assess the rest of the essay, which offered little evidence to support these assertions, preferring instead to vehemently defend Walsh and attack Kellogg (who, by the way, was one of the few Progressives to hold out against intervention as the country moved closer to war). Creel ended by suggesting that by approving the Rockefeller Foundation's plans, Kellogg had become guilty by association, the paid stooge of plutocrats.[35]

Because he had little belief in the independent, disinterested analysis and evaluation of policies and programs apart from those individuals who advocated them, Creel presumed the same must hold true for public figures like Kellogg, who therefore must be tainted by the Rockefellers' blood money. Ideas turn into labels, and personalities are thus polarized into stark binaries that carry symbolic value. Walsh was a cherished friend, he represented the state, he could do no wrong; Rockefeller was an enemy, he was an evil plutocrat, and since Kellogg was taken to be allied with Creel's foe, he therefore became another adversary: end of conversation. While it might be reasonably inferred that Walsh and Kellogg in this feud did hold different positions regarding the redistribution of wealth in the United States, these kinds of ideological niceties were simply not Creel's concern.[36]

In his response to the Creel essay, Kellogg indicated that the *Survey* never received any money from John D. Rockefeller Jr. or the Rockefeller Foundation. He suggested that Creel was guilty of the very thing he was accusing Kellogg of doing in relation to Rockefeller: acting as a proxy or hatchet man for Walsh. "Letting George Do It" was the title of the *Survey*'s rejoinder.[37] The *New Republic* had a slightly different take on the matter. Against the "preposterous" charge that Kellogg was among the "paid apologists of the rich," an unsigned editorial (written by Lippmann) rehearsed the argument between Walsh and Kellogg, and then zeroed in on Creel's suppression of certain passages that would have given a fuller and more accurate picture of Kellogg's mixed attitude toward the Rockefeller Foundation's inquiry. For Lippmann, Kellogg's opinions, Walsh's conduct in running the commission, and the Rockefeller Foundation's plans can all be criticized, applauded, parsed, and debated, since all are subject to reasoned review and analysis—a process of adjudication, negotiation, and discussion, point by point. That is the basis of a democratic public sphere. But not for all-or-nothing Creel. In an uncharacteristic fit of pique, Lippmann exploded: "It is one of the worst cases of brutal stupidity that muckraking has produced, and there is no excuse for Mr. Creel but to state the plain fact that he is a reckless and incompetent person who has at last revealed the quality of his mind. He has shown himself incapable of judging evidence, and determined to make a noise no matter what canons of truthfulness he violates."[38]

To appreciate Creel's great antipathy toward Rockefeller and his equally deep amity toward Walsh, I briefly turn to the Ludlow Massacre itself. On April 20, 1914, the Colorado National Guard and private guards hired by the Colorado Fuel and Iron Company (owned by the Rockefeller family) assaulted an encampment of coal miners and their families who had been on strike since September 1913. The attack resulted in approximately two dozen fatalities and was followed by ten more days of deadly battles, prompting historian Howard Zinn to call it "the culminating act of perhaps the most violent struggle between corporate power and laboring men in American history."[39] This strike is especially crucial for understanding Progressive politics because it cast in bold relief the contending interests of businesses, unions, the policing authority of Colorado's state militia, the federal government, and the press, which were all caught up in trying to manage public opinion while explaining what happened.

At the heart of the strike was the relation between power and property: who ultimately possessed the rights and the means to control the social order. Everybody involved in the tragedy sought to give it a particular spin, including the publicity director of the United Mine Workers of America, Walter H. Fink, who subtitled his account "Revealing the Horrors of Rule by Hired Assassins of Industry and Telling as Well of the Thirty Years War Waged by Colorado Coal Miners Against Corporation-Owned State and County Officials to Secure an Enforcement of the Laws." Major Edward J. Boughton of the Colorado Adjutant General's Office, by contrast, called his official report "The Military Occupation of the Coal Strike Zone of Colorado by the National Guard," perhaps a less provocative title, but no less slanted.[40]

Creel played a minor but significant role in the immediate aftermath of the massacre (dubbed so by the miners), which he recounted on at least three different occasions: in his 1947 autobiography; in a long descriptive article in the popular *Everybody's Magazine* published a couple of months (June 1914) after the tragedy; and, perhaps the most interesting, in a set of articles published in the fall (November 7 and 14, 1914) in *Harper's Weekly* titled "Poisoners of Public Opinion." As with the verb *chloroform*, which opened his "Tainted" essay disparaging the integrity of Kellogg, here too public opinion was imagined as suffering a brutal fate by enemies, not simply contrived or manufactured, but destroyed, debased, polluted, or, as he said elsewhere in another context, "killed" (as if akin to the striking victims themselves).[41]

The *Everybody's* article was ostensibly structured like a conventional piece of journalism, with subheadings titled "Military Oppression," "The Employer's Side," "The Miner's Side," and "The I.W.W. Program" and concluding with the subheading "Which One Is Right?" But it would be very difficult for a reader to weigh the merits or even make sense of the various positions as Creel outlined them, given his overheated rhetoric. For example, this is how he initially described the massacre's resolution: "A weeping, hysterical governor, a blood-drunk soldiery, crazed strikers, an armed working class, and a passion-swept people — these were the conditions on April 28 when President Wilson ordered Federal troops into Colorado for the restoration of peace and the preservation of order." All we can take away from the "bedlam" (Creel's word for the event itself) of this prose is that Wilson and government-sanctioned order saved the day. Creel was especially prone to stylistic excess when describing the rhetoric of the speechmakers: "Seven thousand citizens stood for hours in the drenching rain on the State House lawn, crying out against the Ludlow horror, and branding [Governor Elias] Ammons and the Rockefellers as accessories to the slaughter of babes."[42]

The curious thing about this "slaughter of babes" phrase is that in his autobiography, he retrospectively credited the over-the-top line to himself, not others, as he painted himself into the scene that he had only described as an observing journalist in the much earlier article. In *Rebel at Large* Creel was the oratorical hero of the historical moment, standing in front of a crowd of "ten thousand" (an exaggeration we can generously chalk up to a faulty memory). "[A]ll of the speakers were miners except myself, but according to press report[s], I outdid them in violence of attack," he proudly remarked, adding that on top of calling Rockefeller and his henchmen "traitors to the people and accessories to the murder of babes," he was able to put forward some "constructive" policy suggestions, such as the immediate "seizure of the coal mines by the state" (128). This retrospective account, published more than thirty years after the event, was actually closer to the truth: Creel did help to organize the rally and was its first rousing speaker (if only to a crowd of 4,000–5,000, according to contemporaneous newspaper stories).[43]

Clearly, since he was claiming to examine the various sides of the incident for the *Everybody's* article only two months after the assault, he decided that it would not look good to fervently belong to one of the very sides being analyzed, and so to preserve the pretense of journalistic impartiality, he falsely attributed his own words to others. Besides himself, Creel identified another hero in his autobiographical recounting of the Ludlow affair and its aftermath: his intimate "comrade" from their "Kansas City days" Frank P. Walsh, who as chair of the Commission on Industrial Relations subjected John D. Rockefeller later that year to "merciless questioning" about his role in the massacre. And there was also a second culprit in this version, Ivy Lee, a secretly employed "publicity man for the Rockefellers," who flooded the state and nation with falsehoods (according to Creel) in defense of his corporate client. We thus have two friends fighting fiercely against two foes, with the complex issues raised by the strike itself tending to fall by the wayside.

But what he knew in 1947, Creel did not seem to know when he published "Poisoners of Public Opinion" thirty-three years earlier in *Harper's Weekly*, which was already filled in November 1914 with account after account of the horrors of the war raging in Europe.[44] Somebody was expertly propagating devastating lies about the labor violence at home, including slandering the icon Mother Jones (known as "the angel of the miners"), but who? Part of the fascination of the piece is to see Creel spar with an invisible opponent, as his attention shifts from the plutocrat Rockefeller to the techniques deployed to keep his reputation and the reputation of his business clean. In a tactic that Creel later directly borrowed for the Committee on Public Information, Lee had saturated the country with anonymous, numbered "fact" bulletins purporting to give disinterested information about the strike while erasing all traces of any ties to Rockefeller. Lee's work in Colorado still remains something of a textbook case for how to run an effective corporate public relations campaign, making the operations of the Boston Publicity Bureau in favor of the railroads look modest by comparison. A few years after the Ludlow Massacre the socialist writer Upton Sinclair would wittily riff on Creel's venom metaphor by nicknaming the Rockefeller publicist "Poison" Ivy Lee.[45]

Describing the clever machinations of this master manipulator, Creel could not help but show a begrudging admiration for his rival, much as Twain's Hank Morgan envied Merlin's popularity, Philip Dru sought the advice of the conniving Senator Selwyn, and Ray Stannard Baker in his muckraking exposé of the railroads marveled at the publicity strategies of former newspaper men (see chapter 1). This process of identification cuts across competing interests; it takes one to know one, in other words. But whereas Baker understood the Publicity Bureau as making or engineering public opinion, Creel in a cruder way depicted the work of his dark double as totally destructive. The toxic lies spread by his competitor had to be purged from the polis in order to allow public opinion to return to its pristine, uncontaminated state.

This is the logic of scapegoating, which fits hand in glove with Creel's friend-or-foe psychology.[46] Appreciating that his own publicity was inadequate to combat such poisoning, Creel in the first of these articles called on the federal government "to enter the courtroom with its wealth of discovered and established fact" (438), so that the Commission on Industrial Relations (led by his comrade-in-arms Walsh, whom he does not mention by name) can set things straight. But rather than view the commission's role as merely an extension of the government's creation and enforcement of legislation, Creel quoted President Wilson to insist that "the Colorado dispute must be adjudicated in the court of public opinion."[47] Arguing that corporations such as Rockefeller's "pillage the natural resources of the State," Creel was less interested in defending the rights of labor than in affirming the authority of the state. He therefore called on the federal government to reclaim by publicity (not by law) what had been taken away by the "debauching influences of those sinister aggregations of capital," including hidden propagandists such as Ivy Lee. Creel continued by praising the progress that had already been made in this "struggle for freedom," such as referendums and initiatives for direct recall. "One by one the State has gained the weapons of democracy," he declared, leaving us with a perfect description of his militant brand of Progressive propaganda.[48]

The same year that Creel coined the memorable phrase "weapons of democracy" to describe the reformist state in action, he co-authored a muckraking exposé called *Children in Bondage* (1914), which gives us a hint about the kind of activist administrator he would become during the war. As the book title indicates and with chapters such as "Sacrifice of Golden Boys and Girls," "The Crimson in Our Cotton," "Little Slaves of the Lamp," and "The Sweat-Shop Inferno," this was a scathing attack on child labor that drew on powerful tropes of sentimentality for its persuasive force, along the lines of the "slaughter of babes" remark he made during his Ludlow speech.[49] In an interesting shift near the end of the book, the authors moderated their harsh tone in order to detail some laws, commissions, and agencies that had been established to save children. Suggesting that "the State's interest in the home . . . is a very new thing" (320), the authors bluntly asserted that "the burden of this fight, in the last analysis, will rest upon the women" (317). In a fleeting return to the book's prior rhetorical mode, they continued, "the two million little ones that are caught in the jaws of the remorseless machine that drags them down to darkness and despair, lift their frail hands in pathetic appeal to the daughters of the Divine Mother" (320). This evocation of female agency was in keeping with Creel's long-standing advocacy for women's rights, including the right to vote; in 1911, for example, he and his co-author, Benjamin Lindsey, published an essay extolling the political virtues of equal suffrage in the state of Colorado.[50] And the same year that *Children in Bondage* appeared, Creel gave a talk at a feminist mass meeting (February 17, 1914) organized by the Greenwich Village Heterodoxy Club on the subject "What Feminism Means to Me."[51]

It is not surprising, then, that Creel would put women on the forefront of the battle to abolish child labor. *Children in Bondage* concluded by singling out for "fervent reference" (397) one federal agency and one woman in particular, Julia Lathrop, who so "brilliantly" headed the Children's Bureau. As I briefly mentioned in the previous chapter, Creel drew on a common analogy by comparing the conservation work of Lathrop's bureau with the stewardship of the nation's natural resources undertaken by other federal agencies, such as the Bureau of Fisheries and the Department of Agriculture. What especially impressed Creel about the Children's Bureau was its emphasis on infant mortality and birth registration, a campaign that he urged be enforced by law "in every city and every state" rather than applied piecemeal, as was currently the case. Although Lathrop in 1912 disavowed that birth registration had anything to do with military conscription, the bureau's campaign offered a model for the mass mobilization required for universal service, which Creel urged in 1916. The national reach of the Children's Bureau, combined with its myriad publicity techniques and its calculated arousing of emotion for a common good (saving children) clearly appealed strongly to Creel in both 1914 and a few years later, when he headed his own federal agency.

This brings me to reconsider Woodrow Wilson's decision to appoint Creel to head the Committee on Public Information: Why did he prefer the intemperate muckraker (brokered by Daniels) over the better known and more respected candidates suggested by Lippmann (brokered by House)?[52] The president's biographers are relatively silent on the subject. It might have been, as Sullivan wryly surmised, that Wilson simply was not paying close attention. Or perhaps Wilson wanted to repay loyalty with loyalty, letting the position at CPI (which was no cushy sinecure, to be sure) serve to reward Creel for his Democratic Party campaign work, including his writing of *Woodrow Wilson and the Issues* and his long-standing support of the president. Obviously Wilson would have felt flattered to be lauded as a "visionary," which is how Creel had publicized him since 1914.[53] Or perhaps, to conjecture along psychological lines, selecting the aggressive dynamo Creel allowed Wilson to channel his own inner Teddy Roosevelt, Wilson's archrival for years, whose effusive energies (rhetorical and otherwise) resembled the bluster and swagger of the muckraker. Creel was a man with "a passion for adjectives," as Wilson praised the CPI chair.[54] Characteristic as well of many women reformers, such compassionate fervor would be vital to stir the entire nation to fight, Wilson might have understood, even if the president remained lukewarm about suffrage itself. Or perhaps Wilson intuited that Creel's friend-foe approach was exactly what America needed during a time of war, not the nuanced, civil (and civic) rationality of a Lippmann. Whatever his reasons, at this decisive moment Wilson unleashed through the Creel Committee the most complete and extensive marshaling of public opinion that the citizens of the United States had ever experienced, and arguably ever would until the twenty-first century.

CHAPTER 3

The Conscription of Thought

This chapter focuses on how the Committee on Public Information was built and run, rather than on the ideological content of its propaganda. In addition to Creel, President Wilson in April 1917 appointed to the committee Secretary of State Robert Lansing (who disliked and distrusted Creel), Secretary of the Navy Josephus Daniels (a friend in his debt), and Secretary of War Newton D. Baker. This trio of cabinet members had jointly written a letter to Wilson on April 13 urging him to set up "an authoritative agency" that would combine the two related functions of "censorship and publicity."[1] But Baker, Daniels, Lansing, and their cabinet staffs played little active role in the day-to-day operations of the agency managed by the exuberant former muckraker. As soon as Creel was appointed, he took over,[2] and he was given great latitude on the job. The CPI was initially funded with $5 million, which directly came out of a $50 million wartime discretionary budget that Congress allocated to President Wilson to use as he wished on an emergency basis. Only after the CPI was well up and running, in June 1918, did Creel have to appeal to Congress for continued funding.

With the United States at war, Wilson and Creel understood that there would be no shortage of patriotism. The question was how best to harness and manage this patriotism, how to mobilize citizens on the home front to fight for a common goal. As I suggested in previous chapters, one example of a federal agency before the war that had already effectively united citizens was Lathrop's Children's Bureau, which Creel in his muckraking days had highly admired for its mission to sustain and nourish America's human resources. While caring for infants and embracing war might seem drastically different, President Theodore Roosevelt in a special message to Congress on the eve of his departure from office made this very comparison, declaring in support of such a bureau that "the interests of the nation are involved in the welfare of this army of children no less than in our great material affairs."[3] And so it should come as no surprise that during the war, Wilson too made the connection between aiding the military and saving babies: "next to the duty of doing everything possible for the soldiers at the front, there could be, it seems to me, no more patriotic duty than that of protecting the children who constitute one-third of our population."[4] Lathrop's highly capable, pragmatic administration, her enormously popular government pamphlets and innovative publicity techniques, and her largely successful unification of national interests would serve as one Progressive model for Creel to emulate.

Given Creel's proclivity for aggressive bombast, it is surprising to discover how canny and responsible an administrator he was, as indicated by an examination of the vast CPI archives, consisting of hundreds upon hundreds of boxes (roughly 180 cubic feet) of letters, reports, memoranda, record cards, and other documents amassed during nearly two years of operations. Surveying Creel's voluminous general correspondence reveals a far more restrained and moderate style of prose, that of a high-ranking civil servant pragmatically responding to all kinds of inquiries: dispelling rumors; writing letters of introduction for various petitioners, including members of Congress; patiently fielding advice from "cranks" (as one correspondent put it) who wrote to propose new publicity strategies; replying politely to irritated complaints about long-winded CPI speakers; giving approval to publish potentially controversial opinions; and firmly pressuring (but not absolutely forcing) some publishers to revise or remove certain items from public circulation that he deemed detrimental to the war effort. There are cordial exchanges with former enemies (such as Paul Kellogg) and measured responses to impassioned pleas from writers such as Amos Pinchot, who understood that Creel had special access to President Wilson and therefore was in a position to shape war policy.[5] Of particular note is Creel's repeated refusal to endorse or condemn particular political organizations, as he took care not to appear partisan or divisive while the war was being intensely pursued with a single-minded unity against the country's adversaries abroad (the Central Powers).[6]

Creel's correspondence is restrained compared to the more histrionic *How We Advertised America*,[7] which is peppered with metaphors such as "paper bullets" (11, 323; see also 94) and the penetrating "shrapnel" (7, 285) of effective words, underscoring that Creel understood his primary mission as a battle for the "hearts and minds" (3) of citizens at home and abroad. For the CPI that ideological conflict was as important as the physical war taking place on the ground in Europe. As Creel construed and created it, the CPI was a "plain publicity proposition, a vast enterprise in salesmanship, the world's greatest adventure in advertising. . . . We did not call it propaganda, for that word, in German hands, had come to be associated with deceit and corruption. Our effort was educational and informative throughout, for we had such confidence in our case as to feel that no other argument was needed than the simple, straightforward presentation of facts" (4–5). But as we have already seen, and as Creel himself suggested in quickly shifting back and forth among martial, commercial, and pedagogic metaphors to describe the CPI's mass persuasion, even if never downright devious, there was little "simple" or "straightforward" about how the former muckraker wielded facts, which were propagated through every available medium: "the printed word, the spoken word, the motion picture, the telegraph, the cable, the wireless, the poster, the sign-board" (5).

As if to affirm the primacy of disinterested information, Creel also presented in his book a detailed record, worthy of the most efficiency-minded Progressive bureaucrat, that specified how the CPI was managed as an organization. On page after page he offered lists of numbers, dozens and dozens of them, down to the dollar (sometimes the penny!). And the numbers are staggering: 5,428,048 copies published in English of the pamphlet *How the War Came to America*, with an additional 292,610 copies of the German edition; 1,203,607 copies of *Conquest and Kultur*, edited by two University of Minnesota professors; 570,543 copies of the "loyalty leaflet" *Friendly Words to the Foreign Born*; 13,126,006 copies of the *War Publications Bulletin*; $101,555.10 spent on the Four Minute Men speakers program; and so on, with well over a hundred individual titles (pamphlets and films) documented in the appendix to his volume.

Yet even here Creel's presentation of data had a pointed agenda, since from the very first words of the book, its opening "Dedicatory," Creel in his characteristic combative mode felt obliged to defend the CPI against "the general slaughter" that his political enemies had instigated in order to prevent the organization from gaining its due recognition. The next five chapters, before Creel gets around to describing how the CPI was put together, were devoted to rebutting particular charges made against him in the press and in Congress. And so Creel's detailed accounting in 1920 functioned to justify in the court of public opinion the entire propaganda enterprise, including that money was spent wisely and well and that the CPI had a tremendous impact in helping to win the war.

There is little doubt that the CPI was instrumental for the war effort, bringing the state to the doorsteps of ordinary Americans as never before, and arguably never since. Creel made the case in *How We Advertised America*, as well as in his *Complete Report of the Chairman of the Committee on Public Information*, an official account directly addressed to President Wilson, not a general readership, where the author's self-congratulatory hyperbole (publicity about publicity) was kept to a minimum. The report went over essentially the same ground as the book, both of which were published in 1920. If anything, it offered more facts and figures, allowing us, in conjunction with the archives, to trace and untangle the complicated web of roughly two dozen divisions and bureaus that proliferated once Creel took charge.

In keeping with the approach to propaganda outlined in the introduction, my analysis here concentrates on the "how" (the means of propaganda) rather than the "what" (its content). Such an approach entails examining how the CPI was organized, how it was run, and whom Creel picked to help him run it. But we need to begin by appreciating the amazing (yes, Creel's adjective is deserved here) scale and scope of this governmental operation. Assessing the CPI some twenty years after it disbanded, on the eve of the Second World War, historians James R. Mock and Cedric Larson open their account by offering a wonderful hypothetical case of a midwestern family, circa 1917–1918, whose quotidian experiences graphically illustrate the reach of the CPI. Even though this family lived on a remote farm removed from railways, telegraph, post office, and roads; even though they had no phone and no local newspapers to read, Mock and Larson showed how on a daily basis they would have encountered the work of the CPI: "every item of war news they saw—in the county weekly, in magazines, or in the city daily picked up occasionally in the general store—was not merely officially approved information but precisely the same kind that millions of their fellow citizens were getting at the same moment."[8] As the French social scientist Gabriel Tarde in the late 1890s and Benedict Anderson well after him argued, this simultaneous widespread dissemination of print with identical content is how an imagined national community takes shape.[9]

These publications were filled with "patriotic advertising" prepared by the CPI, which also sponsored war exhibits at the state fair for Mock and Larson's hypothetical family to see. The county movie house screened engaging action films produced by the CPI, interspersed with short talks by CPI-approved speakers. And "[a]t the township school the children saw war photographs issued by the Committee, recited war verse[s] from a Committee brochure, learned current events from a Committee newspaper, studied war maps with a teacher who had acquired her knowledge of international politics through the Committee's pamphlets, and when they came home at night [the children] bore more literature for their parents." Mock and Larson continued in this way for three more paragraphs, covering among other things posters, church services, foreign language newspapers, patriotic buttons, and brochures designed to be given out by traveling salesmen—all the work of the CPI. It would be difficult to assess what the family actually thought about all this material, of course, but they certainly were not lacking in motivational messages to absorb.[10]

The mundane domestic scenario that Mock and Larson eloquently depicted clearly does not carry the drama and mythic symbolism of a mass spectacle, which might be the first thing we imagine when we hear the dreaded word *propaganda*. But the CPI's more commonplace approach to large-scale persuasion was effective in its own way. How was this level of uniformity and saturation achieved? How was the CPI able to penetrate and affect virtually every American cultural institution, from education to commerce to arts and entertainment? It started at the top. There is little indication that Creel was a serious student of propaganda administration, but as America waited on the sidelines to enter the war some thirty months after France and Great Britain, he certainly benefited from seeing how the Allies organized their publicity efforts, which were largely haphazard and ad hoc, and he learned from their mistakes.

The key was keeping everything under a single roof. In his report (and repeated in his book), Creel remarked early on: "In no other belligerent nation was there any such degree of centralization as marked the duties of the Committee on Public Information. In England and France, for instance, five and more organizations were intrusted [*sic*] with the tasks that this committee discharged in the United States."[11] Political scientist Harold D. Lasswell confirmed this insight in his pioneering comparative study *Propaganda Technique in the World War* by pointing out the confusions and disunity that resulted when publicity was not centrally coordinated. Given its elaborate state bureaucracy, German propaganda was especially disjointed, Lasswell indicated, with each department going its own way, sometimes at odds with one another.[12] In *Mein Kampf*, published about two years before Lasswell's study, Adolf Hitler notoriously blamed Germany's ineffectual war propaganda efforts for contributing to the nation's defeat.

But centralization does not necessarily entail a rigid, top-down hierarchy. Here is Creel's genius as an administrator. For all of his efforts at political self-aggrandizement, linked to his passionate endorsement of Wilson's executive leadership, Creel nonetheless understood that there were multiple channels through which power could effectively flow and operate in an American democracy. In a time of war, the state and its weapons were supreme, subsuming all other interests. But using this arsenal (both who and how) was an open-ended process subject to constant revision. Just as Wilson adopted a hands-off approach to the CPI once he picked Creel to head the agency, so Creel understood how to delegate authority to each unit of the organization, and he allowed the divisions to run with relative autonomy. Even the way these units were structured in relation to one another had an "improvised" feel, as Mock and Larson described it.[13] There was actually more logic to the agency's development than might appear at first glance, but it is certainly true that Creel was receptive to new ideas coming from the outside, including from civilians, and could therefore quickly respond accordingly. It was precisely because he was clearly and absolutely in charge that he was able to be so flexible in his planning and implementation.

Rather than follow conventional government, military, or corporate models of organization, the CPI resembled Wilson's other emergency wartime agencies, such as the Food Administration, led by mining engineer Herbert Hoover, and the War Industries Board (WIB), led by financier Bernard Baruch. As historian David Kennedy explained, these temporary agencies were run by a mixture of civilian employees, volunteers, and federal officials, and they tried to strike a balance between the public and private domains, so that "the state's formal power should be small, but its services placed at the disposal of those private interests working to coordinate and rationalize the nation's economic life."[14]

In practice this meant that these agencies rarely invoked coercive state authority as a mandate, preferring a softer compulsion (like the "voluntary censorship" of the press) that relied on "cajolery, exhortation, intimidation, and negotiation," as another historian described the "salesman's methods" of the WIB. Such persuasion depended on the self-discipline and self-sacrifice of patriotic citizens dedicated to the national good—a previously amorphous ideal suddenly given tangible meaning and force with the onset of intervention. Mobilization, to recall James's 1906 essay proposing a moral equivalent of war, constituted the "essence of nationality," and Wilson's administrators pursued large-scale mobilization with such energy and efficiency that these managers, "not the military figures, ended up being the heroes of the war."[15]

Creel's early choice of civilian assistants reveals a great deal about how he conceived of the committee, especially in contrast to Britain's counterpart, which was known as Wellington House. From its inception in September 1914, Britain's secretive War Propaganda Bureau relied heavily on well-known authors such as Arnold Bennett, John Buchan, Arthur Conan Doyle, Ford Madox Ford, Thomas Hardy, Rudyard Kipling, and H. G. Wells, along with journalists, to help covertly direct public opinion (mainly abroad) in favor of Britain's cause against Germany. Wellington House's primary publicist in the United States, for example, was Gilbert Parker, a Canadian author of bestselling historical romances. This was a model that privileged literary eloquence: the men of letters most highly skilled with words, including modernist novelists like Ford, so the government's reasoning went, would be most adept at persuasion.[16] But Creel from the beginning understood propaganda differently, as an enterprise at once less highbrow and less surreptitious. As we might anticipate, he started with what he knew, selecting a couple of muckrakers as his associate chairs: Harvey O'Higgins, a minor essayist and playwright, and Edgar Sisson, an editor at *Cosmopolitan*, a Hearst magazine that had infuriated Roosevelt in 1906 when it published the inflammatory series "The Treason of the Senate."

But then, to Creel's credit, within a few months he reached out in two different directions, drawing on talent from academia and business. Based on a patriotic speech he had come across, Creel recruited Guy Stanton Ford, a well-connected professor of European history at the University of Minnesota who had studied in Germany, like many other American scholars. Ford would lead the highly influential Division of Civic and Educational Cooperation, working with hundreds of professors across the country who eagerly volunteered to produce dozens and dozens of pamphlets in various formats and languages and for various target audiences: workers, German-Americans, schoolchildren, and so on. Ford farmed out these assignments piecemeal to help keep his overhead down and his permanent staff in Washington, DC, minimal.[17]

A university professor who favored the war, as most did, might have found writing for the CPI a great way to reach a mass public far beyond the students enrolled in class—an online, long-distance learning program *avant la lettre*. But this was no mere academic exercise, and Ford early on (July 13, 1917) took pains to systematically contact various organizations and companies, such as the many local branches of International Harvester, to discover what questions about the war were being asked "in the street, in stores, on the train, from school children, from your own children," so that he could then use this feedback to help craft the content of certain leaflets.[18] At the direct urging of the National Education Association (NEA), representing some 600,000 public school teachers and the interests of some 22 million children, this division later began publishing a newsletter "recognizing the power and influence of the teachers and schools in training in patriotism" so that "propagandas" could effectively be spread, as the NEA press release with the title "Coordinate Government Activities thru Schools" proclaimed.[19]

Creel's pick for a third associate chair is even more interesting and perhaps unexpected, given his professed aversion to commerce, at least of the plutocratic (Rockefeller) kind. At Sisson's suggestion, he hired Carl Byoir, who would quickly assume a central role in the running of the CPI. Byoir's background was impressively varied: he had graduated from the University of Iowa, where he profitably managed several campus publications; he held a law degree from Columbia; he was the exclusive American sales representative for the Montessori educational system recently introduced into the United States; he was co-founder of a magazine for young children; and then he held a variety of positions in the Hearst publishing empire, including—and this is absolutely crucial—head of circulation for *Cosmopolitan*, which in three months saw an increase from 790,000 to more than 1 million readers, thanks to Byoir's innovative and aggressive sales methods. Unlike his muckraking associates, Byoir was less focused on what the magazine said than on how many paying readers it had. Here was a Republican businessman well versed in law, publishing, childhood education, and advertising, who most of all understood how to promote and sell ideas or, better yet, packages of ideas. After his tenure at the CPI he would become one of the most important public relations counsels in the United States, along with Ivy Lee and Edward Bernays.[20]

The fact that Creel in the title of his book chose the verb *advertise* to summarize the activity of the CPI testifies to Byoir's profound influence on the agency. The word signaled a subtle expansion in Creel's thinking from martial and pedagogical metaphors for mass persuasion to the broader and perhaps deeper modes of influence developed by public relations experts. In a chapter discussing the CPI in an engaging social history of public relations, or "spin," the historian Stuart Ewen concentrated on Creel and, surprisingly, did not even mention Byoir's administrative position as associate chair.[21] But a close look at the archives reveals that Byoir, not Creel, took increasing responsibility for the day-to-day operations of the agency. As Creel himself praised Byoir, "he soon came to be known among us as 'the multiple director,' for I used his organizing ability in division after division, moving him from one to the other, and, whether the activity was domestic or foreign, he showed equal skill in giving it efficiency, force, and direction" (*HWAA*, 248).

Freed from micromanaging, Creel served as the public face of the CPI, responding personally to thousands of letters from individuals; appearing before Congress to take heat, ask for funding (after June 1918), and defend the committee's actions; and meeting frequently with his friend and supporter President Wilson to consult on matters of publicity and policy. He was the cheerleader, whipping boy, and executive liaison, serving as one of Wilson's main links or "personal representative[s]" (as Wilson put it) to the postmaster, the Justice Department, military and naval intelligence, and the Censorship Board.[22] Byoir, meanwhile, was the primary in-house administrator whose work behind the scenes "held unbroken the inner lines" of the agency, to borrow Wilson's famous phrase describing the mission of the CPI on the home front.

One example will illustrate this division of labor between outer and inner duties. On June 8, 1918, Creel was sent a letter co-signed by Emmett Scott, a special assistant to the secretary of war, and J. E. Spingarn of military intelligence, who expressed concerns about "Negro public opinion," which in their view "should be led along helpful lines rather than lines that make for discontent and are calculated to breed indifference or disloyalty." They proposed bringing to Washington "fifteen or twenty editors of the most important colored newspapers and magazines" for a conference that would persuade them to more enthusiastically back America's war effort. The letter ended up in Byoir's files in a thick folder simply titled "Negroes," with a penciled jotting on top: "Mr. Byoir—Looks good to me. GC."[23] Creel, with this approval, had passed on to Byoir the task of actually organizing said conference. Once the conference was scheduled, Creel wrote a letter to Wilson (dated June 17, 1918) suggesting that it would be a good idea for him to invite these editors to the White House as part of their visit to Washington, DC. But Wilson declined, writing back to Creel the next day (June 18), "It probably would do no good for me to receive them." He bluntly continued, "I have received several delegations of negroes and I am under the impression that they have gone away dissatisfied. I have never had an opportunity actually to do what I promised them I would seek an opportunity to do."[24] So, views on the nagging problem of black public opinion were exchanged between the Department of War, Creel, and President Wilson, while Byoir actually invited the editors and organized the conference.

It is not surprising that Byoir was delegated this particular task, given that he took a special interest in managing the CPI propaganda designed to "Americanize" foreign-born residents and members of ethnic groups in the United States. He promoted foreign-language pamphlets and newspapers, which were at once informally monitored by the CPI for disloyal content and targeted to receive pro-war material. In addition to the Foreign Language Division, Byoir also worked for the Foreign Section, which was set up in October 1917 to disseminate propaganda abroad, and directed the foreign operations of the Division of Films. In January 1918 he helped establish and appointed the directors (but did not run) the Division of Advertising, whose work would have long-lasting implications for public relations control of the media after the war (see chapters 5 and 6). This division not only encouraged publishers to voluntarily donate free advertising space for the CPI, but actually designed war propaganda that would include the name of the sponsoring businesses right on the patriotic advertisements themselves, thereby merging commercial and government interests, as if the government were actively endorsing the business and its products (and vice versa). The CPI essentially operated as an advertising agency for the state.

Here it is instructive to briefly look at a sample CPI advertisement, an especially self-reflexive one, which appeared in a variety of magazines as the war drew to a close. Perhaps because this was the fourth and final drive for Liberty Bonds, issued in October 1918, only weeks before the war ended, the wording of the ad and its imagery seem lax, betraying a certain exhaustion or exasperation. On the visual side is the familiar patriotic female Columbia garbed in a flowing tunic, but she is curiously allegorized not as Lady Liberty but rather as Public Opinion, which is announced by the headline "I Am Public Opinion." Drawn in a rather aggressive pose, with one hand clenched into a fist and the other held up in warning, Public Opinion is in a censorious, browbeating mood, declaring, "All men fear me!" Belligerence once reserved for the enemy was now redirected toward American consumers.

This is quite a strange and striking way to think about public opinion, which was no longer regarded as a reflection of popular sovereignty or the common will, as in standard notions of democracy, but as a club to pressure people into buying bonds. Beyond the illogic of the allegory (how can "all men" both be the public and fear it?), the ad openly deploys a conformist intimidation that Creel and the CPI otherwise sought to mask by an ethos of volunteerism. For all those who do not comply, "I will make this No Man's Land for you!" The lethal, terrifying ground between enemy trenches in the field of battle is weirdly invoked as a site of non-citizenship, or at least the threat of social shunning. How was this menacing appeal received? We might also wonder at the reaction of the various advertisers that sponsored such patriotic appeals; in keeping with Byoir's innovative scheme, these sponsors paid for space in magazines such as the *Poultry Item* as a way of tying their products to the products that the CPI was pushing, in this case shame and Liberty Bonds. The government's propaganda bullets might have been made of paper, but they were clearly capable of wounding its own citizens.

This curious "I Am Public Opinion" advertisement was a far cry from most other wartime propaganda imagery (both still and moving), which aimed to stir Americans to patriotic duty and self-denial, or rouse them against the Hun, but did not try to shame them into submission. Another fourth Liberty Loan effort, *100% American* (Famous Players–Lasky, 1918), for instance, featured Hollywood movie star Mary Pickford as a cute-as-a-button shopaholic who is inspired by a (CPI?) speaker at a crowded amusement park to forgo pleasure and instead save

Lady Public Opinion as an intimidating browbeater. This was a fourth Liberty Loan advertisement sponsored by the Committee on Public Information and published in a number of magazines, including the *Poultry Item* (October 1918).

her money for the war cause. The short film ends with Pickford getting her fun by knocking a cartoonish Kaiser Wilhelm into a tank of soup with a Liberty Loan baseball (as if war were a Coney Island arcade game), followed by "America's Sweetheart," as Pickford was called, smiling at the camera and imploring us with pointed finger to buy Liberty Bonds. Her direct address was an inclusive gesture appealing to us to become, like her, 100% American, defined here strictly by how to spend (and not spend) money, rather than by the Americanization plans Byoir installed at the CPI to help the foreign-born appreciate their place while the nation was at war.

Tracing Byoir's various positions in the CPI helps us to grasp the multifaceted complexity of the organization. Rather than try to examine all the divisions and bureaus one by one, I will instead focus on some overarching principles that governed the development of the committee, which although improvised was certainly not arbitrary in its administrative logic and structure. The committee relied on two related analytic schemes, one based on media and the other on functions. In a series of expansions, the CPI started by focusing on print, and then added voice (speakers), followed by images (mostly moving, but also cartoons). The one major exception to this tripartite succession was the immediate founding of the Division of Pictorial Publicity, led by the famous artist Dana Gibson (creator of the "Gibson Girl"), a bureau based on Creel's "conviction that the poster must play a great part in the fight for public opinion" (*HWAA*, 133). We will see why posters were so crucial from the start when we shift from media to the development of the CPI in terms of function.

Certainly categories and concepts here overlap, but it is clear that Creel understood his first role as that of censor (recall his letter to Daniels even before the CPI was created), making sure the press did not publish anything that would aid the enemy or, more accurately, anything that might be considered to do so, as determined by the censors themselves. After controversial censorship provisions attached to the Espionage Act failed to pass in Congress in the spring of 1917, Creel issued a broadside titled "What the Government Asks of the Press," which listed eighteen kinds of information to be kept secret, such as troop movements. In keeping with his faith in voluntary censorship, these were "requests to the press . . . without larger authority than the necessities of the war-making branches."[25] His second priority beyond censorship was entreaty, mobilizing the public to take particular action. This was entreaty of two sorts, for enlistment and for financial support. Debated both before and during the earliest stages of the war, a compulsory draft required a voluntary registration drive with local service boards, which were then able to enforce mandatory conscription and to authorize exceptions from military duty. Raising money for the war cause took the form of Liberty Loan campaigns (note the military metaphor), which were created by the Department of the Treasury but required continual monitoring and publicizing by the CPI. For both recruitment and selling war bonds, Creel understood the poster as an essential instrument of visual rhetoric, which is the reason Gibson was brought on board so quickly.[26]

Beyond censorship and helping to mobilize men and money, the uncertain path to winning the hearts and minds of citizens might have seemed wide open to Creel and his committee, which at this early stage was just an executive division. Here the chair resembled Mark Twain's Connecticut Yankee (see chapter 1), who tasked himself with civilizing and modernizing King Arthur's medieval subjects from the ground up. Hank Morgan's progressive formula for manufacturing democratic citizens started by establishing a patent office and then systematically created schools, followed by newspapers. Creel slightly altered this scheme: having the technological means of dissemination already at his disposal, he started with the news and soon after (roughly a month later) moved to education, setting up the Division of Civic and Educational Cooperation run by Guy Stanton Ford.[27]

And so from two initial pragmatic primary functions, censoring and entreating, the CPI quickly expanded to a second phase, informing and educating. Carrying both the promises and problems of rule by public opinion, news was at the absolute center of American democracy. If citizens were given free and open access to unbiased information, they would collectively come to make the best decisions about their governance. Progressives like Dewey early on pinned their hopes on this ideal (see the introduction); Lippmann more skeptically examined it (see chapter 4); the political scientist Wilson expressed it in his long-standing call for a national newspaper; and Creel embraced some version of this dream as well. Recall, for instance, his 1908 involvement in *Newsbook*, a publication linked to the "University Militant" project, which his friend Walsh compared to a town hall meeting and which promised to give the journalist the "sovereign power" that he so desired.

When the CPI created the Division of News, both President Wilson and Creel in effect got what they had wished for, in two different ways. First, they established a bureau that turned the federal government into a national news syndicate, disseminating thousands of items to city and regional newspapers in all parts of the country for uniform publication, just as the Boston Publicity Bureau was hired a decade earlier by the railroad trusts to feed local newspapers items favorable to their interests. Second, starting in May 1917, they published an *Official Bulletin* that without any private subscribers still became the most widely distributed newspaper in the nation, with a daily circulation of more than 118,000 copies at its peak.

As Creel grasped, this "official machinery" of information, standardized and centralized, worked hand in glove with his notion of "voluntary censorship" by meeting the "legitimate demand" of the self-censored press "for all war news that contained no military secrets." Rather than dwell on the content of this "free and continuous flow," which Creel mostly described as impartial "facts" (although he did offer some extended, more complicated examples), the chair in his postwar accounting proudly emphasized the rapid deployment and comprehensive scope of the mass operation. The division "became the sole medium" for the dispersal of war news "not only for the Army and Navy, but for the White House, the Department of Justice, the Department of Labor, the National War Labor Board," and he continued, listing one government agency after another. Creel described the speed with which "live news" releases—more than 6,000 of them during the course of eighteen months—were delivered to the press, information that he conservatively estimated amounted to 20,000 columns per week. The *Official Bulletin*, distributed to newspapers and mailed to post offices across the country for public perusal, achieved a similar scale of propagation. In the case of post offices, however, it is worth pointing out that citizens would have been able to clearly discern that the government was directly publishing news, whereas when they read CPI material mediated by their local newspapers, it was more difficult to tell that the information was coming from a single governmental source (*HWAA*, 70–83).[28]

Truth be told, despite this governmentalizing of a compliant free press, browsing through the CPI's news flow reveals little that was sinister or even very interesting. Unlike a publicity bureau for corporate hire, the committee was not in the business of planting fake stories, or spreading misinformation, or even deliberately exaggerating enemy losses or downplaying Allied casualties for the sake of keeping up morale. After three years of absorbing various semi-official propaganda publications, which belligerent nations tended to label by color (white books, blue books, yellow, and so on), including reports like the Bryce Committee's, which luridly described atrocities (both real and imagined) perpetrated against innocent civilians, Americans had grown dubious about the veracity on both sides of the conflict, and the CPI wisely resisted the urge to play to the sensational. A forerunner to the *Federal Register*, the *Official Bulletin* mainly stuck to a dry recital of war items pertaining to various government agencies, although there might occasionally be an inspirational piece about Secretary of the Treasury William Gibbs McAdoo thanking an elderly widow for buying a Liberty Bond.[29]

Reading through this bland and relatively benign material, we might be inclined to yearn for the good old days when Creel the rabid muckraker made unfounded assertions and railed for and against various causes in colorful prose that at least had the merit of conveying a powerful personal voice.

With this allusion to Creel's voice, I now turn to a less metaphoric kind of speaking that marked the third and most complex phase of the CPI's activities: a broader, ongoing cultural saturation by way of speeches, moving pictures, cartoons, advertising, and other activities, including the Division of Women's War Work. While it might seem that speaking would mainly serve as a supplement to print, it actually can work quite differently, as Creel quickly understood. By the fall of 1917 the CPI had established a conventional speakers bureau, sending out at the request of various venues and organizations well-known figures such as Jane Addams, who spoke on behalf of Hoover's Food Administration even though she continued to oppose the war. But months earlier Creel had hit upon a far more original and profound program to marshal voice: the Four Minute Men (4MM).

Everybody who writes on the Committee on Public Information singles out the 4MM for special comment, and with good reason. It was the most brilliant and innovative contribution of the entire state propaganda enterprise, unprecedented and with implications far beyond the war effort itself. Unlike the top-down formation of most of the other divisions in the CPI, which were created by either Creel or one of his associates, the 4MM had a grassroots origin outside the agency. A few days before the United States declared war on Germany, a Chicago businessman by the name of Donald M. Ryerson, at the suggestion of Senator Joseph McCormick, had made a brief speech between screenings in a local movie theater on behalf of the pending Chamberlain bill, which called for compulsory, universal military training (Creel had endorsed this bill the previous year). In the weeks that followed, with America now officially at war, Ryerson organized a number of like-minded volunteers to make similar speeches with the permission of area movie theater managers, and the speakers dubbed their group the "Four Minute Men of Illinois" after the patriots of the American Revolution. "Four" referred to the short duration of their speeches, which quickly became the main incontrovertible rule of the program.

When Ryerson came to Washington, DC, to meet with Creel that spring, the rest was history, or at least legend, as Creel retold this impetuous encounter: a "rosy-cheeked youth burst through the crowd" of supplicants assembled outside Creel's office, and after "ten minutes" of discussion, Ryerson "rushed out" as the national director of the new program. "Had I had the time to weigh the proposition from every angle," Creel admitted, "it may be that I would have decided against it, for it was [a] delicate and dangerous business to turn loose on the country an army of speakers impossible of exact control and yet vested in large degree with the authority of the government" (*HWAA*, 84–85).

Creel's administrative savvy led him not only to immediately recognize the extraordinary potential of Ryerson's proposal, but how to closely manage it as well. By the end of the war, Creel estimated that at a total cost of a little more than $100,000, the Four Minute Men program numbered 75,000 volunteers, who had delivered 755,190 speeches to a recorded aggregate of 314,454,514 Americans (more than three times the nation's population). He rounded up in his report: "a million speeches heard by four hundred million individuals during the 18-month life of the organization."[30] The CPI accomplished such astonishing saturation with an impressive degree of control by way of a series of interrelated measures regarding speaking venues, the selection and preparation of the volunteers, the program's nimble plan of organization, and its administrative apparatus, including precise record keeping, topical bulletins sent to each speaker as talking points, and a quarterly Four Minute Men newspaper.[31]

I will start with the audiences. Movies were enormously popular, arguably already the most central cultural medium in American life by 1915, when full-length narrative features, silent but almost always accompanied by music, began to hit the screen at ever-accelerating rates. Unlike crowds sharing similar opinions who gathered for a specific purpose, to hear a sermon or attend a political rally, here was a captive audience representing an enormous cross-section of the public, rich and poor, black and white, rural and urban, segmented and segregated in many aspects, but all united in their weekly or biweekly addiction to movies. By keeping the speeches short and by making the 4MM volunteers exclusive, the CPI gained the cooperation of the National Association of the Motion Picture Industry (and its theater owner members), which allowed these speakers — and these speakers only — to address audiences during intermission on matters of national importance pertaining to the war.

Accredited as the only "authorized agents" speaking on behalf of the US government, the Four Minute Men introduced themselves by a slide stamped with a 4MM logo, which the CPI actually took the trouble to trademark and copyright in order to prevent pretenders from taking the stage. This promotional slide was projected at the start of each presentation, lending visual flair to the performance. Although the CPI established a Division of Films, which was especially influential abroad and quickly became financially self-supporting, most of the movies shown in conjunction with the 4MM were entertainment, not overt propaganda, and so were all the more effective in creating a receptive attitude on the part of

the listeners, who were treated to a multimedia experience combining words, images, and even sing-alongs in some cases. Aside from the occasional group singing
session, audience members were expected during these four minutes to sit quietly
and attentively, ask no questions, and engage in no discussion with the speakers.[32]

Because the Four Minute Men acted as official government representatives,
they had to be carefully selected, trained, and monitored. The national division
was responsible for picking a state chair, who operated in coordination with that
state's council of defense. These state chairs in turn worked with the chairs of
local branches to pick and oversee the volunteers, usually in groups of ten, to
assure adequate geographical coverage. Each speaker's final approval (and possible removal) came from the central CPI office in Washington, DC. As interest
in the program grew rapidly, the chairs were able to be more and more selective
in their choices, preferring prominent community leaders with some oratorical
experience, such as lawyers, bankers, and businessmen, who were rotated among
different venues to avoid repetition. A professor of rhetoric from the University of
Chicago, S. H. Clark, volunteered to help train many of these men, the content
of whose speeches were closely guided by bulletins that the CPI issued to each
of them, detailing specific organized campaigns: the Liberty Loan (May 1917),
Food Conservation (July 1917), the Nation in Arms (August 1917), and so on. In
preparing a speech, each Four Minute Man was to rely on the information contained in these guiding bulletins, yet give his own perspective and use his own
words. After each performance, an evaluation report card was filed, which listed
the venue, date, and audience figures, which is how Creel could be so precise in
his calculations.

Marveling at the 4MM propaganda network, Mock and Larson described it as a
national broadcasting system before the widespread commercial advent of radio.[33]
The comparison is apt but inadequate. When introduced in the 1920s, American
radio quickly settled into a one-to-many pattern of delivery: disembodied music
or voices carried wirelessly to millions of largely passive listeners in their homes.
Just as far reaching, if not more so, the 4MM as a medium of transmission was
more flexible and effective, enabling face-to-face encounters with members of
a community who were respected and perhaps even personally known by some
in the movie audience. The 4MM was also tweaked in another direction and
engaged in a bit of presidential ventriloquism, with all its speakers instructed to
recite Woodrow Wilson's Flag Day message on that holiday, and even Lincoln's
Gettysburg Address for Memorial Day. The 4MM dialectically cut across all sorts
of binaries and tensions challenging wartime America: between the federal and
the local, between the traditional (oratory) and the modern (its scheme of organ-

ization), between voice and print (the bulletins), between control and freedom, between conformity and originality, between presence and absence, between the one and the many, between the organic and the mechanical, between ethnic/ racial identity and national identity.

The 4MM was so dazzling and unparalleled in its conception and execution, and remains so endlessly fascinating to contemplate as a mode of broadcast, it is easy to forget that all those spoken messages strictly regulated by the clock were essentially monologues, not dialogues, made in the service of a horrendous war that led to millions of deaths. In her thorough and largely admiring account of the 4MM, for instance, Lisa Mastrangelo concluded by applauding the program's encouragement of civic activism, which shifted the attitude of many citizens from pacifism to "preparedness."[34] But that term only applies to the buildup to war, not the war itself, which saw more than 323,000 American casualties (including 116,000 deaths, the majority killed not in battle, but by the 1918 influenza pandemic),[35] or about one casualty for every two or three 4MM speeches given. To put it another way, by the time the war ended, dead American soldiers far outnumbered the entire impressive "army" of 4MM volunteers.

The 4MM was the CPI's most innovative contribution to the technology of mass persuasion, and its in-house organ, *Four Minute Men News*, offers the most interesting insights into the ethos of its speakers. At roughly quarterly intervals starting in November 1917, the division issued to its volunteers a small gazette (16–32 pages in editions A–F) designed to keep the Four Minute Men informed about the program as a whole. As was made clear in the first line of the first page of the first edition, written by its then-director, William McCormick Blair, this news was authored by and for the men themselves: "Do We Four Minute Men all realize the tremendous growth of our movement?" He then indicated that the purpose of the newsletter was to compile "helpful suggestions and comments" that would lead to an "interchange of views" among Four Minute Men all across the country. "Criticism" was invited: Are the bulletins too long? Did they want more facts? Or pithy phrases? Should the 4MM county branches have more authority? Are the sample scripts valuable or not, given that "it is much better for a speaker to prepare his own speech entirely in his own language so long as he does not digress from the general tone desired by the Government"?[36]

These were not rhetorical questions but substantive ones, posing legitimate alternatives that required deliberation. Along with practical advice (what every speaker should bring with him) and excerpts from speeches, the *Four Minute Men News* also selectively reprinted report cards submitted by speakers, with comments such as "Crowd not attentive"; "had to speak between reels in second show. No bond salesman showed up"; and "Manager extremely courteous . . . Audience, 200 or 250, mostly children and negroes." Letters were printed from members coast to coast complaining about the ignorance of people from the rural districts, praising the power of motion pictures, and calling for experts in public speaking to tutor the Four Minute Men on matters of oratorical style (a suggestion subsequently acted upon, as mentioned above). And near the end of this first edition, a giant collage of clippings about the 4MM was pieced together from different regional newspapers (Atlanta, Bayonne, Newark, Providence, Portland, Charlestown, and so on), not only to signify the national impact of the program, but to give the impression of the *Four Minute Men News* itself as a meta-newspaper that encompassed the whole country.

In short, this was the kind of publication that encouraged serious self-reflection —the only one put out by the CPI—and so constituted news in the profound sense imagined by Lippmann and Dewey. The second and third issues grew even more self-aware, discussing, for example, the role of hatred and fear in stirring up citizens during war, and whether and how to appeal to emotions in laying out a case against Germany. Certainly these questions were pondered by the writers of the CPI's many bulletins (both in this division and others), and even George Creel might have given them some thought. But what is remarkable is that the speakers themselves—no mere parrots of the government—were being invited as readers to consider these issues. Sometimes these exchanges went beyond print, since many local branches of the 4MM scheduled weekly luncheons for their members so that they could directly share their experiences with one another. Trading rhetoric tips (400 words is enough, know your audience, do not say "I") and offering criticisms of the program from many points of view (no highbrow stuff, give more authoritative citations), these men were "free to talk from the heart" even as the CPI was "mildly insisting that [they] adhere to the general plan of each bulletin," as Professor S. H. Clark, who was schooling the men, remarked in a speech reprinted in edition B, aptly titled "Greater than the Fourth Estate."

As part of its domestic mission, the Committee on Public Information sought to create the semblance of a public national culture. It is not difficult to see how a volunteer reading through the pages of the *Four Minute Men News* with pride and pleasure would feel himself a significant part of a synchronized collective dedicated to a monumentally important cause. Director Blair expressed this sense of unified belonging in a lead editorial in edition C that realized the full implications of these simultaneous acts of elocution: "A mental picture of this army all speaking the same evening on the same topic baffles the imagination. . . . Thus, your individual four-minute effort means all the more because it reflects credit or discredit upon 25,000 other men's work. . . . Results have shown what each thought wave means when it is started by these speakers from coast to coast. Do we then all, each of us, recognize the importance of individual quality for the sake of mass momentum?" Here was Dewey's *Thought News* (discussed in the introduction) in the flesh, although confined to a single subject, the state at war, and delivered in four-minute bursts of speech.

Of course audiences on the receiving end of these "thought wave[s]" might have felt more drowned or drowned out than positively inspired by the mass momentum, as a brief "field note" from Olympia, Washington, in the same edition C suggested: "One evening I was addressing an audience at this theater in the interest of the Red Cross; I was just finishing when a man in the audience took exception to my remarks and voiced his sentiments as follows: 'Cut out the bunk on the Red Cross and go on with the show.'" A crowd gathered and the man and his wife were "in a gentle way" escorted outside the theater, even as the wife "called me names that wouldn't look good in print," leaving the speaker (and his news readers) to surmise that perhaps the couple mistakenly thought the Four Minute Man was being paid for his speaking. Clearly these particular citizens were not buying what the CPI was selling, and yet the fact that the altercation was included as a piece of news served to acknowledge them as part of the national polity.

Later editions of the *Four Minute Men News* were not so self-inquiring and inclusive, marked by a subtle shift in emphasis from second person ("you") to third person ("them") by which 4MM activities were largely described from the outside, with such conventional headlines as "Famous Blue Devils of France Welcomed by Four Minute Men." There were still some interesting features: Yiddish-speaking Four Minute Men were organized by a rabbi to address Jewish audiences in New York City theaters and playhouses; a "full-blooded" Sioux was serving as a 4MM for his people in South Dakota; and 4MM addressed audiences in Italian, Polish, Lithuanian, Magyar-Hungarian, and three other languages during a Fourth of July celebration in Hartford, Connecticut (edition E, 20). There was also mention of the "first organization of colored Four Minute Men under a colored chairman," but the racist explanation given for this group's founding in Georgia—active work was needed "among the colored people to counteract vicious propaganda, to which they appear to be peculiarly susceptible"—strongly indicates that these black volunteers ("they") were merely objects of curiosity for (white) readers, not subjects helping to make the news themselves (edition D, 20).[37]

Perhaps the most poignant moment in the six editions was the lead article "What Shall the Four Minute Men Do in the Future?" This essay was printed in the final keepsake edition of the *News*, published on Christmas Eve 1918, a month after the armistice. Along with President Wilson and Progressives across the country, who were contemplating postwar reconstruction, the national 4MM director, William Ingersoll, struggled to imagine some future for the organization that would allow it to continue to contribute to "the needs inherent in our condition of national existence." The primary plan would transform each branch into "a local forum to hold open public meetings once a week or once a month at which public questions of the hour would be discussed and debated." As in the case of the 4MM bulletins, these topics would be centrally dictated, so that

> by having the same matters of public interest thrashed out in open discussion everywhere throughout the country at the same time a tremendous impetus would be given to national unity, so greatly needed in American life. This, of course, would not in any sense be propaganda; it would not be partisan, but it would focus the public thought nationally on matters of universal public interest, and we can in this country safely leave it to the people to arrive at sound and just conclusions when the merits of both sides of popular questions have been put before them.

Keeping intact the simple yet elegant administrative apparatus of the 4MM, this was a beautiful idea for nourishing a robust democracy that was worthy of Lippmann or Dewey.[38] But of course nothing came of the plan, and the 4MM quickly vanished into thin air, as did the rest of the CPI. As soon as the war ended, the state moved to relinquish its control of publicity, which reverted back to more private competing interests. And because neither Lippmann nor Dewey were Four Minute Men (what a thought!), they probably never came across Ingersoll's essay, although it was reprinted in the *Quarterly Journal of Speech Education*, an academic publication combining Dewey's two central concerns, but without his impact.[39] That such a suggestion emerged from the CPI itself would have been especially ironic to Dewey, who before, during, and right after the war wrote more than a dozen articles in the *New Republic* on what he came to understand as America's "conscription of thought." While he did not call out the CPI by name in this series of more and more pessimistic essays, it is clear that the CPI was partly responsible for the climate of intolerance that he so deplored. Conscription, of course, was not simply a convenient metaphor; a few months before Creel in mid-1916 published his essays calling for universal military training, Dewey was deriding such proposals, arguing in "Universal Service as Education" that nationalizing education, not the military, was needed. He posed rhetorically the dark question that the political theorist Schmitt would answer in the affirmative: "[S] hall we deliberately proceed to cultivate a sense of the danger of aggression, shall we conjure up enemies, in order to get this stimulus to unity among ourselves?"[40]

But once the United States went to war, or once "the war came to America," as the popular CPI pamphlet would have it, Dewey, like so many other Progressives, more or less reluctant, more or less eager, saw the conflict as a historic opportunity, a way to unify and collectivize the nation. Still speaking in the future tense five months after Congress's declaration (and therefore more prescriptive than descriptive), Dewey worried in the essay "The Conscription of Thought" that because the public was increasingly being directed in how to feel and act, rather than thinking for themselves, citizens would inevitably "miss the contribution which the war has to make to the creation of a united America."[41] In these wartime essays, Dewey was fighting a battle on two fronts. He not only was trying to resist "the expert manipulation of men en masse for ends not clearly seen by them"[42] (such as Creel's brand of propagandizing), but also was defending the government's intervention against the withering criticism of Randolph Bourne, a self-professed "malcontent" who in article after article accused his former teacher and other intellectuals of complying with an unbridled militarism for the sake of democratic ideals that could only be bogus under the oppressive, regimenting conditions of state-sponsored war. As Bourne succinctly put it, "If the war is too strong for you to prevent, how is it going to be weak enough for you to control and mould to your liberal purposes?"[43]

In his unrelenting attacks on American intervention, Bourne adopted a range of positions, from a philosophical sort of secular pacifism to a more pointed condemnation of Progressivist and pragmatist thinking, which had led intellectuals disastrously astray, according to him, and the vast majority of American citizens along with them. To argue that "war always undermines values" (61, "Twilight of Idols") might be too blanket a claim: Would Bourne, for instance, have dismissed Lincoln's Gettysburg Address as merely empty rhetoric? But his seething anger at Dewey and Lippmann seems right on target, especially a hundred years in retrospect, after a succession of wars the United States has undertaken ostensibly to preserve and defend democracy around the globe. Stressing that the organizing of opinion about the war was left largely to "professional patriots, sensational editors, archaic radicals" (60, "Twilight of Idols"), Bourne noted how justifications for going to war, both moral and practical, quickly "petrified into a dogma to be propagated. Criticism flagged and emotional propaganda began" (11, "The War and the Intellectuals"). The result, Bourne predicted, would be a wholesale destruction, not an enhancement, of Progressive ideals: "The war—or American promise [Croly's phrase]: one must choose. One cannot be interested in both.

For the effect of the war will be to impoverish American promise" (46, "A War Diary"). Whether this stark binary would hold true for all wars, or only for this one in particular, was a question that Bourne finessed by referring to "the inevitable chaos and disillusionment of adopting a war-technique" (23, "The Collapse of American Strategy").

Technique is a word that shows up dozens of times in Bourne's essays, not only in references to war, but also in references to contemporary administrative, artistic, and educational procedures. When technique predominates in a society, the means to an end tend to become ends in themselves. Rather than residing in people and social relations, values are displaced or "deranged," as Bourne put it, onto methods and things. The rise of technocratic thinking, practice, and feeling on a massive scale was not unique to the twentieth-century United States, Bourne understood, but was a broader symptom of Western modernity that was accelerated by the Great War. In his penetrating, posthumously published essay, "The State," Bourne described how "modern nations" are organized by "death-dealing energy and technique" that is "not a natural but a very sophisticated process" designed to meet the demands of the state above and beyond any specific "religious, industrial, political group" (81, "The State"). "Essentially a concept of power" (68), the modern democratic state, according to Bourne, achieves its maximum health during war, which represents the ultimate sovereign instrument (or weapon) at its disposal to manage public sentiment (a "terrorization of opinion," 79), maintain orthodoxy, and keep its citizens obedient.

Dewey never arrived at his former student's brilliant perspicuity or historical grasp of modernity, but by the end of the war, he had pretty much come around to Bourne's point of view about the conflict. In his essay "The Cult of Irrationality," published on the eve of the armistice, now speaking in the present (or past) tense, Dewey decried "the present cultivated propaganda of the irrational" by which war emotions were being deliberately converted into "fear, suspicion and hatred."[44] While he primarily held the propagandists responsible, he also blamed the "unexpected voluntary docility in the American people to submit to limitations." Ever the innocent, Dewey seemed genuinely surprised by his compatriots' willing passivity and conformity, behavior that challenged his abiding faith in (or naïveté about) a vibrant, engaged, self-aware citizenry. Americans and American democracy, it would seem, were perhaps not so special after all. In another essay ("The New Paternalism") he remarked on the "effect upon collective action of opinion when directed systematically along certain channels," wondering if the "word 'news' is not destined to be replaced by the word 'propaganda.'" Noting that "the governmental control demanded by the exigencies of war has in part merely revealed the scope of influential forces previously operative in private hands" (the contending interests shaping public opinion, discussed in chapter 1), Dewey went on to assert, "But the war has also increased the prior centralization, and created an atmosphere of feeding the people with just those things and only those things which the authorities believe that is good for them to know." This "paternalistic care for the sources of men's beliefs, one generated by war, carries over into the troubles of peace."[45] Clearly this was not the sort of Progressive public that Dewey envisioned before and during the conflict, but he was determined to confront and try to rehabilitate the public in the war's aftermath. The war to save democracy had been fought and won, but what kind of democracy exactly was it now?

CHAPTER 4

Searching for a Public (to Educate)

In his proclamation on May 18, 1917, establishing conscription, Woodrow Wilson eloquently declared, "It is not an army that we must shape and train for war; it is a nation."[1] Wilson's contrast between army and nation emphasized that America's commitment to the world war would be a total one, as the large-scale, state-sponsored efforts of George Creel's Committee on Public Information (examined in the previous chapter) make abundantly clear. Less well noted, however, is the way this nationalizing of martial energy and ethos depended on another crucial phrase embedded in Wilson's statement: "shape and train." The word *shape* echoed the directing of public opinion that Wilson early in his political career grasped as a crucial feature of executive leadership. Combined with *train*, the two verbs suggested that the former political science professor and college president understood this process of mustering fundamentally as a program of education.

Of course Creel too referred to the propaganda work of the CPI as a matter of pedagogy, a metaphor that he frequently mixed in (or mixed up) with religious and commercial tropes, such as spreading the gospel and advertising. We might be inclined to be skeptical that Wilson's "shape and train" exhortation signaled a serious dedication to edification, especially since the specific occasion at hand was the mandatory mobilization of soldiers to fight the war. As I previously indicated, the vast majority of Progressives supported US intervention, thinking that entering the conflict would help unify America and bolster the government's authority to provide for its citizens.

But thanks to the state's "weapons," to borrow Creel's resonant word, instilling patriotic consensus at the expense of dissent also created an increasingly compliant citizenry. The public's ready acquiescence to mass persuasion effectively amounted to a "conscription of thought" (not just bodies), in the telling phrase of John Dewey who, along with Walter Lippmann, warned about this chilling of free expression in essay after essay in the *New Republic*. Wartime propaganda was a symptom of something more profound plaguing the nation. Long after the fervor for war had subsided, these two prominent intellectuals during the 1920s would each deeply ponder the prospects for rejuvenating American politics, publishing a series of studies that offered penetrating analyses of democratic publics: what, who, how, and when such a thing (or things) came into being or ceased to be vital.

First there was a trio of books by Lippmann—*Liberty and the News* (1920), *Public Opinion* (1922), and *The Phantom Public* (1925)—which were followed by Dewey's response, *The Public and Its Problems* (1927). It has become common to treat this exchange as an academic set piece or debate, which allows scholars to condense and simplify the nuanced positions of these two thinkers in order to line up for or against one or the other. "The Battle for America's Political Mind: Lippmann Versus Dewey," one noted historian melodramatically headlined it, as if this were the boxing match of the century, Frazier versus Ali.[2] As a result, we have been forced to choose between ostensibly stark oppositions as a litmus test for our intellectual allegiances. Do you prefer Dewey the optimistic egalitarian to Lippmann the pessimistic elitist? Or is Lippmann's hard-nosed realism more compelling than Dewey's romantic idealism? Pitting these two important public philosophers against one another then seems to produce a "winner" (usually Dewey) triumphing over his rival.

Such reductive labeling has tended to encourage partisan analysis, to the point of contributing to factual errors on one side or the other (no, Lippmann never worked for the CPI).[3] The approach is also misleading, as scholars such as Sue Curry Jansen and Michael Schudson have vigorously argued. They show how such a warped view of the supposed conflict or contest between Lippmann and Dewey served for media historian James Carey, among others, as a convenient myth to explain the origins of communication studies in the United States.[4] For one thing, although *The Public and Its Problems* was clearly spurred by Lippmann's two books on public opinion, which Dewey positively reviewed in the *New Republic*, Lippmann never replied to Dewey's book, and so there was no debate as such. More important, casting these two as opponents or competitors ignores the fundamental convergence between the Progressive beliefs of Dewey and Lippmann. As we shall see, Dewey actually built his extended argument by teasing out one of Lippmann's central but fleeting insights in *The Phantom Public*, which did not shut down possibilities but indicated a positive way forward for Dewey.

It is worth summarizing here some general points of the philosophers' convergence. Both Dewey and Lippmann firmly believed in science and the experimental method, not in any narrow sense of technocratic instrumentality, but rather as a broad means to rationally solve social and political problems in a communal setting that encouraged the collective accumulation of knowledge. This was the pragmatist legacy they both took away from C. S. Peirce and William James. The ultimate goal of such Progressive pragmatism for both Lippmann and Dewey was the radical reconstruction of American democracy. Seeking directly to influence politicians in power (including presidents from Woodrow Wilson to Richard Nixon), Lippmann additionally approached this task of reconstruction by way of political commentary aimed to enlighten a broad audience of citizens. Dewey's mode of influence was by way of an accessible philosophy, which he came to construe less as a fixed system of thought than as a general theory of education. In theorizing about democracy, both Lippmann and Dewey endeavored to bring that very democratic public into being. In his first book (1913) Lippmann put it simply: "to govern a democracy, you have to educate it."[5]

Understanding their reformist missions as essentially instructional, both Lippmann and Dewey (more gradually) appreciated that from a pragmatist, functional perspective, social facts were contextual, neither neutral, transparent, nor inert, so that there was no categorical or absolute way to determine a priori the intrinsic value of information as it circulated and flowed in a democracy. As Dewey noted in 1916, "[P]ublic agitation, propaganda, legislative and administrative action are effective in producing the change of disposition which a philosophy indicates as desirable, but only in the degree in which they are educative—that is to say, in the degree in which they modify mental and moral attitudes."[6] Requiring the active, constructive participation of citizens, such ongoing modification was crucial for democracy to flourish. But even well before the war, as the belief in self-evident rule by public opinion began to wane, the question became not whether the American public needed to be directed, but how and who would guide it (see chapter 1). Here is where education (in both informal and formal institutions) comes into play: How should information be organized and disseminated to allow citizens to freely and openly interpret, deliberate, and act upon knowledge?

In this regard we can begin to detect crucial differences between Dewey and Lippmann. Despite their similarities, there are key points of divergence that need to be examined, even if not in the terms of a contest or debate. These divergences center on their respective assumptions about education and communication, assumptions that in turn shape the way they each conceive of a public. To summarize the argument of this chapter in a somewhat schematic fashion, if we imagine a primary (primal?) scene of instruction at the center of each of their theories of democracy, for Lippmann it would be a solitary citizen reading a newspaper (including an opinion piece by Lippmann himself, no doubt), whereas for Dewey that scene of instruction would be two people conversing, perhaps a husband and wife or a student (singular) and a teacher. Given Lippmann's background as a journalist and Dewey's as a professor, such a distinction may not be surprising, but these two scenes create two different understandings of publicness, each attenuated or comprised in particular ways.

Between the two of them, Lippmann and Dewey raised but could not solve the problems at the heart of democracy. As we will see, Lippmann was more interested in results, and therefore focused on ideology, power, and politics, whereas for Dewey democracy was primarily a state of endless aspiration without particular content. In neither case did the collective fully enter: Lippmann aligned the national interest with an individual's (his own) sense of it, until he grew so disenchanted about his ability to definitively locate a unifying good that he replaced this ideal with a set of rules or tests dictating that the only common interest was regulating how special interests operate. These rules resembled Dewey's looser notion of education as a means to partake in community, although the philosopher did not seem to care much about specific outcomes of this participation beyond self-realization; for him ethical value resides in the process of growth itself, a perspective that suggests the shortcomings of his brand of pragmatism.

In order to work through this argument, this chapter will rely on a slightly convoluted scheme of organization. Rather than simply compare Lippmann's three 1920s books to Dewey's response, an approach that tends to stress contestation, I take a longer view of each intellectual. It is now routine to claim that their mutual "search of a public" (Dewey's phrase) stemmed largely from their disenchantment during the First World War, part of the larger cultural discontent that would spell the end of American Progressivism. While it is certainly true that propagandists like Creel affected their thinking, Dewey and Lippmann became disillusioned for different reasons, differences that will become clearer once I establish the strong continuity between their prewar Progressive ideas about democracy and their postwar thinking. In other words, the war did not mark a complete rupture.

Because Dewey was born thirty years before Lippmann, he had a tremendous head start in publishing, even factoring in Lippmann's remarkable precociousness. Their generational difference also leads to an imbalance when comparing the development of their ideas, which arose out of different historical moments. What Lippmann could pretty much take for granted in 1914—the loss of traditional authority, or the emergence of "modernity" (to rely on a shorthand term)—Dewey in the 1890s would have needed to take some pains to work out and explain to his readers.[7]

Following a chronological organization, I trace Dewey's developing ideas about the public and politics in the late 1880s and 1890s, then move to his growing interest in pedagogic theory around the turn of the century, and end the first section with a look at his ambitious *Democracy and Education* (1916). This classic Progressive text will function as a hinge as I examine in the second section Lippmann's prewar writing (including books published in 1913, 1914, and 1915). I next turn briefly to Dewey and Lippmann's wartime essays in the *New Republic*, where they were pretty much on the same page (literally), both endorsing Wilson's foreign policies and deploring the curtailing of domestic civil liberties that accompanied the war effort. In the third and concluding section, having taken the long view, I then address Lippmann and Dewey's 1920s ruminations on the public.[8]

I

In an excited memo (April 22, 1889) to his University of Michigan colleague Henry Carter Adams, John Dewey explained what was at stake in the *Thought News* project he had recently embarked upon:

> That which finally touches everybody is the public thing—politics—the state of the social organism. The newspaper in giving publicity to public matters (not for reform, or for any other purpose excepting that it is its business to sell facts) becomes the representative of public interest. . . . No paper can afford now to tell the truth about the actual conduct of the city's business. But have a newspaper whose *business*, i.e. whose livelihood, was to sell intelligence, and it couldn't afford anything else, any more than any genuine business can afford to sell spurious goods.[9]

As I discussed in the introduction, Dewey saw *Thought News* as embodying an ethics of democracy whereby the nation as a social organism would be enriched by "publicity," which Dewey equated to disseminating facts. Oddly, for Dewey the commercial aspect of the news venture freed it from bias and dishonesty, so that the political business of selling "intelligence," like any "genuine business," simply could not survive if it traded in "spurious" products. For such an economic analogy to work, Dewey had to assume that Americans were smart consumers, that whether goods or facts were genuine or worthless would always be perfectly obvious on the face of things for both buyer and seller. (His trust is a bit ironic given that a major thrust of Progressivism was to regulate deceptive sales practices.) Obviously there would be no need for persuasion in this seamless transaction of commodities or thought, much the way that Edward Bellamy simply banished advertising from his utopia *Looking Backward* (1888). This bestselling novel was a favorite of Dewey, who later deemed it one of the most important American books ever published.[10]

In the years to follow, partly in response to the fiasco that the *Thought News* endeavor turned into, Dewey amended his assumptions about the transparency of social facts and the public's ability to consume them without guidance. But such revision took time, given the philosopher's profound faith in America as a unified organism. In his essay "Christianity and Democracy" (delivered 1892, published 1893), for instance, Dewey offered this account of truth:

> It [truth] is freed only when it moves in and through this favored individual to his fellows; when the truth which comes to consciousness in one, extends and distributes itself to all so that it becomes the Common-wealth, the Republic, the public affair. . . . It is in the community of truth thus established that the brotherhood, which is democracy, has its being. . . . It is no accident that the growing organization of democracy coincides with the rise of science, including the machinery of telegraph and locomotive for distributing truth. (EW 3:8–9)

In his characteristic fashion, always mixing description with prescription, Dewey moves rapidly in a single sentence from religious revelation to national politics. These two are linked, as his pun "common-wealth" suggests, by the presumed identity between Christian brotherhood and an equally rich democratic brotherhood. Truth, the public, democracy, the republic, and Christianity all stand for one and the same. But the final sentence of this passage signals something of a shift from his previous thinking, since the sharing that constitutes democracy is no longer static and self-evident, but depends on a "growing organization" that Dewey associates with scientific innovation. Even though he does not go on to articulate exactly how the telegraph and the locomotive ipso facto distribute truth, his reference to technologies of communication and transportation at least grounds his metaphysics in some material mode of organization. News, even or especially "thought news," requires a packaging and delivery system, what he suggestively calls "machinery."

We can see how this machinery began to figure into Dewey's account of the American public by turning to another early essay, "Austin's Theory of Sovereignty" (1894), a little-noted work (perhaps because it was ostensibly a book review) that was one of Dewey's longest and most explicit excursions into political theory (EW 4:70–90).[11] As in the case of "The Ethics of Democracy" (discussed in the introduction), Dewey's argument here was similarly galvanized by his reaction against an opponent of American democracy. This time Dewey's nemesis was not Sir Henry Maine, but another British jurist, John Austin, whose early nineteenth-century legal positivism posed a direct threat to Dewey's belief in the organic unity of the United States. Since Austin's subject was sovereignty, that is, how to locate and define the authority of the state, this is an especially intriguing essay because Dewey so rarely confronted this key question head on. Distinguishing between positive and moral law, Austin insisted that the former depends on the force of command, arguing further that such sanctioned sovereignty can only reside in a very limited number, the legislators who make the laws, precisely because the body politic as a whole cannot be definitely enumerated. In effect Austin dismissed the concept of a ruling public as a fiction without any empirical basis, akin to Rousseau's overly vague notion of a "general will."

As we might expect, Dewey right off the bat rejects the distinction between moral and positive law, but perhaps more telling is his realization that Austin's theory remains "of special interest in this country" (76) because it challenges the very possibility of popular sovereignty. Dewey's most pointed defense of an exceptional American democracy is not theoretical, but practical. "To one surrounded with institutions of a 'popular" character," he contends, "accustomed, almost every day, to see government affected and controlled by various agencies of clamor, mass meeting, petition and newspaper writing" (76–77), it is not clear that "this inability of a body numerically uncertain to express itself" automatically meant that it could not have "the force of a command" (77). With that happy phrase *agencies of clamor*, Dewey pinpoints how the machinery of public opinion might indeed control and affect government, and therefore secure sovereignty above and beyond those few who govern. Sovereignty, Dewey goes on to argue, resides in public institutions, which he concedes (contra Rousseau's belief in a general will) must be linked to "definite and definable modes of expression" or "operation" (90).

Here is where Dewey's essay ends, by insisting on specific modes of expression, no longer simply undifferentiated organic unity, but then he characteristically refuses to spell out any of these institutions. The only clue we have is the wonderful *agencies of clamor*, which is not exactly a flattering way to describe how public opinion works. Between positive command and unruly clamor, Dewey was faced with figuring out a middle ground to allow for some definable and definite organization of democracy and social intelligence that could effectively and rationally disclose and distribute the truth. That is one reason that by the mid-1890s he increasingly turned his attention to public education as a primary way of guiding an American public. "Education," he said bluntly in "My Pedagogic

Creed" (1897), "is the fundamental method of social progress and reform" (EW 5:93). While education as a definable set of institutions bears an uncomfortably close resemblance to propaganda as a mode of indoctrination, for Dewey the crucial difference resided in whether learning was primarily inner- or outer-directed —not such a clear distinction to maintain, as we will see.

Dewey's growing interest in the practice and theory of pedagogy during this decade derived from multiple sources, including his move away from Christian brotherhood to entertain more secular concepts of association and his gradual abandoning of Hegelian idealism in favor of a more flexible pragmatism that emphasized experimentation and the contingency of values. If we shift from Dewey's evolving philosophy to his active engagement in social reform, then his strong reaction to the Pullman Strike in 1894 can also help explain his increasing focus on education. Even though the strike was broken with the arrest of Eugene V. Debs and other leaders, Dewey took away from this dramatic defeat one of his signature "make lemonade from lemons" lessons. He wrote his wife, Alice, that the violence and suffering of the strike were worth it, since they provided "the stimulus necessary to direct attention, and it might easily have taken more to get the social organism thinking."[12] Although he was still imagining the nation as a single "social organism," Dewey here at least acknowledged that this organism is not entirely self-motivated, but needs prodding to get it "thinking." Turning to Dewey's research in development psychology, I might even cite his pioneering 1896 essay, "The Reflex Arc Concept in Psychology" (EW 5:96–109), which challenged the prevailing stimulus-response model to argue that a child's interplay with her environment works more as a circuit or feedback loop than in a unilateral direction. If I substitute *student* for child and *school* for environment, we quickly find ourselves in the field of education.

Presumably the major impetus for Dewey's concentration on public education was the fact that in 1894 he moved from the University of Michigan to the University of Chicago, where he headed not only the Department of Philosophy, but also the Department of Pedagogy. From the start of his tenure at Chicago the two academic disciplines were completely intertwined in his mind, so much so that he wrote Alice in the fall of 1894, "I sometimes think I will drop teaching philosophy directly, and teach it via *pedagogy*."[13] His dual positions enabled him to put theory into practice by starting the Laboratory School, his famous experiment in education that in turn spurred new ideas based on his observations and interactions with the children enrolled in the school.

As this brief reference to the reflex arc essay suggests, with Dewey categories of knowledge always remained remarkably fluid. Whether he began with aesthetics, psychology, theology, politics, pedagogy, ethics, or epistemology, he frequently ended up in the same place: a meditation on American democracy, his insistent theme or "god-term," as Kenneth Burke might have called it, a way of generalizing a wide array of particulars with seemingly infinite variations. That is why any specific path taken by scholars to address the question of publics and public opinion for Dewey feels arbitrary.

In one of the most rigorous and sustained examinations of Dewey's political philosophy, for instance, Matthew Festenstein found the key to be Dewey's ethics, arguing persuasively that at the center of his understanding of politics was "an ethical account of individual self-realization through participation in collective forms of life."[14] To support this critical insight, Festenstein cited a passage from the early *Outlines of a Critical Theory of Ethics* (1891) that Dewey set off in uppercase: "IN THE REALIZATION OF INDIVIDUALITY THERE IS FOUND ALSO THE NEEDED REALIZATION OF SOME COMMUNITY OF PERSONS OF WHICH THE INDIVIDUAL IS A MEMBER; AND, CONVERSELY, THE AGENT WHO DULY SATISFIES THE COMMUNITY IN WHICH HE SHARES, BY THAT SAME CONDUCT SATISFIES HIMSELF" (EW 3:322). This idea, clearly inspired by Emerson, recurred as a mantra with various iterations over the next sixty years, suggesting that for Dewey "a good" that is "realized by the will of one is made not private but public," and therefore by this reciprocal process becomes a common good.[15]

To grasp more precisely how Dewey construed democratic publics as emerging from negotiations between self and society, we need to look closely at his Progressive theories of education rather than analyze his more abstract ethics or psychology. Dewey's views on pedagogy mark his clearest and greatest impact on American culture at large, although Dewey the lifelong academic never attained the cultural and political influence that Walter Lippmann was able to wield through the press. Yet within a year after founding the Laboratory School, his ideas carried sufficient weight for him to issue "My Pedagogic Creed" in a national journal widely read by thousands of educators, most of whom had never heard of a reflex arc.

In addition to helping Dewey rapidly attain cultural prominence, his pedagogical theorizing carried certain advantages over more direct and explicit political theorizing. While Dewey did not make any sharp distinction between children and adults in terms of cognitive or moral potential, he saw children as plastic and more open to positive change and new ideas than were adults, whose habits had already hardened. Second, as an institution the school for Dewey represented a "simplified social life" (EW 5:87, "My Pedagogic Creed") that grew naturally out of home life, mediating between values learned in the family and social values at large. The school's simplified or purified environment therefore held great promise for experimental reform, especially as it was partially removed from the pressures of industrial capitalism. Refusing to limit public education to a strictly utilitarian, technical function that would merely perpetuate the status quo, Dewey in this regard consistently rejected both occupational training and studies in citizenship as overly narrow ways to prepare children for their futures.

Since "My Pedagogic Creed" is less a coherent argument than a series of pithy (for Dewey) declarations grouped under five general "articles" of belief, it is relatively easy to locate passages that have particular implications for his notions of democracy. Early in article I, Dewey proposed that education has two sides, the psychological and the sociological, and he insisted that the psychological is the basis, so that only if the pedagogical process coincides with the individual child's activity will it gain "a leverage." This curious word borrowed from physics was one of Dewey's favorites, showing up over and over in his work. In a letter (June 3, 1891) to James about *Thought News*, for instance, he asserted that "intellectual forces" would get their "physical leverage in the telegraph and printing press,"[16] and in a subsequent pedagogical tract, "The Child and the Curriculum" (1902), he contended that however important as a starting point, a child's "interests in reality are but attitudes toward possible experiences; they are not achievements; their worth is in the leverage they afford, not in the accomplishment they represent" (MW 2:280). In all three cases, *leverage* was Dewey's preferred term for a manifest influence or power put to effective use for the common good, as opposed to the child's own intrinsic capabilities, which to grow need to be "stimulated and controlled" through "the life of the community" (EW 5:88, "My Pedagogic Creed").

But what did Dewey exactly mean by "control"? In "The Child and the Curriculum" he explicitly rejected the notion of "guidance" as a form of "external imposition," defining its work instead as *freeing the life-process for its own most adequate fulfillment*" (MW 2:281, emphasis in original). In other words, as he explained in his credo, "The teacher is not in the school to impose certain ideas or to form certain habits in the child, but there as a member of the community to select the influences which shall affect the child and to assist him in properly responding to these influences" (EW 5:88, "My Pedagogic Creed"). Focusing on the interaction between child and teacher, Dewey sketched out a two-stage process: the teacher first selects certain influences in keeping with that particular child's interests, and then helps him respond "properly" to these influences. Less an individual in her own right, the teacher as a member of the community represents social life; therefore the influences she selects are also socially mediated, however tailored to the specific psychological interests and needs of the pupil, whose responses must then be interpreted by the teacher to assure maximum self-realization.

What is missing in this pedagogic model? Leaving aside the question of how to determine what is "proper," Dewey hardly touched on the child's interactions with other children. Even though in *The School and Society* (1899, MW 1:1–109), Dewey's famous account of the Laboratory School, he described how students formed teams to work on solving problems together, his emphasis was on how each individual possesses a strength or talent that contributes to the overall solution, not on any group dynamics themselves. It is striking in this book and in his other education essays of this period how frequently Dewey referred to "the child" in the singular and hardly ever to "children" plural, even when he imagined the activity of play. Community for Dewey meant the social life already in place, not the associations built and shared among pupils. Because his ethical imperative was the democratic self-realization of each individual, the student remained a psychological entity plugged into the social organism only by way of the mediation of an impersonal teacher who seeks to discover and adapt a distinctive set of influences or "social situations" for each of her charges. The student is unique but, paradoxically, like everybody else in this respect, while the undifferentiated school faculty simply belong to the commons.

Other related questions, both practical and theoretical, follow from this model, as a closer look at "The Child and the Curriculum" suggests. Arguing that the opposition between the "old education," which emphasized traditional curricular content, and the "new education," which emphasized the student's individual development, was a false binary, Dewey neatly collapsed the two, showing how one must entail the other. But he was so intent on overcoming dualism, here and elsewhere, that his rendering of the dilemma risked oversimplification, replicating the very either-or mentality that he sought to defeat. "There are those who see no alternative between forcing the child from without, or leaving him entirely alone" (MW 2:282), he explained, only to show that personal growth depends on particular knowledge of the world. Subject matter serves as a particular phase or stage in the child's experience.

Yet this sensible conclusion did not really probe or engage any dialectical relation between external ("from without") and internal, but simply asserted their integration as a given. Unable to fully conceive of a self always already social (as George Herbert Mead sought to articulate in some detail), Dewey took for granted as a starting point the opposition between the sociological and the psychological—the latter being his consistent origin and end. As a result, each of his two poles of analysis, child and curriculum, remained a static, homogenized monolith. For example, he never discussed how a curriculum is constituted beyond assuming that disciplines or branches of learning possess some inarguable permanence, what he called the "formulated wealth of knowledge" or "race-experience" (MW 2:291, "The Child and the Curriculum").[17] This last phrase curiously echoes Matthew Arnold's fixation on cultural authority, although presumably Arnold would not have endorsed cooking as a way to teach chemistry, as Dewey did. Yet Dewey's pragmatism tended to blind him to matters of ideological strife, or at least allowed him to mainly overlook contentious problems. There certainly were strains and debates in America circa 1900 about what to include or exclude in the school curriculum, tensions that Dewey simply ignores here.

On the other side, the side of the child, I detect a similar inflexibility in Dewey's approach. He passionately insisted that subject matter "must be restored from which it has been abstracted," so that it will become "*psychologized*; turned over, translated into the immediate and individual experiencing within which it has its origin and significance" (MW 2:285, "The Child and the Curriculum," emphasis in original). This is an admirable goal, no doubt, but practically speaking, how would a teacher standing in front of a classroom of twenty-five students eager (for the sake of argument) to learn about the Civil War go about imparting twenty-five different lessons on the subject depending on the experience and interests of each individual? And even if this were possible, would not such an approach atomize the classroom, isolate students from one another rather than encourage them to collaborate in learning and to share their insights?

For all of Dewey's talk of social life at the heart of his educational theories, there is something oddly vague and abstract about his construing of community, which he constantly referred to, but did not vividly render. Why is this so? One clue can be found in another brief declaration from his educational credo. Before going on to praise "the image" as "the great instrument of instruction," Dewey first turned his attention to language, which he described as "the device for communication; it is the tool through which one individual comes to share the ideas and feelings of others" (EW 5:90, "My Pedagogic Creed"). Admittedly this bland insight belongs to an early work aimed at a general audience, but looking high and low throughout his entire oeuvre, I am hard-pressed to find any detailed discussion of metaphor, ambiguity, rhetorical tropes, conventions of meaning, or how language does (or does not) materially work as a "device" or "tool."[18]

Dewey's thin instrumental view of language is not very illuminating. Jürgen Habermas, by contrast, in trying to articulate a basis for deliberative democracy, devoted two thick volumes to spelling out an elaborate account of communicative action drawing on a multitude of twentieth-century language theorists. And if we might be inclined to let Dewey off the hook by thinking that no American pragmatist before Richard Rorty seriously attended to the role of language, consider the complex semiotics of Peirce (one of Dewey's teachers at Johns Hopkins) and the equally complex social dynamics of "the vocal gesture" elaborated by Mead (Dewey's student at Michigan and his friend and colleague at Chicago).

Without a nuanced perspective on language, accounts of communication will tend toward abstraction, as Dewey's often did.[19] If we jump forward a decade to the eve of America's entry into World War I, we can see how Dewey was able to articulate the significance of communication more concretely and robustly in relation to his deepening conviction that education represented "the supreme human interest" for all of philosophy. Unlike his earlier piecemeal essays, his classic *Democracy and Education* (1916, MW 9:1–402) ambitiously aimed to offer a wide-ranging theory of social knowledge, including its foundations and conditions for democratic thriving, in twenty-six interlocking chapters that move (as we have come to expect) back and forth across various discrete disciplines such as ethics, psychology, epistemology, politics, the history of ideas, and sociology. It is among his greatest and most comprehensive studies. In the intervening years between his earliest forays into pedagogical theory and this mature work (his personal favorite, he would later declare), Dewey benefited greatly from the arguments of Progressive social scientists such as Edward Ross, Charles Cooley, and Mead, whose ideas were partly shaped by Dewey's influential publications during the 1890s.[20]

Progressive social science, in fact, serves as Dewey's launching pad in *Democracy and Education*. Opening on a Darwinian note, the "renewal of life by transmission," Dewey quickly converts this biological meaning of reproduction into a social one—transmission as communication—which he then connects to education. Given Dewey's tendency to rapidly link concepts across disparate fields, especially in a volume that purported to treat virtually everything under the sun, this matter of organization is telling. While his earlier theories of education were grounded in and took off from the psychological experience of the individual, Dewey here instead emphasizes from the beginning social life, which is no longer assumed to be an organic yet essentially inert given, but rather is something actively construed as a process:

> Society not only continues to exist *by* transmission, *by* communication, but it may fairly be said to exist *in* transmission, *in* communication. There is more than a verbal tie between the words common, community, and communication.

Men live in a community in virtue of the things which they have in common; and communication is the way in which they come to possess things in common . . . aims, beliefs, aspirations, knowledge—a common understanding—like-mindedness, as the sociologists say. Such things cannot be passed physically from one to another, like bricks. . . . Consensus demands communication. (MW 9:7–8)

From this promising start, Dewey turns to "Education as Direction," one of the longest and most important chapters in the book, followed by "Education as Growth"; this sequence (moving from society to self) again suggests a significant reversal of Dewey's priorities. And in *direction*, Dewey hits upon the exact same word that Wilson used to describe a political leader's relation to public opinion. Dewey prefers "direction" over social "control" because it smacks less of coercion or compulsion, which, interestingly, he explicitly associates with "systems of government and theories of the state" (MW 9:28).

Dewey's struggle in the chapter "Education as Growth" is to articulate precisely the difference between benevolent direction and coercive control, a distinction with an immediate bearing on his understanding of democracy. Arguing that direction is both spatial and temporal, a matter of focusing and ordering the activity of a subject (student), Dewey insists that "purely external direction" is therefore impossible, since the self over time is responding not only to the environment, but to its own prior accumulating dispositions. In this way Dewey seeks to counter mechanistic accounts of behavior: "The difference between an adjustment to a physical stimulus and a *mental* act is that the latter involves response to a thing in its *meaning*; the former does not," and so in the former case, "there may be training, but there is no education" (MW 9:34).[21]

While Dewey links meaning to mental acts, this mentality is not an internal, private affair, but belongs to a common mind that becomes what he calls "*the method of social control*" (MW 9:38, emphasis in original): "To have the same ideas about things which others have, to be like-minded with them, and thus to be really members of a social group, is therefore to attach the same meanings to things and to acts which others attach. Otherwise, there is no common understanding, and no community life. But in a shared activity, each person refers what he is doing to what the other is doing and *vice-versa*" (35). To illustrate his last point, Dewey then gives a number of examples heavily indebted to Mead's social psychology (a game of ball rolling, a child wanting to be fed, and so on). But whereas Mead tried to work out the precise relations and tensions among mind, self, and society, Dewey was content for the most part simply to invoke the "objective likeness of acts and the mental satisfaction found in being in conformity with others" (39).[22] Because he did not specify the tangible means by which meanings are socially negotiated, including instances of dissonance, not just consonance, his rapid back and forth synthesizing of physical activity, ideas, meaning, and community begins to seem a sleight of hand, a circular set of assertions not all that different from his 1891 declaration that the realization of individuality automatically must (somehow) entail the realization of a communal good. Although in the remainder of his study he valiantly sought to overcome a series of conventional dualisms, such as mind and world, authority and freedom, discipline and interest (the index of one edition of the book lists more than thirty of these binaries),[23] Dewey had yet to carefully articulate how democratic publics might come into being and maintain themselves. Such a consideration would require a more direct, fuller engagement with political theory rather than the more indirect route of pedagogy.

II

On July 15, 1915, the *New Republic* published an excerpt from John Dewey's latest book, followed by a thoughtful review, and then a footnote of appreciation for "Professor Dewey" penned by Walter Lippmann. The work in question was *German Philosophy and Politics* (1915, MW 8:135–204), one of many such books published at the start of the First World War by scholars (many of whom had studied in Germany) intent on explaining the peculiar characteristics of a nation engaged in brutal conflict with Britain, France, and Russia. Dewey's particular task was to make sense of an apparent contradiction between German philosophy and politics. How could a culture that produced in Immanuel Kant and his followers the most powerful and influential champions of Enlightenment freedom of thought, so the paradox goes, be dominated by the rigid and ruthless autocracy of Kaiser Wilhelm? Dewey resolved the paradox quite effortlessly by suggesting that both Kant's idealism and the kaiser's autocracy operated by a similar logic, what he called a "traffic in absolutes," so that for Kant universal freedom rested on a lifeless systematic abstraction that had little to do with the lived experience of democratic citizens.

Applauding Dewey's notion of American philosophy as a "radical experiment," Lippmann in his note cited with approval one passage in particular from *German Philosophy and Politics*: "every living thought represents a gesture made toward the world, an attitude taken to some situation in which we are implicated." He then supplemented this quintessential pragmatist insight (which echoes Emerson's great essay "Circles") with his own poignant twist, suggesting that such a "gesture can represent a compensation for a bitter reality, an aspiration unfulfilled, a habit sanctified." This was certainly not the sort of dark direction that Dewey would be inclined to take, yet it suggested how both men understood American philosophy not as a presentation of eternal truths or fixed principles, along the lines of German idealism, but rather as expressing a "human being's adjustment of his desires to his limitations," as Lippmann elaborated, although he wisely refrained from delving into any autobiographical specifics concerning the author, Dewey. As we shall see, the eloquent phrases "compensation for a bitter reality" and "an aspiration unfulfilled" may in the end tell us more about Lippmann and his philosophy than illuminate Professor Dewey's gestures.[24]

It is surprising to hear Lippmann, already a distinguished author and editor at the tender age of twenty-five, refer to reality as bitter. The precocious cultural critic had been addressing broad political questions for some time, with two influential books published in quick succession already under his belt when Dewey's first piece appeared in the *New Republic*. Scholars tend to treat Lippmann's *A Preface to Politics* (1913) and *Drift and Mastery* (1914) as a pair, with most preferring *Drift and Mastery* as the more mature and significant work, less prone to name-dropping and less enamored of the trendy new ideas of Henri Bergson and Sigmund Freud, not to mention those of William James, Gabriel Tarde, Graham Wallas (Lippmann's mentor), and a host of others. But I beg to differ. In many ways *A Preface to Politics* is the far more interesting and important of the two books, not so much for what it positively proposed in the way of Progressive reform, but rather for how it so exuberantly and intemperately thumbed its nose at received wisdom, tearing down one commonplace after another to clear the ground for a wholesale reconstruction of American politics. It therefore needs to be read with some care, not glossed over quickly in favor of *Drift and Mastery*, which in its logical plan of organization and chapter-by-chapter delineation of particular problems and familiar topics (big business, consumer affairs, the labor movement, the women's movement, scientific methods, and so on), conformed more closely to a standard political treatise.[25]

A Preface to Politics, by contrast, is more wild and unpredictable, taking surprising turns and tacks. Still vital a full century after publication, its central iconoclasm is to argue for and restore individual human agency at the center of American politics, pushing aside the rotting props of various systems—parties, ideologies, utopian schemes, moral absolutes. Challenging the system of checks and balances enshrined in the Constitution, for instance, Lippmann simply remarks that "power upsets all mechanical foresight" (14), castigating the founding fathers for naïvely contriving such a false symmetry of governing branches. Practical power, in fact, remains the one and only true standard for Lippmann, giving rise to the reign of "invisible government," an "empire of natural groups about natural leaders" (18). In a contrarian move that aimed to unsettle and scramble Progressive orthodoxy, Lippmann unabashedly applauds Tammany Hall as one great example of "invisible government," "an accretion of power around a center of influence, cemented by patronage, graft, favors, friendships, loyalties, habits,—a human grouping, a natural pyramid" (ibid.).[26]

Despite such brashness, a close reading of Lippmann's first book suggests that he was quite ambivalent about the exercise of natural power untethered to any sanctioned legislative authority. Lippmann credits Senator Albert J. Beveridge with the phrase *invisible government*, which was excerpted from the Progressive Party's Declaration of Principles issued during the election campaign of 1912: "Behind the ostensible government sits enthroned an invisible government, owing no allegiance and acknowledging no responsibility to the people. To destroy this invisible government, to dissolve the unholy alliance between corrupt business and corrupt politics is the first task of the statesmanship of the day."[27] As in the case of President Roosevelt's railing against both trusts and muckraking journalists back in 1906, the Progressive Party's attack against abuses of power centered on the legitimacy of influence, that is, who can or cannot presume to represent the people. But both Lippmann and Roosevelt seem to have grasped that without the charisma and force to back it up, sanctioned authority by itself cannot automatically translate into effective political action.

Given Lippmann's valorizing of individual agency, it comes as no surprise that Teddy Roosevelt in the young man's account assumed the stature of a "colossal" hero, the greatest American example of a natural leader, who was remarkably "sensitive to the original forces of public opinion" and who "haunt[ed] political thinking" by virtue of his energy and drive. "Government under him," Lippmann wrote, "was a throbbing human purpose" (99). Yet this was visible, perhaps all too visible, government, not the invisible sort deplored by Roosevelt. Just a few pages after praising the Tammany bosses, Lippmann would appear to have changed his mind, now indicating that "invisible government is malign." But not for the reasons we might expect, that is, not for disrupting the formal legitimacy of political systems, which he continued to mock as "the Newtonian theory of the constitution." The problem was elsewhere, in the simple fact that such power was not transparent: "what is dangerous about it is that we do not see it, cannot use it, and are compelled to submit to it" (21). Because it stayed hidden, this power worked on citizens without their knowledge or participation, and therefore could not be "harness[ed]" to "the nation's need," which (good Progressive that he was) remains "the object of democracy."

But Lippmann's distinction between formal legitimacy (not important to him) and democratic transparency (important) was difficult for him to maintain. Take, for instance, his understanding of propaganda, about which he has a fair amount to say in his first book, declaring near his conclusion that "all propaganda, is, of course, a practical tribute to the value of culture" (312). As this line indicates, Lippmann deploys the concept in its most expansive, nonpejorative (prewar) sense to mean any partisan advocacy, appreciating that exerting influence over public opinion required effective mass persuasion. "The task of reform," he remarks a few pages earlier, "consists not in presenting a state with progressive laws, but in getting the people to want them" (298). Although he sometimes chides "the reformer bound up in his special propaganda" (68) who inflexibly insists on content over method, at other times he actively praises propaganda as a mode of communication for its tendency to deviate from orthodoxy. In a fascinating discussion of Marx and his followers, for instance, Lippmann calls attention to "the importance of style, of propaganda, the popularization of ideas" (237) precisely because such reinterpreting for a wide audience of a seminal thinker like Marx prevented his theories from turning into fixed dogma. The writings of Marx then become less significant than the notions subsequently attributed to him by propagandists, who are not "automatic transmitters" (237–238). Against the certainty of an authentic or true Marx, people (presumably without their knowledge) have not been given the letter but the spirit, "living ideas," although it is a fair question whether such creative transmission, however legitimate in Lippmann's eyes, depended on a lack of transparency.

One reason that transmission was not automatic for Lippmann is that language itself remains an imperfect means of communication, "grossly inadequate," as he concedes (170). Citing Freud, Lippmann observes, "unconscious casuistry deceives us all. . . . between ourselves and our real natures we interpose that wax figure of idealizations and selections which we call our character." (By contrast, Dewey mentions Freud only four times in his collected thirty-seven volumes, and only starting in 1932; the self for Dewey always remains transparent to itself and to others.)[28] Lippmann goes on to point out self-reflexively that his own use of expressions such as *wax figure* in this analysis mistakes metaphor for reality, concluding, "all language can achieve is to act as a guidepost to the imagination enabling the reader to recreate the author's insight" (170). With these few sentences, Lippmann suggests an opacity bedeviling communication that Dewey never seriously considers, given his unwavering faith that meanings will be shared by a community of the like-minded, such as a classroom of students listening to a teacher. In Lippmann's more fraught model of edification, we should further note, his specific frame of reference for partial understanding (or misunderstanding) remains the medium of print, a "reader" trying to decipher an author's insights.

We are now in a better position to see how Lippmann and Dewey diverged on crucial matters having to do with democracy, education, and communication. Although he was anything but consistent at this very early stage of his thinking, at the center of American politics Lippmann located pragmatic power, which he saw operating in both sanctioned and indirect or hidden ways; both kinds of power effectively depended on human individual agency, getting things done, not on abstract systems. The natural leaders and groups influenced opinion and policy by persuading and transmitting beliefs to others, however imperfectly. This public in turn instructed those governing, so that the "contact with great masses of men reciprocates by educating the leader," which is the second half of the sentence I quoted near the beginning of this chapter: "to govern a democracy, you have to educate it" (116). That back and forth between governing and governed constituted democracy, which Lippmann defined in the lowercase: "There is no such thing as Democracy: there are a number of more or less democratic experiments which are not subject to wholesale eulogy or condemnation" (294). What counted for Lippmann were tangible results, grounded in the premise that the "one thing that no democrat may assume is that the people are dear good souls, fully competent for their task" (302).

For Dewey of course Democracy was spelled with a capital D. Less a form of government or even a normative ideal, democracy served as a limitless prospect calling forth the infinite growth and potential of each citizen. That was the exceptional promise of America. While this ethics of self-realization according to Dewey demanded full participation in a collective life, even after pondering this reciprocal relationship between self and society for nearly thirty years (since his 1888 essay, "The Ethics of Democracy"), he still seemed reluctant, as if by a studied refusal, to spell out the particular dynamics of this mutual interplay. As we have seen, his notion of a common mind characteristically took the form of an abstract, theological assertion. Even if no longer linked to notions of Christian brotherhood, community for Dewey remained an article of faith in the absence of a specific account of how people build and maintain associations with each other.

Social intelligence for Dewey was self-evidently organic, not actively organized, as Lippmann would have it.[29] The younger man's key term *power*, for instance, hardly ever entered the lexicon of Dewey, who preferred the word *leverage*, it would seem, because it allowed for an individual's advantage or gain over circumstances without implying one person's power over another. Such external control (as opposed to direction or guidance) threatened to violate the ethical imperative of self-realization at the heart of Dewey's understanding of democracy and education. Such an imperative outweighed other sorts of utilitarian schemes for organizing society, as Hilary Putnam trenchantly observed: "One of Dewey's fundamental assumptions is that people value growth more than pleasure."[30]

While it is common in comparing Lippmann with Dewey to deem Lippmann more individualistic, less committed to the well-being of a community, quite the opposite is true. Lippmann was more concerned with human agency than with each individual's infinite expansion, which always had to originate from within for Dewey; given Lippmann's belief that natural leaders can exert positive influence, he was quite able and willing to say in no uncertain terms what it would take to reform the commonwealth: "The politics of reconstruction require a nation vastly better educated, a nation freed from its slovenly ways of thinking, stimulated by wider interests, and jacked up constantly by the sharpest kind of criticism" (305). And anticipating the concerns of his later books published in the 1920s, Lippmann identified a crucial obstacle to such Progressive enlightenment (Dewey would soon arrive at a similar recognition): "Ours is a problem in which deception has become organized and strong; where truth is poisoned at its source; one in which the skill of the shrewdest brains is devoted to misleading a bewildered people" (105).

At this point in his career, Lippmann himself was anything but bewildered. *A Preface to Politics* gives us a very smart and very young man excitedly sharing his insights with his readers. Conceived as a preface, the book aimed to lay the groundwork for reform by knocking down stultifying conventions, rather than to offer a detailed blueprint for reconstruction. Yet given Lippmann's emphasis on natural leadership, it is not difficult to infer his overall solution: If politics is made up of "routineers" as opposed to "inventors" (like him, we presume), what needs to be done is simply to get rid of one group and replace it with the other. Yet there are passages in the book—such as the one quoted above suggesting that American politics could not so easily be reformed by a change of personnel—that indicate that power resided in structures and institutions, not just in individuals who were more or less innovative, more or less competent. As the title of his next book, *Drift and Mastery* (1914), implied, Lippmann's emphasis shifted from a binary polarizing two types of political agents to a binary indicating two opposing directions for the nation. Such a shift speaks to Lippmann's growing appreciation that "the modern world is brain-splitting in its complexity."[31] This realization paradoxically both diminished Lippmann's confidence that he could offer comprehensive solutions *and* increased his willingness to try to point the country toward mastery, not drift.

My aim here is not to examine the specifics of these proposals, which tended to be tied to particular topics and policies and thus seem somewhat dated. More at issue is Lippmann's new rhetorical stance, which was less iconoclastic than his previous study, more measured, respectful, and mature in seeking to directly weigh in on matters of state. Flushed with the success of his first book, Lippmann was no longer just coming up with brilliant insights, but saw himself as giving tangible advice, not just to readers at large, but specifically to Progressives in power. In short, he had turned himself into a political commentator, a maker of opinions aimed at influencing policy decisions.

An extended discussion in *Drift and Mastery* centered on Woodrow Wilson, for instance, reads as if it were not simply analysis *about* the president, but actually addressed *to* him, even though it was harshly critical of Wilson's New Freedom, which Lippmann dubbed "an unworthy dream" (141), especially as it neglected the role of administrative expertise and refused to engage modern complexities. Dream bigger and take charge, Mr. President, Lippmann seems to be saying. Rational enlightenment remains for Lippmann the primary path toward Progressive mastery: "You have in a very literal sense to *educate* the industrial situation, to draw out its promise, discipline and strengthen it" (165). But following this declaration with four more pages oddly apostrophizing a disembodied series of *you*'s, Lippmann signaled that it was the entire structure and system that was in need of edification, along with the people in authority who governed it, not just run-of-the-mill citizens, who somewhat receded into the background in this book.

By the time *Drift and Mastery* came out, Lippmann had already joined the editorial staff of the *New Republic*, a new journal dedicated to opinion and interpretation that quickly became the magazine of record for serious Progressives. As we have seen, Dewey also signed on as an early contributor, which encouraged him to articulate political positions and arguments more concretely than he was in the habit of doing. The journal's cultural and political influence was so great that by January 1917 Lippmann and his co-editor and co-founder, Herbert Croly, were meeting weekly with Wilson's chief adviser, Colonel Edward House, and so helping to shape national policy in person (if behind the scenes) as well as in print.[32] This is not to say that the *New Republic* was a shill for the Wilson administration; starting with a very strong enthusiasm for the decisive leadership of Teddy Roosevelt, Lippmann and his co-editors only gradually came around to Wilson, reluctantly backing his reelection in 1916 as the United States struggled to stay out of war even as it painfully inched toward intervention month by month. After America entered the conflict, both Lippmann and Dewey used the pages of the *New Republic* to support the war effort, but they decried the Wilson's administration harsh crackdown on civil liberties at home. As I previously discussed, Dewey also faced a withering series of attacks from his former student Randolph Bourne, who accused him of betraying his pragmatist philosophical principles in endorsing Wilson's war and in vainly pursuing a chimera of national unity.[33]

While Lippmann and Dewey basically appeared to be in agreement in their *New Republic* articles, it is important to appreciate how the underlying reasons for their positions differed and therefore so did the reasons for their disillusionment after the war ended. Take the question of civil liberties. In a letter to House dated October 17, 1917, Lippmann explained that "men like Prof. Dewey who represent the warmest kind of faith in the war and in the President" were so fed up with Postmaster Burleson's suppression of the socialist press that these men would actually vote the socialist ticket. But then Lippmann continued, "So far as I am concerned I have no doctrinaire belief in free speech. In the interest of the war it is necessary to sacrifice some of it. But the point is that the method now being pursued is breaking down the liberal support of the war and is tending to divide the country's articulate position into fanatical jingoism and fanatical pacifism."[34] This practical emphasis on method diverged from the more ethically inclined arguments of Dewey, who insisted in article after article that the stifling of dissent violated the core values of American democracy.[35]

It remains an open question if President Wilson believed and how he understood his own sloganeering about going to war to make the world safe for democracy. But even if benighted and blinkered, as Bourne might have it, Dewey did seem to find the defense of "Democracy" a compelling, transcendent reason to intervene in the conflict. Lippmann was another story. Years later, writing in the midst of the Second World War, Lippmann flat out asserted that the United States did not go to war to make the world safe for all democracies, nor to overthrow the kaiser and make Germany a democratic republic, nor to establish the League of Nations, but rather more simply and concretely to preserve its security. If Germany had defeated Russia, Britain, and France, it would have been very bad news for the United States, and so to protect the nation's interests the United States entered the war, even as Wilson and publicists like Creel sold the American people a high-minded but false bill of goods about democracy.[36] We might be inclined to doubt Lippmann's revisionist account, especially since it slighted his own promotional role in that sales job. In other words, Lippmann's own justifications for the war, published in the *New Republic* between 1916 and 1918, if not couched in the far cruder rhetoric of Creel and the CPI, still did echo Wilson's tendency to emphasize nationalistic ideals over practicalities. But Lippmann's tilt toward real-politik well after the fact did at least offer an alternative explanation that Dewey would not or could not entertain, either during the war or afterward.

There is no doubt that Lippmann, like Dewey, was disturbed by the crass appeals of Creel, but that does not mean he was above practicing a softer sort of propaganda linked, as he put it in *A Preface to Politics*, to broad cultural values and aimed at shaping opinion. Toward the end of the war, he signed on with the Military Intelligence Bureau as an army captain and produced leaflets urging German soldiers to surrender. Lippmann saw this position as an opportunity to engage in a kind of public diplomacy, to drastically change the attitudes of a defeated enemy toward America. He was largely motivated by his disgust at what he considered the Committee on Public Information's clueless and ineffective propaganda efforts in Europe. When he complained about this to House, the colonel told Wilson, who sided with his favorite, Creel, and asked Secretary of War Newton Baker to marginalize Lippmann's efforts: "I want to keep the matter of publicity in my own hands." As a result, Captain Lippmann ended up doing very little abroad. Pointing to Lippmann's failure, Sue Curry Jansen wittily dismissed this episode as "much adieu about very little."[37] Yet the salient point is not what Lippmann was actually able or not able to accomplish—circumstances were outside his control, after all—but rather his willingness to voluntarily take on the assignment with his eyes wide open, knowing full well what this propagandizing would inevitably entail. His disenchantment was not focused on propaganda as a mode of persuasion per se, as Jansen would have it, but rather because he had once again lost out to Creel, who at the beginning of the war had bested Lippmann in an indirect power struggle to decide the future course of the CPI.

III

After the war ended, there was plenty of blame to go around. Appalled at the draconian measures imposed on Germany in the Treaty of Versailles, the editors of the *New Republic* in May 1919 denounced Wilson's agreement and urged its rejection, finding that as it stood, it could only portend "the future specifications for revolution and war."[38] Having helped draft the Fourteen Points, Lippmann was especially stung, and he began to seriously (re)consider how in a democracy information is produced, is organized, flows, and is received. As early as 1915, in his third book, *The Stakes of Diplomacy*, Lippmann had devoted an entire chapter to public opinion, specifically how to get apathetic Americans to pay more attention to foreign affairs. He proposed, "In brief, to have public opinion there must be interest, and this can be created not by preaching but by making the subject of it part of the business of life."[39] But his solution was still relatively simple because he had not yet recognized the urgency and complexity of "the crisis of western democracy," as he would call it soon after the war ended. Whatever else can be said about the Committee on Public Information, there is no doubt that Creel's massive propagandizing did manage to make the war a part of the daily "business of life" for virtually all American citizens, but with obviously less than ideal results.

Dewey for his part located the futility elsewhere, holding war itself responsible for the catastrophe that led to millions of pointless deaths around the globe with nothing to show for all the horror. In the early 1920s, opposing the League of Nations, he hitched his wagon to the outlawry movement, a utopian scheme (not quite as farfetched as *Thought News*) that sought to reduce international conflict by legally making warfare a crime. The plan gained some support among US politicians, notably Senator William Borah, but was quickly derided by a host of commentators, including Lippmann. He attacked the plan as naïve and blind to diplomacy, a position Dewey rebutted point by point in an article published in 1923, "What Outlawry of War Is Not" (MW 15:115–121). If there was any true debate between Dewey and Lippmann, it would be on this issue of outlawry, not about the continuing vibrancy of public opinion.[40]

Just as Dewey early on sought to locate democratic prospects in the free circulation of "social facts," Lippmann three decades later began to offer his own darker reassessment of the relationship between news and democracy by way of a practical demonstration co-authored with fellow journalist Charles Merz and published as a supplement to the *New Republic* (August 4, 1920). Analyzing how the *New York Times* reported on the Russian Revolution between March 1917 and March 1920, this detailed empirical study, "A Test of the News," was accompanied by a more theoretical short book, *Liberty and the News* (1920), which consisted of two chapters previously published as articles plus an introductory chapter, "Journalism and the Higher Law," which clearly laid out what was fundamentally at stake for Lippmann in his examination of news coverage.

Sharply distinguishing between news items and editorials (which were largely excluded from their study) and steering clear of nebulous matters of interpretation to focus on "a few definite and decisive happenings about which there is no dispute," Lippmann and Merz showed in convincing detail how *New York Times* reporters gave American readers a highly inaccurate account of key aspects of the revolution.[41] The reporting had more to do with the journalists' own

hopes—namely, that the revolution would fail or was failing—than with the ver-
ifiable facts on the ground. As a method and model of rigorous analysis, "A Test
of the News" remains indispensible, but of greater interest here are the broader
implications Lippmann drew from his study, which he elaborated in *Liberty and
the News*, particularly in the first two chapters, which sketched out a diagnosis,
and the concluding chapter, which offered a few tentative solutions. Characteristically for Lippmann, these solutions are weaker and less compelling than his
presentation of the problem.

Even though *Liberty and the News* was conceived in the disillusioning wake
of the war, a close look reveals that certain important themes and preoccupa-
tions that ran throughout Lippmann's prewar writing have become amplified,
narrowed, and foregrounded in striking, sometimes contradictory ways. After
quoting a passage from the editor of America's first newspaper (1690) decrying
the spreading of "False Reports," Lippmann quickly gets down to business:

> Everywhere to-day men are conscious that somehow they must deal with
> questions more intricate than any that church or school had prepared them to
> understand. Increasingly they know that they cannot understand them if the
> facts are not quickly and steadily available. Increasingly they are baffled because
> the facts are not available; and they are wondering whether government by
> consent can survive in a time when the manufacture of consent is an unregulated
> private enterprise. For in an exact sense the present crisis of western democracy
> is a crisis in journalism.[42]

There are a number of key assumptions that undergird this dense passage,
which begins with a familiar refrain, the increasing complexity of modern life.
Despite this complexity, Lippmann presumes that the matter of "facts" is neither
an ontological nor an epistemological question, but mainly a matter of availa-
bility. Later in the book, he suggests otherwise, that information (almost always
reading and writing for him) may not be such a self-evident thing: "it is difficult
to decide just what reporting is—where in the whole mass of printed matter it
begins and ends" (81). In other words, is the difference between a "fact" and an
"opinion" always clear? This kind of epistemological puzzle would dominate the
first half of his next book, *Public Opinion*. But at this point his primary concern
centers on what happens to democracy when access is denied, or replaced by
a manufactured consent. Lippmann's crucial phrase echoes prewar muckrakers
like Ray Stannard Baker who exposed how trusts such as the railroads sought to
make or manufacture public opinion (see chapter 1). But Lippmann marks a
subtle difference, suggesting not just that certain opinions may be produced in

others, but that "consent" or agreement can be produced, so that people not only believe, but come to accept these beliefs as their own in a mockery of the consent of the governed.

It is difficult here not to think of the Committee on Public Information and George Creel, especially his mass orchestrating of compulsions that would seem to come from within each patriotic citizen. Yet unlike the CPI's wartime propaganda apparatus, these weapons of democracy were no longer manufactured, assembled, and controlled by a centralized state, for better or worse. Now information was in the hands of "unregulated private enterprise," which for Lippmann was not so much big business intent on profit, but journalists who were simply too incompetent or overwhelmed to tell the news straight. Or else they smugly assumed that they already understood what was good for their readers: "So long as there is interposed between the ordinary citizen and the facts a news organization determining by entirely private and unexamined standards, no matter how lofty, what he shall know, and hence what he shall believe, no one will be able to say that the substance of democratic government is secure" (12–13).

This is a curiously mixed position on Lippmann's part, still expressing a Progressive faith in public oversight and rational standards for governance, but also castigating the reform-minded inclinations of reporters for slanting the news. I can trace a similar narrowing of the Progressive agenda by turning to Lippmann's new understanding of "propaganda," which "especially since the outbreak of war" had taken on solely negative connotations (49–50). The word in its more restricted meaning now signified a mode of lying and deception for Lippmann, who reserved the proximate concepts of "advertisement" and "advocacy" for more benign uses (we might ask, why not "education"?). But this categorical moral distinction between the "sins" and "virtues" of the term is compromised by Lippmann's insistence, over and over again throughout the book, that the primary threat to democracy is not deliberate malfeasance on the part of journalists, but the drastic curtailing of the sort of individual agency that had figured so prominently in his thinking since A Preface to Politics. Civilization is "too extensive for any man's personal observation" (14); "nobody knows enough, or can know enough" to put a universal ideal into political practice (22); "[t]he world about which each man is supposed to have opinions has become so complicated as to defy his powers of understanding" (37); an editor "can hardly be expected to know all about everything" (46); and so on.

Such a fixation on personal limitations complicates Lippmann's brief but pivotal analysis of John Milton, John Stuart Mill, and Bertrand Russell, all proponents of classic doctrines of liberty and free speech. Such doctrines cannot be sustained, Lippmann argues, because these thinkers invariably posit some escape or "weasel clause" that allows them to make exceptions to their absolutes. Fair enough, but to explain this discrepancy between theory and practice, Lippmann speculates that the "omnipotence" denied to men "in action, nevertheless illuminates activity with a sense of utter and irresistible value" (23): hence the thirst for universals such as liberty. But why assume this is an issue of "omnipotence" and an individual one, no less? How the question of power exactly intersects with the question of knowledge, he does not make clear. In an oblique reference to liberalism's enshrining of freedom as a negative condition (e.g., freedom from restraint), Lippmann reasonably concludes that "liberty is not so much permission as it is the construction of a system of information increasingly independent of opinion" (96–97). Only by the independent search for truth, not the application of theories, would these systematically constructed facts become positively "educative"—an adjective right out of Dewey.

Yet he is hard-pressed to say how this reorganized public liberated from misleading opinion would work, given his worries about each citizen's restricted knowledge. In one of his most interesting analogies, he compares the "public affairs" of a nation to the operations of a jury, "the whole community . . . everybody who creates public sentiment—chattering gossips, unscrupulous liars, congenital liars, feeble-minded people" (39), who are compelled without clear guidelines to assess evidence and testimony much the way a newspaper reader is compelled to evaluate and assimilate the information she scans in the press. But Lippmann's comparison falls short, since he does not consider the second stage in the juridical process, when the jury begins to deliberate among themselves and share their partial impressions. Persuasion (dare we still call it propaganda?) in this regard is not strictly unilateral, streaming from reporters (or attorneys) to individuals, but becomes collectively negotiated by the jury as a group. Even a jury of misfits such as Lippmann has described might reasonably be expected to arrive at a sensible verdict once they had the chance to talk things over.

Along these same lines, Lippmann briefly acknowledges that "the ordering" of information in a newspaper "is not done by one man, but by a host of men," but then he pulls back to observe that these men "are on the whole curiously unanimous in their selection and their emphasis." Why this curiously might be so, as well as "why the editor is possessed by a particular set of ideas," Lippmann continues to ponder: it is "a difficult question in social psychology, of which no adequate analysis has been made" (48–49). Lippmann would attempt just such an analysis in *Public Opinion*. His best known work, *Public Opinion* would seem to give John Dewey a run for his money in scope and ambition, weighing in on aesthetics, morals, psychology, sociology, politics, and just about everything else in twenty-eight chapters arranged in eight sections that consolidated much of Lippmann's previous ideas on modern democracy and developed them in new directions.

What was mainly new was Lippmann's interest in epistemology, his attempt to describe, in the first four sections of *Public Opinion*, where our knowledge comes from or, as his first section famously explained this process, the relation between "The World Outside and the Pictures in Our Heads." Lippmann's epistemology has drawn the greatest attention from commentators, particularly those in communications studies; his thinking in this regard might very well strike a familiar chord, especially for anyone well versed in the neopragmatist and poststructuralist theories of the past four decades. "For the most part we do not first see, and then define, we define first and then see," he claims and then continues, "in the great blooming, buzzing confusion of the outer world we pick out what our culture has already defined for us, and we tend to perceive that which we have picked out in the form stereotyped for us by our culture."[43]

While this line of neopragmatist inquiry might seem fairly standard today, Lippmann's great insight that "opinion" is always already mediated by cultural and ideological structures was quite original and striking in 1922. But at this point in his argument, we still have not learned much about the "public" aspect of this inevitably prepackaged knowledge. Focused on how "signs stand for ideas," which "we fill out with our stock of images" (88), Lippmann's epistemology seems largely derived from William James's psychology of perception. James is the authority most cited in the first half of the book, as if Lippmann dusted off his old Harvard class notes in an attempt to update and apply his mentor's insights to make sense of a disenchanted postwar modernity.[44]

Two ironies in particular attend this effort. What readers mostly take away from this half of the book are not nuances, but a series of slogans and pithy formulations: "stereotypes," "pictures in our heads," and "pseudo-environments," among others. Yet the thrust of Lippmann's argument here was to question this kind of linguistic shortcut as impeding serious independent thinking; for somebody highly suspicious of sloganeering, Lippmann was adept at coining and popularizing such phrases, which quickly threaten to turn into tyrannical intellectual clichés of their own.[45] Second, and perhaps more important, in his concocting of a philosophy that combined and synthesized so many different disciplines, "Analytic psychology and social history" and "Psychology" and "Anthropology," to quote one typical passage (189) (never mind the specific issue at hand), Lippmann appeared to lay claim to being an all-knowing expert on everything. But when he turned to politics in the second half of *Public Opinion*, he explicitly rejected this pretense as American democracy's myth of the "omnicompetent citizen," yet another of his memorable catchphrases.

At the risk of downplaying Lippmann's capacious speculations on the foundations of knowledge, the remainder of this discussion will concentrate on his political analysis in sections 5–8 of *Public Opinion*. How he shifted to this firmer, more familiar ground is itself quite telling. In a chapter titled "The Transfer of Interest," he seeks to show how "self-interest" gets transformed into a larger body of opinion, which he calls "a common will," although he tries to steer clear of the metaphysical, organic overtones associated with a collective soul or a national mind (as Dewey was in the habit of invoking). Asking, "how is it that a vague idea so often has the power to unite deeply felt opinion?" (203), he offers a historical illustration close to his heart, claiming that "without cable, radio, telegraph, and daily press, the experiment of the Fourteen Points would have been impossible" (207–208).

But Lippmann was no technological determinist, and his riveting insider analysis centers less on channels of communication than on the content of the document, which he examines point by point, showing how and why certain individual words were carefully deployed or avoided, even though he does not say that he helped draft the text, assuming perhaps that many of his readers would already know this fact. The goal of the Fourteen Points, according to Lippmann, was to set aside differences to create "the much grander spectacle of a public worldwide debate," yet despite the linguistic care taken to manufacture the grounds for such a public debate, in the end the signers of the Treaty of Versailles could only "realize those expectations which were held by those of their countrymen who wielded the most power at home" (216). Lippmann thus converted a devastating personal disappointment into a lesson illustrating how an "experiment" designed to foster a common international will ("The Rights of Humanity") crumbled in the face of more particular and more forceful national wills shaped by influential insiders within each of the victorious countries.

With that reference to wielding power, Lippmann reintroduces his most persistent and pressing concern. The rest of this section examines how power and privilege in a complex modern democracy necessarily restrict everyday citizens to the role of agreeing or disagreeing with their leaders via a simple binary of yes or no. While Lippmann connects this reduced role to the limitations of inevitably partial knowledge that he sketches out in the first half of the book, the specific implications for democracy he addresses by way of a historical analysis of early national politics. Here is where "the omnicompetent citizen" comes in. According to Lippmann, "the early democrats insisted that a reasoned righteousness welled up spontaneously of the mass of men" (257), assuming (following Aristotle) that citizens must directly know each other's characters in order to govern themselves. And so the founders endorsed a doctrine of popular sovereignty based on rural townships where "not only was the individual citizen fitted to deal with all public affairs, but he was consistently public-spirited and endowed with unflagging interest" (273). As long as twentieth-century Americans still held themselves to this impossible ideal—recall how many times in *Liberty and the News* we are reminded that nobody knows everything—and still clung to this false promise, democracy must remain a sham.

The rest of Lippmann's historical explanation, which slips from describing a doctrine to describing conduct, is remarkable enough to quote at some length:

> This meant that men formed their picture of the world outside from the unchallenged pictures in their heads. These pictures came to them well stereotyped by their parents and teachers, and were little corrected by their own experience. . . . Most voters lived their whole lives in one environment, and with nothing but a few feeble newspapers, some pamphlets, political speeches, their religious training, and rumor to go on. . . . The number of public opinions based on any objective report was very small in proportion to those based on casual fancy.
>
> And so for many different reasons, self-sufficiency was a spiritual ideal in the formative period. The physical isolation of the township, the loneliness of the pioneer, the theory of democracy . . . all converged to make men believe that out of their own consciences they must extricate political wisdom. (273–274)

This is a questionable assessment, to say the least. Were Americans ever as benighted as all this, at once homespun provincial simpletons and yet so self-sufficient? Even if we leave aside the political leaders and thinkers (Madison, Jefferson, Adams, Hamilton) who powerfully shaped public opinion, Lippmann's account borders on caricature. He needs to posit such a prelapsarian past in order to sharpen the contrast between a public based on intimate personal contact among individuals (all intensely civic-minded, naturally) and a contemporary public too large, distracted, and atomized to make sense of politics and too overwhelmed by the complexities of modern life, especially its confusing eddies of misinformation, stereotypes, persuasion, and "official propaganda," which he now defines as a "more or less perfect organization of perception" (208).

But suppose that this doctrine of omnicompetence, this burden of total knowledge, never existed in the first place? This was Lippmann's own myth attributed to others. Nowhere does he cite Thomas Jefferson or any other early leader as claiming that citizens needed to master all aspects of public affairs; they only needed to pay attention. And such attention was clearly mediated, whether in 1790 or 1920. Tom Paine, for one, might have differed about the minimal role Lippmann assigned to "some pamphlets." It is especially disconcerting that one of the most astute theorists on news and newspapers would offer a somewhat misleading account of their "feeble" significance in the early republic, when circulated print media clearly played an important role during the American Revolution, in some ways anticipating the same kind of innuendos, scoops, and leaks that we have come to associate with certain strands of modern journalism. Recall the 1690 newspaper he himself cited in *Liberty and the News*, which decried the spread of false reports. On the brighter side, such Enlightenment publications effectively created a bourgeois public sphere that allowed strangers living miles apart to anonymously share and debate their views with one another, as Habermas and Michael Warner, among others, have argued in convincing detail: multiple authors, multiple readers, building and sustaining a shifting community of interests out of which an imagined publicness emerges.[46]

Understood as a discursive formation, a public or publics, in other words, need not depend, cannot depend, upon a solitary citizen or groups of citizens trying to understand and keep track of everything. Such a dubious model, channeling all information through a single point of reception, assumes that at the core of democratic deliberation a unitary subject is situated in an already established set of social arrangements. Lippmann construed the goal of this deliberation to be the solving of political problems, an assumption Dewey found too limiting. In the absence of any transcendental general will organizing politics, moreover, the citizen for Lippmann was basically on her own. He most frequently figured this subject as a reader scanning printed news, part of the great emphasis on visuality running throughout his book. It is no coincidence that the term *stereotype* originally referred to a metal plate cast from a printing surface that could make multiple copies of a text. In his penultimate section on the press, Lippmann turned directly to scenarios of print circulation, distinguishing between truth and news (as he had not done in his previous work) and concluding with some practical suggestions for producing more effective "organized intelligence," most notably greater transparency and a greater reliance on expertise, core Progressive values.

Who would be Lippmann's ideal omnicompetent citizen? Why Walter Lippmann himself, of course, and if he cannot adequately do the job, nobody can. He says as much in his next book, *The Phantom Public*, which was more polemical and brisker than *Public Opinion* (no excursions into epistemology or American history, for one thing), but darker in its implications. In the first chapter, "The Disenchanted Man," Lippmann claims sympathy for the baffled and apathetic individual who has been "saddled with an impossible task" and "asked to practice an unattainable ideal": "I find it so myself for, although public business is my main interest and I give most of my time to watching it, I cannot find time to do what is expected of me in the theory of democracy; that is, to know what is going on and to have an opinion worth expressing on every question which confronts a self-governing community."[47] The human agency so celebrated in A *Preface to Politics* is still valorized, but now by way of negation and limitation.

Pushed to its logical extreme in this book, Lippmann's assumption that democratic doctrine burdens unitary subjects with the impossible task of containing all knowledge renders the conventional notion of a public, not just public opinion, something of a phantom. In *Public Opinion* he still maintained that a common interest, understood as a fluid set of political and social arrangements, could be aroused and managed by "insiders" or experts with access to power, if not by "outsiders," the public at large. But such a prospect appeared dimmer in *The Phantom Public*, moving him closer it would seem to the position of political scientist Arthur Bentley, who well before the war argued that there was no such thing as a common will or good, only special interests controlled by various pressure groups exerting influence on specific issues (see chapter 1). But while Lippmann recognized this "deep pluralism" (97) at the center of democratic governance, he refused to accept the inevitability of relentless partisanship; and so increasingly he advocated for impartial expertise, which his critics crudely stereotype as a form of elitism. They are fond of quoting provocative passages such as this: "The public must be put in its place, so that it may exercise its own powers, but no less and perhaps even more, so that each of us may live free of the trampling and the roar of a bewildered herd" (155).[48]

But Lippmann meant *place* precisely, just as he deployed the spatial metaphors of *inside* and *outside* precisely in a process of understanding where power is located in a democracy. A close examination of the second section of the book, hardly ever touched upon by commentators, reveals his rather rigorous account of how the public can indeed exercise its own powers, which for Lippmann centered on the need to "purge itself of the self-interested groups who become confused with it" (112). In a brilliant stroke Lippmann observes, "there is only one common interest: that all special interests shall act according to settled rule" (106). What may seem like a narrow formalism actually opens up a series of strenuous and exhilarating tests of this rule that allow, indeed compel, citizens to engage in debate. One test, for example, would gauge the extent to which a partisan would be willing to submit his claims to inquiry. These deliberations restore a "true public" (112) constituted by outsiders who may not be competent to weigh in on the substance or intrinsic merit of policies, but who can determine "whether the actors in the controversy are following a settled rule of behavior or their own arbitrary desires" (144). Such adjudication requires paying close attention to the behavior of the insiders ("sampling," Lippmann called it) and diligently applying criteria to assess their behavior—becoming enlightened bullshit detectors, in short, which is no mean or trivial task.

Some of the more technical aspects of this argument in *The Phantom Public* appealed to Dewey, as we will soon see, but in his *New Republic* reviews of two of Lippmann's books, he confined himself to admiring summary, followed by a few modest caveats. Calling *Public Opinion* "perhaps the most effective indictment of democracy as currently conceived ever penned," praise he repeated near the end, Dewey rehearsed without reservation Lippmann's (dubious) account of eighteenth-century political ideals, which led to a "break down in the theory of a government worked by spontaneous public opinion." As Dewey framed it, the central problem was how to disentangle "the dogma that individuals can of themselves get the knowledge required to render democratic government effective and competent" from "the need that every human being rise to his fullest stature."[49] This last clause tells us more about Dewey than Lippmann. As I have suggested throughout this chapter, Dewey more than Lippmann defined democracy in terms of such profound self-realization, although Lippmann in describing the motives of the founders did remark, "They had themselves felt the aspiration of democracy, which is ever so much deeper, more intimate and more important than any theory of government" (*Public Opinion*, 256).

Dewey's long review of *The Phantom Public* was similarly filled with glowing respect. But because Lippmann had seemed to shut the door on Dewey's most cherished value, insisting early in the book that "the usual appeal to education as the remedy for the incompetence of democracy" was "barren," the philosopher was harder-pressed to make lemonade from Lippmann's sour lemons. Dewey certainly appreciated that sourness, quoting, for example, Lippmann's acerbic assertion that "the making of a general will out of a multitude is not a Hegelian mystery," but rather practically depends on "the use of symbols which assemble emotions after they have been detached from their ideas." But Lippmann pitched his argument too generally, Dewey suggested, sometimes taking "an accident for the essence." In other words, "the inherent problems and dangers" of modernity might extend well beyond the "weakness of democracy," a system of governance whose problems in Dewey's view were perhaps "symptomatic rather than causal."[50]

But symptomatic of what? Delivered as a series of lectures before appearing in print in 1927, Dewey's *The Public and Its Problems* offered one sort of answer, strongly prompted by Lippmann's two books but drastically reconstructing both Lippmann's ideas as well as his own previous understanding of politics.[51] Even by the standards of Dewey's notoriously awkward prose, it comes across at first glance as a "maddeningly obscure book," to cite the view of James Carey, who would seem to do us a favor by "mercifully" presenting only a rousing snippet of the concluding three pages rather than engaging with Dewey's full argument.[52] But Carey's little joke backfires, since how can we accept that Dewey in effect won the "acute conflict" with Lippmann, as Carey would have it, if he did not even bother to closely follow what Dewey was saying? We might very well prefer where Dewey ended up, as most commentators do, duplicating Dewey's habit of frequently substituting upbeat exhortation—wishful thinking—for detailed analysis. Here and in his other works, all too often Dewey seemed more intent on talking about philosophical ideas than in constructing rigorous philosophical arguments. But we need to figure out how *The Public and Its Problems* arrived at its conclusions, especially since in the first two chapters of the book (infrequently discussed), Dewey did attempt to lay the foundations for a new way of construing the public, well before the question of democracy was even introduced.[53]

As if to correct the mistake he made years earlier in pursuing the *Thought News* project, Dewey begins by insisting that facts are never self-evident but must be interpreted, so that a gap opens up between the practice of politics and political theory. Against abstruse theories of the state that all depend on some abstract causality to explain how a state comes into being, Dewey shifts "in a flank movement" (241) to a pragmatic definition based strictly on consequences. Here he follows Lippmann in *Public Opinion*, who urged that the "origin of government" was less important than understanding "processes and results" (312). As Dewey posits, there is a transaction between A and B. If the consequences of that exchange or "conversation extend beyond the two concerned, that they affect the welfare of many others, the act acquires a public capacity."[54] If not, the transaction is private, which, like "public," does not operate as an essential category, but serves as a fluid, relational concept based on function. What is refreshing about this approach is that Dewey, spurred on by Lippmann, seems to abandon, once and for all, his long-standing belief in organic unity: no Hegelian mysteries needed. Dewey's distinction between direct and indirect consequences, moreover, takes its inspiration from an early passage in *The Phantom Public* where Lippmann argued that a public official was better "placed" to understand and address a political problem than "a reader of newspapers" (there is that trope again) because this official, holding an "indirect" view, remained "external" to the problem (72).

In a reverse engineering of Lippmann's insight, Dewey posits a primary distinction between direct and indirect consequences, out of which emerge third-party officials or officers who collectively constitute the state: "The public consists of all those who are affected by the indirect consequences of transactions to such an extent that it is deemed necessary to have those consequences systematically cared for. Officials are those who look out for and take care of the interests thus affected" (245–246). Given Dewey's characteristically attenuated grasp of agency, signaled by passive voice constructions such as "deemed," we might be inclined to dismiss such a strange proposition. But it does have the merit of allowing Dewey to imagine associations of people by way of function, not metaphysics. Defining the state as "the organization of the public effected through officials for [its] protection" (256), Dewey is then able to more specifically describe "the democratic state" (with a lowercase *d*), which he argues is a mode of governance in which the public recognizes itself as such: the greater the recognition, the stronger the democracy.

It might be objected that all Dewey did was smuggle into this argument his familiar ethics of self-realization, now magically applied to a personified, transcendental Public (with a capital *P*). Yet that is not necessarily so, since the public's "discovery and identification of itself" (351), as Lippmann demonstrated, can operate by a series of analytic rules and tests. But instead of articulating, along the lines of Lippmann, what such self-conscious recognition might entail, Dewey in the third and fourth chapters of *The Public and Its Problems* swerves into historical analysis: an account of the development of political democracy, both in contingent practice and in ideas (Locke, Smith, Mill, Wallas). This is followed by a loose account of the broad historical and technological forces or causes—note that he is no longer talking about consequences—that have contributed to the "eclipse of the public," as he calls it. In the fourth chapter, explicitly acknowledging Lippmann's influence in a footnote (308), Dewey seems to outdo Lippmann in his own harsh assessment of a befuddled contemporary public, although of course we intuit that he does so in order to restore and celebrate the "Great Community" in the final two chapters of the book. And so in tracing the fate of a democratic public, Dewey has given us a three-act drama: rise (first two chapters), then fall (middle two), and resurrection (last two).

With his introduction of the concept of community, Dewey drifts from analysis to amelioration, and therefore seems to go astray. The fourth chapter closes with a passionate call for communication, which he claims "can alone create a great community" (324). But what happened to the state? It seems to have become eclipsed, along with the public; now "government exists to serve its community" (327), a decisive shift from his earlier assertion that the state exists to serve its public. This slippage suddenly triggers an odd reversion on Dewey's part to ideals that he held since the 1880s.[55] "Wherever there is conjoint activity whose consequences are appreciated as good by all singular persons who take part in it," he claims, "there is in so far a community. The clear consciousness of a communal life, in all its implications, contains the idea of democracy" (328). He goes on to define "liberty" as "that secure release and fulfillment of personal potentialities which take place only in rich and manifold association with others" as if the social were only a setting for self-realization.[56] But if personal potential were an end in itself (even if situated in a social setting), would there necessarily be indirect consequences that would give rise to a public? By contrast we might recall Lippmann's definition of liberty as "a construction of a system of information," a proposition that foregrounds social intelligence, not personal consciousness or growth, as the basis for democracy.

Dewey seems to right himself later in the chapter when he explicitly returns to Lippmann, responding to the impossible burden of "the omnicompetent citizen" by insisting that "knowledge is a function of association and communication" (334). Yet he never really explains how this communication works except for some vague references to shared signs and symbols. Nor does he say how local communities could turn into a national one, beyond wishing it were so.[57] He prefers instead to devote far more energy and space to questioning in his final chapter the notion of an "intellectual aristocracy" (362), which for some reason he does not openly attribute to Lippmann. But those arguments of Dewey that do not actively misrepresent Lippmann end up pretty much in agreement, since Lippmann even at his most pessimistic would not have denied that citizens "have the ability to judge of the bearing of the knowledge supplied by others upon common concerns" (365). If this was a debate, it was not an especially illuminating one.

The Public and Its Problems closes with another implicit rejoinder to Lippmann, but this time usefully highlighting a key contrast between the two thinkers. Seemingly out of the blue, Dewey poetically remarks that "the wingèd words of conversation in immediate intercourse have a vital import lacking in the fixed and frozen words of written speech" (note the oxymoron). Disseminated print might be a "precondition of the creation of a true public," but the "final actuality is accomplished in face-to-face relationships by means of direct give and take . . .

dialogue." He continues, "[T]he connections of the ear with vital and out-going thought and emotion are immensely closer and more varied than those of the eye. Vision is a spectator; hearing is a participator. Publication is partial and the public which results is partially informed and formed until the meanings it purveys pass from mouth to mouth" (371).

Remembering that Dewey first delivered these words as a lecture, and leaving aside the impracticalities (to be polite) of founding a "Great Community" on millions of citizens directly talking to one another in person, this distinction between seeing print and hearing speech does help us appreciate how different modes of communication shape different versions of a public and vice versa.[58] Lippmann's persistent evocation of newspaper reading as the scene of education was clear enough, but where did Dewey's emphasis on speaking come from? While its sudden appearance at the end of *The Public and Its Problems* might seem gratuitous, it actually followed directly from the way he constituted a public at the start of the book. Recall that the transaction between A and B was described by Dewey not as a contract but as a "conversation," and it was from the consequences of this ground zero conversation that he spun out the rest of his argument. It might seem that Dewey's notion of a public is triadic, depending on an impartial third party who oversees, or rather, overhears dialogue. But this superintending official other only emerges for Dewey when the intercourse between two persons—his foundational model—carries indirect consequences.

To conclude, Dewey offered a model for publicness based on harmonious dialogue working toward a common good, while Lippmann gave us a solitary reader of news who was expected to know everything about current events. Living in the present tense, Lippmann's overwhelmed citizen (a version of Lippmann himself) must contain and totally answer for the public. Dewey by contrast grasped the public not as an actuality but rather as a potential to be realized, yet he (mis)located these aspirations in face-to-face communities. Lippmann more realistically appreciated the necessity of mediation, especially print, but confined himself to the world as it is. Their ideas are not entirely incompatible, but beyond these two unsatisfying alternatives perhaps there might be other ways to imagine how a democracy could organize information.

CHAPTER 5

Public Relations as Social Relations

Whatever John Dewey and Walter Lippmann might have disagreed about, they did seem to agree that "publicity men" were harmful for democracy. As Lippmann emphasized in *Public Opinion*, what counts as news is not a self-evident, spontaneously appearing set of facts, but derives from a complex process of editorial selection and arrangement. To influence this process, pressure groups, trade organizations, and corporations often hired agents to represent their positions by feeding items (press releases) to newspapers: "But it follows that the picture which the publicity man makes for the reporter is the one he wishes the public to see. He is censor and propagandist, responsible only to his employers, and to the whole truth responsible only as it accords with the employers' conception of his own interests. . . . since there is little disinterested organization of intelligence, the need for some formulation is being met by the interested parties."[1] A need is exploited and an opportunity seized by "unregulated private enterprise," the means by which consent is manufactured in a democracy, as Lippmann first identified right after the war in *Liberty and the News*. Business fills the vacuum left by the failure of intelligence to organize itself. In his prewar (1911) muckraking exposé of the newspaper business, Will Irwin put the point more simply and crudely, calling press agents "the only group of men proud of being called liars."[2]

As early as 1908, John Dewey had expressed similar concerns: "It is scarcely more satisfactory to leave all the education of public opinion to commercial control than to leave all elementary education to private interests."[3] This analogy makes explicit Dewey's long-standing tendency to see news, publicity, and educational institutions as part of a large single system of social intelligence, although given the American government's virtual monopoly on information during the war, it remained an open question whether the state would necessarily be a better curator of such intelligence than was big business. Dewey returned to this question in *The Public and Its Problems*. While he insisted (contra Lippmann) that it would be a "mistake" to assume that the conditions "which limit free communication" and "thereby arrest and pervert social thought" are mainly "overt forces" or external obstacles (as opposed to internal habits of thinking and feeling), he did admit that there were currently those "who have the ability to manipulate social relations for their own advantage." And he knew what to name these people: "We seem to be approaching a state of government by hired promoters of opinion called publicity agents" (LW 2:340–341). He defined "publicity" as "advertising, propaganda, invasion of private life," arguing later that such propaganda offered "at least the simulation of general consultation in arriving at political decisions" (348).

Beyond the matter of "simulation" (softened by the silver lining "at least"), Dewey's charge that publicity invades privacy was puzzling, since earlier in his book he argued that "public" and "private" were strictly functional categories that depended on whether social interactions had extensive indirect consequences or not. In this regard anything private could be made public, and there could be multiple publics. But Dewey's subsequent call "to penetrate and saturate" individuals "with a sense of local community life" (367–368) suggested that it might not always be so easy to distinguish between the external directives shaping how and what people believe and value—the province of publicity or public relations agents—and more inwardly induced education. If any social intelligence managed to systematically "penetrate" and "saturate" the daily lives of citizens during the war, after all, it was George Creel's Committee on Public Information, including its targeting of local communities via patriotic media like the Four Minute Men (see chapters 2 and 3).

What are the effects of such penetrating publicity in the absence of war and in the absence of state-controlled and state-organized information? Although the unregulated private enterprise of publicity bureaus distinctly emerged around the turn of the twentieth century (clearly predating the war), the business of public relations dramatically accelerated during the 1920s, just as intellectuals like Dewey and Lippmann were contemplating the ever-dimmer prospects for democratic publics. In this chapter I consider what public relations in practice and theory might contribute, if perversely, to these prospects, particularly what happens when governmental agency gives way to corporate clients and when deliberating citizens are reconceived as desiring consumers. I concentrate on two key public relations purveyors, Ivy Lee and Edward Bernays, who wrote a pair of books in the

1920s, *Crystallizing Public Opinion* (1923) and *Propaganda* (1928). These books by Bernays shadowed or, we might even say, mimicked the more famous pair that Lippmann published.

Earlier, I mentioned Lee in his (largely covert) role during the 1914 Ludlow Massacre when he propagated and defended the perspective of his patron, John D. Rockefeller Jr., against the striking miners and the muckraking attacks of George Creel. Like Creel and many other publicity agents, Lee began his career as a newspaperman. But Lee's background more closely resembled that of Creel's friend and supporter Woodrow Wilson: a devoted son of a southern minister who traveled north to attend Princeton. Lee in fact fondly recalled long walks with his teacher Wilson during his Princeton days, although he did not specify what he might have taken away from his professor's lectures on political science.[4] Because publicity at the start of the twentieth century was a relatively new field of endeavor, it is instructive to follow the career paths of these ambitious young men (and they were virtually all men) to trace how they helped forge and define an emerging lucrative vocation combining politics, journalism, and business.

After graduating from Princeton in 1899, Lee seemed to have no difficulty moving back and forth across the porous boundaries of reporting news for a variety of papers, including Hearst's *New York Journal,* the *New York Times,* and Pulitzer's *New York World,* and making news as a press agent by helping run the political campaign of New York mayoral candidate Seth Low. During his stint as a reporter, Lee specialized in covering Wall Street, gaining an insider look at American corporations as opposed to adopting the investigative practices of a muckraker like Creel. We can gauge his attitude toward big business and its public by turning to an early freelance article he published in 1902 (at age twenty-five) titled "Savings Banks." Here he argued that "teaching the working classes to save is of vital importance, especially in a country with a free ballot," and he continued, "it is essential to the development of good citizenship that the savings of the poor should be invested for them."[5] Offering advice couched as news, the orientation of the article is unmistakable, directed toward banks not so much in order to help them increase their profits (the amounts would have been paltry) as to enhance their standing in the community by encouraging virtuous habits among the poor. These customers were patronized and treated as an afterthought, the object of the banks' goodwill and educational endeavor. That bankers would clearly know what was best "for them," Lee simply accepted as a given.

Lee was among the first to pioneer this brand of paternalistic Progressivism, burnishing the image of corporations by pushing for greater civic engagement, including refreshing gestures toward liberalism and accountability that could be seen as fostering democracy. Little wonder that he soon left newspaper reporting to work more directly for these powerful corporations, which became his clients when he co-founded a publicity bureau in 1904. For big businesses that had shown little but contempt for public opinion throughout the nineteenth century, Lee's endeavors marked a crucial shift, effectively deflecting or even preempting the negative press of muckrakers and politicians that accompanied any agitation for economic reform. Rather than withdraw from such agitation or defiantly try to combat it head on, Ivy Lee recast corporations in a favorable light by emphasizing the social value of their services. With a list of clients that included dozens of giants of industry (Chrysler, General Mills, Bethlehem Steel, and so on),[6] Lee sought to give each of these businesses a coherent and appealing story to present to the American public—a key PR approach still effective today.

While skeptics might be inclined to dismiss Lee's efforts as cynical lip service, merely superficial window dressing, he did profoundly help transform the ethos of American corporations by teaching his clients how to carefully attend and overtly respond to public sentiment. This was an ethical matter for Lee, as he made clear in his "Declaration of Principles," which he issued to newspaper editors in 1906 to explain his work as a new kind of press agent:

> This is not a secret press bureau. All our work is done in the open. We aim to supply news. This is not an advertising agency; if you think any of our matter ought properly to go to your business office, do not use it. Our matter is accurate. . . . Upon inquiry, full information will be given to any editor concerning those on whose behalf an article is sent out. In brief, our plan is, frankly and openly, on behalf of business concerns and public institutions, to supply to the press and public of the United States prompt and accurate information concerning subjects which it is of value and interest to the public to know about. . . . I send out only matter every detail of which I am willing to assist any editor in verifying for himself. I am always at your service.[7]

First, Lee emphasized the transparent dissemination of information, which he defined as news; second, such information was not disguised advertising aiming to sell something; third, as news, it was accurate; fourth, he worked "on behalf of business concerns and public institutions"; fifth, the information he provided would be of "value and interest to the public"; and sixth, he personally would vouch for and stand by the veracity of this information.

In seeking to affirm the integrity of his agency, Lee's logical sequencing was striking, leading with news and only mentioning the detail about his clients in the middle of the declaration. But what made such information valuable to a news-

134   WEAPONS OF DEMOCRACY

paper reader, let alone the "public of the United States"? By strategically inserting the phrase "public institutions" to supplement "business concerns," Lee would seem to broaden the appeal and interest of this information, although he was vague about what he meant by "public institutions"—regulated communication, utility, and transportation companies, we might reasonably infer. As if to counterbalance the grand scale and scope implied by this large subject matter, Lee closed on a personal note ("I"), reassuring editors that he himself took full responsibility for the information provided by his bureau. As the agent of publicity (a word never used in the declaration), he had become the face of the corporation.

Lee's declaration was reprinted in an article titled "An Awakening in Wall Street" that appeared in the September 1906 issue of *American Magazine*, a fascinating venue considering that journalists Ray Stannard Baker, Lincoln Steffens, and Ida Tarbell had recently helped found and then joined this periodical after leaving *McClure's* earlier that year. Baker that spring in *McClure's* had published his exposé "How Railroads Make Public Opinion," an article that seems to have provoked Teddy Roosevelt's famous rant against muckrakers (see chapter 1). It is surprising, to say the least, to find corporate press agents lauded in a magazine that prominent muckrakers had helped establish. But the thrust of the article was a Progressive one: times are changing and instead of keeping silent or secretly planting news items, "masters of finance" now finally understand that they need to be responsive and open in dealing with the public.

To prove his point, the author of the article, Sherman Morse, contrasted corporate behavior during the coal strike of 1902 with the one looming four years later. In 1902, the Coal Trust stonewalled reporters, whereas the miners union representative, John Mitchell, gladly shared information, and as a result "the public was influenced to sympathize with the miners, rather than with the operators."[8] This time around, however, former reporter Ivy L. Lee, "knowing just what the newspapers want," was "openly employed" by the trust to carry on "a campaign of education on behalf of the operators." According to Morse, even the miners were compelled to acknowledge the effectiveness of Lee's campaign, which they deemed "the most ready weapon against them." Publicity was both an "education" and a "weapon," as Creel would reiterate a few years later.

Like Lippmann, Lee took as his primary communication model news and newspapers, which typically in various campaigns took the form of bulletins or a series of short pamphlets that outlined specific issues from the corporation's point of view. Of course this information was partial and selective—how could it not be?—but Lee always insisted that businesses get their facts straight and present nothing overtly fraudulent or misleading. His definition of news, as opposed to mere advertising, offered the same year that Lippmann published *The Phantom Public*, was less complicated than Lippmann's: "news is that which the people are willing to pay to have brought to their attention."[9] In his persistent focus on the corporate bottom line, he understood his own role as an advocate, or "counsel," a word that Edward Bernays would quickly take to heart soon after the war in promoting his own public relations mission. But while a prosecutor or a defense attorney would always be clearly identified in a court of law, on whose behalf a commercial agent spoke in the court of public opinion was not always as transparent as Lee claimed.

In an interesting article he published in *Moody's* in November 1907, for instance, Lee sketched out a variety of "indirect" services provided by the Pennsylvania Railroad for the common good: giving community aid, creating municipal parks, endowing scholarships, and so on.[10] But at no point in this recital of "enlightened self-interest" benefiting the public did Lee stop to identify himself or his publicity bureau as having been hired by this railroad. The article may indeed be considered newsworthy and factually accurate, but given his valorizing of corporate disclosure, Lee owed it to his readers to clarify that his authorship was specifically motivated, not disinterested. Who paid you determined what you said, or at least Lee's readers should have been given the chance to freely deliberate that possibility.

Lee consistently seemed far more committed to managing his clients than to managing a public or publics, far less interested than Bernays, for example, in trying to figure out the mindsets and dispositions of those on the receiving end of publicity or the receiving end of corporate largesse. His major published effort at such an analysis was reductive and unconvincing. On May 19, 1914, Lee delivered an address to the American Railway Guild called "The Railroads and Human Nature" which was much sharper on the issue of railroads than on "human nature." The address began with an analogy. Although some railroad men preferred to keep their business as a "house without any windows," Lee suggested an alternative course: many more windows, the clearer the better, in order to disabuse the American people of some "deeply sinister" ideas about railroads. Asserting that "you cannot argue with the public," Lee counseled a careful reframing of terminology, so that what labor called "full crew" laws, the operators renamed "extra crew," among other examples of semantic tweaking.[11]

This was shrewd advice, but when it came to depicting the public itself, Lee was on shakier ground. Comparing this public to a "crowd on the streets" suspiciously milling about the windowless building, Lee remarked, "the people now rule. We have substituted for the divine right of kings, the divine right of the multitude" (8). Delving into the psychology of this multitude, Lee listed four elements:

crowds do not reason, crowds are led by symbols and phrases, crowds possess a will to believe, and strong leaders can organize this will.

Stuart Ewen rightly pointed out that Lee "filched" these observations, without attribution, from Gustave Le Bon, who had published his popular account of irrational crowd behavior in 1895. Stressing the impact of Le Bon's work on American social science and public relations, Ewen surmised that "Lee was haunted by the historical nightmare that had been outlined by Le Bon," so that the practice of public relations for Lee became a way "to establish a critical line of defense against the crowd."[12] This proposition is a bit melodramatic and overly adversarial. For one thing, it is hard to imagine the patrician Lee "haunted" by anything, except perhaps during the last year of his life (1934), which is discussed at the close of the next chapter. Second, twenty years after its initial publication, Le Bon's sensationalistic raising of the specter of class warfare might have felt even to big business like an unhelpful cliché since public relations typically aimed to increase the satisfaction and compliance of consumers, not banish them from the market. Many of Le Bon's speculations had been challenged when the book first came out as exaggerated and simplistic, especially when situated in an American context. The "crowd" implied an unreflecting mass, while "the public" was a more deliberative social body, as social scientists like Robert Park took pains to make clear.[13] And yet when we (over)hear Lee's harsh address to railroad men concerning the unruly mob they must contend with, it is difficult to fully accept J. Michael Sproule's far more benign assessment that Lee's "philosophy of communication" was "based on an extreme version of intellectual democracy" that put "extreme faith in the morality of institutional leaders."[14]

A clue to Lee's stridency, which was unusual in comparison to his other publications, resides in the timing of this address, less than a month after the Ludlow Massacre of striking miners and only a few weeks before Rockefeller would officially hire Lee as public relations counsel to represent his corporation in the aftermath of the killings. In other words, in this specific context, Lee was not thinking about the crowd as a potential buying public or a democratic "we the people," but rather more urgently and narrowly as a threat to the stability of big business. Although Lee did not directly mention the violent episode in his address to the railroad executives, who were closely associated with the coal mining industry, in so castigating crowd behavior, it is as if he were gearing up for the publicity campaign of his life. This campaign was fought with news bulletins that his nemesis, journalist George Creel, would decry as misleading, but not with bullets. In practice, if not in his weak theorizing, Lee sought to reach his target audience (not the miners themselves) by largely rational means rather than the demagogic methods suggested by Le Bon.

For a far richer and capacious appreciation of the public, I turn to Edward Bernays, who was happy to put himself forward as the father of public relations, even though he clearly came on the scene a full decade after Lee. Considering influence rather than seniority, I would again insist that Lee remains the more important figure in the history of public relations, despite Bernays's relentless efforts to toot his own horn. The simple fact is that Bernays was more fun and flamboyant than Lee. He was also a far better self-promoter and propagandist for propaganda. He publicized his profession more widely than did Lee, writing in a self-aggrandizing vein that exaggerated the power of his type of public relations; academics studying Bernays rarely have questioned this power since buying into Bernays as a master manipulator enhances the significance of their own analysis of this particular brand of mass persuasion.[15]

What is most interesting about Bernays was his construing of consumers as a new kind of citizenry. Lee never took this route, loyally promoting his corporate clients as trustworthy sources of information and aiming to present an attractive picture of big business to an otherwise fairly indistinct public. In this way he resembled Lippmann, who assumed news to be the primary channel of communication for a democracy, with a befuddled mass of individuals tasked with the impossible burden of trying to offer opinions about an overwhelming cascade of information. But Bernays imagined this public, or publics, in far greater detail and nuance, with desires and identities and subgroupings that could be aroused and exploited in particular ways, sometimes by precise targeting and sometimes by trying to build communities of interest. It might be difficult to fathom, but in this specific regard his communication model resembled Dewey's, although of course the ends of Bernays's participatory spin differed starkly and drastically from the philosopher's emphasis on self-growth.

Bernays embarked on this path before the war, well before he would assume the professional mantle of public relations counsel. Even though after his death in 1995 (at the age of 103) more than 800 boxes of material consisting of 227,000 items were deposited in the Library of Congress, and even though a popular biography made some use of this massive archive, the main source of information about his life remains his 1965 autobiography, which he gave the intriguing title *Biography of an Idea: Memoirs of Public Relations Counsel Edward L. Bernays*.[16] Bernays cleverly sought to depict his life as a narrative allegory ("idea") about the profession of public relations itself. After quickly skimming through early family matters, Bernays introduces this professional allegory by recounting his involvement in the US production of the play *Damaged Goods* in 1913. Working as an editor for a couple of obscure medical journals, Bernays received through the mail "an unsolicited manuscript that influenced my life" (53), an article about a daring French drama that sought to portray the scourge of syphilis, especially for women, in a forthright and educational manner. American citizens might be receptive to a frank treatment of the subject, Bernays calculated, realizing that not only sexually transmitted diseases were spread by social contact: "Progressivism was [also] in the air" (59), a contagious spirit of reform rapidly sweeping across the nation.[17]

To make a long story short, Bernays quickly abandoned a career in journalism to become a theater and music promoter, concentrating at first on productions that promulgated serious and enlightened reformist agendas. To capitalize on Progressives' crusading impulses, he publicized the play by soliciting positive responses from corporate leaders and medical authorities, setting up a "Sociological Fund Committee" (57) of philanthropists and experts to sponsor the drama. Featuring a well-known actor (Richard Bennett) who had just starred in a play about women's suffrage, his co-produced *Damaged Goods* ended up being performed before the "austere" (61) President Wilson in the White House. This Progressive spectacle was followed a year later by the Broadway comedy *Daddy Long Legs* about poor orphans. For both dramas Bernays described how he had "taken the socially significant idea in the play and associated with it a newsworthy group that supported it" (79). Such an approach gathered politicians, reporters, actors, social workers, concerned Vassar College coeds, and specialists from a variety of fields, inspiring the formation of *Daddy Long Legs* support groups, along with fundraisers for orphans, human interest magazine stories, *Daddy Long Legs* cartoons, and even a *Daddy Long Legs* doll promoted by a famous race car driver. In short, Bernays was able to build up a whole *Daddy Long Legs* culture and context surrounding and sustaining the play. In this manner the public relations counsel became a "creator" of news,[18] or rather news events, promiscuously circulated through a variety of media for a coordinated effect.

If Lee's brand of Progressivist propaganda was paternalistic, assuming the point of view of his corporate clients, we might call Bernays's version performative Progressivism. This is absolutely crucial. It is not simply that Bernays's liberal credentials were more bona fide than Lee's (they were), but that he imagined a different way that political awareness might be aroused and enacted. Up to this point in my book, Progressivism has been entirely defined by the medium of print, with an occasional speech by Roosevelt or Wilson thrown in for good measure. But

Bernays intuited that reformist ideas could be disseminated theatrically, not just literally by way of the stage, but also by his own staging of events—arranging charity benefits, forming sponsoring committees, planning symposia and community meetings—that would be both socially valuable and pleasurable for the participants. Audiences were not simply passive recipients of inert information or befuddled news readers, but more engaged partakers in what might cynically be viewed as shallow spectacle, but that offered citizen-consumers a shared focal point for collective action. Bernays gave desire a spatial dimension: in his famous illustration, you do not sell a piano by listing its attributes, but rather by inviting consumers to imagine the musical instrument situated in a cozy parlor that would bring a family together.[19]

Who and what inspired Bernays to develop this style of performative Progressivism as the basis for his public relations practice? An infamous PR campaign orchestrated by Bernays after the war offers a telling clue. In 1928 Bernays was hired by George Washington Hill, the head of the American Tobacco Company, to encourage more women to smoke cigarettes, specifically Lucky Strikes. We need to give Bernays the benefit of the doubt and assume that medical science in the 1920s had not yet conclusively linked smoking to cancer; when such reports emerged decades later, Bernays vigorously sought to publicize smoking as harmful and destructive. A more central issue surrounds the social value of Bernays's publicity, which focused on making the green color of Lucky packages more alluring and on treating smoking as an appealing mode of dieting. Among other things, he arranged on Easter Sunday (March 31) 1929 for a group of young women to march down Fifth Avenue openly smoking cigarettes. Bernays dubbed this parade "The Torches of Freedom" and publicized it as a feminist demonstration aimed to combat discriminatory social conventions that frowned on such liberated behavior by women.

Bernays borrowed the clever phrase *torches of freedom* from psychoanalyst A. A. Brill, a colleague of Freud, who had argued that smoking cigarettes might help to emancipate women by encouraging their "feminine desires."[20] This is where conspiracy theories about corporate-directed propaganda kick in, melding together Freud, Marx, and the puritanical distaste for spectacle. In this view, at the psychological level Bernays was promoting cigarettes by tapping into women's unconscious sexual desires. His motive was profit, to increase the bottom line of his (hidden) client by a kind of fetishizing of a commodity that he endowed with attractive, if not exactly magical, properties. These properties were put on display in a theatrical event that hoodwinked and ensnared an inert audience, masking the truth with a show of hypnotic illusion.

Such an interpretation might have some merit, but seems rather overblown. For starters, cigarette smoking remains a superficial and crude way to access the unconscious. It might be argued that symbolically appropriating the patriarchal phallus could be construed as a path toward women's empowerment, but neither Brill nor Bernays seem up to this kind of subtlety. Bernays instead orchestrated the event to mimic a suffrage march,[21] suggesting that his model of persuasion derived from Progressive Era social reform, not subliminal brainwashing, which is how public relations and marketing commonly came to be regarded during the Cold War. The parade's focus on freedom was collective, overt, and political, rather than isolated, covert, and inward. And while it is true that these marchers were paid actors hired (via a PR specialist) by a particular tobacco company, for Bernays such events always worked to break down the barriers between players and audience, who would be encouraged to participate, if not by marching in the parade itself, then by sharing their opinions of the spectacle in its aftermath.

Of course from the perspective of classic political theory, there is a vast difference between an amusing display of publicity and a rational, critical debate in a public sphere, although there is evidence to indicate that Bernays's PR stunt, which was widely covered in newspapers at the time, did spur some people to talk less frivolously about what women should or should not be doing to enjoy themselves.[22] If we take a broad view about what constitutes political expression, then the parallel that Bernays drew between a woman's right to vote and her freedom to smoke may not be so far-fetched. In itself, the gendering of a public, even if primarily a buying public, deserves serious consideration. Beyond selling cigarettes, beyond accusations of cynical duplicity, and beyond his self-serving affirmations of feminism, Bernays's publicity deserves careful attention as to its causes and effects.

The suffrage movement offers one important source for his brand of PR. That Bernays would stage such a suffrage parade, a full nine years after women nationally won the right to vote, indicates the deep impact the movement had on his way of conceiving of publicity. As historian Margaret Finnegan put it, the suffragists were "among the first political players to fully and eagerly incorporate the methods and technologies of mass culture into their campaigns," thereby contributing "to the commercialized political sphere" that would dominate American culture during the twentieth century. More pointedly, Finnegan continued, "no political party, union, or social cause during the progressive period utilized the advertising potential of public space as fully as did suffragists."[23]

This "advertising potential of public space" included electric billboards, street theater, pageants and parades, sandwich boards (with women's bodies as both the subjects and objects of public spectacle), and the mass circulation of com-modities to be worn or displayed (badges, hats, fans, playing cards, shopping bags with slogans, Kewpie dolls). All of these modes of suffrage propagandizing were well established before Bernays hit the scene and heavily informed the public relations tactics that he would deploy. And the timing here is quite intriguing: only two weeks before the play *Damaged Goods* premiered (March 14, 1913), suf-fragists led a huge and elaborate march (March 3, 1913) in Washington, DC, on the eve of Wilson's inauguration, including the stunning figure of a lawyer, Inez Milholland, astride a large white horse.

In addition to these similar theatrical campaigns that helped sell political re-form, there was an affinity between the agitation for women's voting and Bernays's brand of promotion that rested on ideological grounds. Drawing on his lifelong relationship with his wife and business partner, Doris Fleischman, as a prime example, Bernays in his autobiography repeatedly called attention (as did George Creel) to his feminist sympathies, suggesting that his championing of women's rights helped him better understand the psychology of consumers. Early on, to note one instance of his professed feminism, he stressed that he strongly encour-aged Doris to retain her own surname, bragging that after he made a fuss, "the State Department issued her the first passport ever made out to a married woman in her maiden name, confirming [his] belief that individual action in a demo-cratic society can move even the most hidebound bureaucracy" (218). Bernays was always quick to extract lessons about democracy from his own experience.

Beyond his feminist proclivities and particular techniques, Bernays also bor-rowed something more profound from the suffragists. Historian Stuart Ewen cred-ited Bernays (and Bernays credited himself) with pioneering the public relations strategy of creating circumstances for news. News in this approach (which Ewen deemed "an elitist strategy") was not information reported, but rather something made, a topical event contrived to provoke interest and produce effects.[24] The suffragists understood the need to engineer the newsworthy. Claiming that "the concern of suffragists with organization, with publicity, and with propaganda is one and the same," a feminist strategist, Rose Young, argued, "If you concede that you want to keep suffrage before the public as a live issue, the livest [*sic*] issue of the times, you must concede that you've got to keep it in the newspapers. To keep it in the newspapers you must relate it acceptably to the news of the day."[25] Convinced of the importance of their goal, suffragists by such organized and organizing propaganda confidently pursued their well-defined and well-focused mission, which was indeed the liveliest of the day and situated within the broader but looser agendas of Progressive reform. In doing so, these women may have contributed to the commercialization of the public sphere, as Finnegan indicated, but (marking one end to Progressivism?) they politically succeeded.

The problem, of course, is that compared to the suffragists, Bernays was clearly more enamored with his methods than his causes, and getting people to eat more bacon became just as challenging and compelling a puzzle for him to solve as getting them to fight venereal disease. In his two books written after the war he tried to recast the business of public relations in primarily political terms as a way of giving his profession greater cachet. But reading his enthusiastic accounts of campaigns for hair-net fashions and Ivory soap sculpture contests, which he strained to present as matters of health education, it is difficult not to feel let down, even if his paying clients might have been delighted with the results. Once techniques of mass persuasion are treated as detachable instrumentalities that can be applied to any circumstance, then changing the eating habits of the public or convincing them to go to war operate by the same logic, as propaganda critics are quick to point out, although it remains debatable, as we shall see, exactly how effective these PR methods really are.

As Bernays was starting to promote plays like *Damaged Goods* (and other more frivolous ones), a substantive case for the political importance of consumers was being made by Walter Lippmann and other Progressives. By the early twentieth century "the right to consume became identified as a right of American citizenship," as one historian observed,[26] thereby according these democratic rights anchored in unfettered consumerism a quasi-official status. In response to the proliferation of quack medications and unsanitary processing conditions, legislation such as the Pure Food and Drug Act (1906) was passed to protect consumers. Chartered in 1899 and subsequently led by Florence Kelley, the National Consumers League (NCL) sought to build alliances between workers and consumers by lobbying to improve poor working conditions, especially for women, including sweatshop laborers and department store clerks, and by encouraging female shoppers to avoid establishments that did not meet the NCL's standards.

In his book *Drift and Mastery* (1914), Lippmann took this burgeoning idea of consumer empowerment further. He began by sounding what would become a familiar theme for him, that the consumer is "told what he wants, and then he wants it," and "consumers are a fickle and superstitious mob" who are "at the mercy of advertising" largely because "the scale on which the world is organized to-day" made it "impossible" for "the ordinary purchaser" to exercise "discrimination."[27] This line of reasoning anticipated the arguments about the "omnicompetent" citizen he would make in *Public Opinion*. But then Lippmann noted that "politics is becoming the chief method by which the consumer enforces his interests upon the industrial system," and he asserted that the cry of consumers against the "high cost of living" was "destined to be stronger than the interests either of labor or capital": "With the consumer awake, neither the worker nor the employer can use politics for his special interest. The public, which is more numerous than either side, is coming to be the determining force of government" (72). This was an odd conception of "the public," which was determined numerically but excluded workers and employers as such, suggesting a functional but circular definition. That Lippmann meant a certain kind of public rather than "the public" became clearer when he immediately turned to the crucial role of women in fostering "consumers'-consciousness." Once enfranchised, women "will increase the power of the consumer enormously," because as the family's primary shoppers, "it is they who feel shabbiness and fraud and high prices most directly" (72).

Lippmann did not explain why this female public would be less prone to the blandishments of advertisers, why they were more awake and enlightened than their male counterparts, other than by virtue of their greater exposure and experience as consumers. On this point he displayed a characteristically Progressive optimism in the efficacy of knowledge. Nor did he clearly distinguish between commodities that consumers need ("the high cost of living") and those they might want to purchase with disposable income. Presumably he would regard his cherished news as a necessary commodity rather than a desired one, but it still required consumption (buying and using), just like eggs and butter. He also did not consider that if publics could be divided along gender lines, they could be further subdivided into smaller segments of buyers, a prospect that would call into question his assumption that "the consumer" as a monolithic category represented a common political good without any special interests of her own.

Leave it to Bernays in *Crystallizing Public Opinion* to show how consuming publics can be divided, multiplied, and reconfigured at will thanks to the magic of public relations. As Sue Curry Jansen demonstrated point by point, Bernays in trying to hitch his wagon to Lippmann's star took great liberties with Lippmann's *Public Opinion*, published a year prior.[28] He twisted passages out of context, omitting key qualifying phrases, and deliberately misconstrued Lippmann's arguments, especially his worries about the engineering of consent, which Bernays tried to turn into a necessary virtue. Once business resumed control of the country after the war, corporate public relations did democracy a favor, according to Bernays, by helping to organize its chaos. Such a conclusion was clearly not what Lippmann had in mind. This mangling of Lippmann by Bernays has unfortunately misled many scholars who paint the two with the same broad brush as

anti-democratic elitists. But rather than see Bernays as indulging in malicious fal-
sification, we might more generously treat *Crystallizing Public Opinion* as what
literary critics might call a strong misreading, one that opportunistically developed Lippmann's ideas in particular ways that Lippmann may not have intended
or condoned, but that have a certain logic nonetheless.

Bernays's repeated assertions about the importance of public relations, how
this new field "impinges upon the daily life of the public in an almost infinite
number of ways" (CPO, 64), was driven by his exuberant appreciation for social
complexity, which for him was intensified in the domain of consumption. "Society," Bernays remarked, "is made up of an almost infinite number of groups, whose
various interests and desires overlap and interweave inextricably" (150). Public
opinion, such as it is, consists of interrelated clusters or formations organized
not only by class or political allegiance, but also by a whole series of shifting
affiliations and identities.[29] A silk firm trying to increase its business would need
to realize, with the help of its public relations adviser, that while "fundamentally
women were its potential buying public," not all women were alike: some might
be interested in fashion, others in art (members of art or museum clubs) or education (school teachers), so the trick for the PR counsel would be to rearrange
"the thought of the individuals in these groups with respect to each other and with
respect to the entire membership of society" (152).

Everybody who writes about Bernays points out that he was the nephew of Sigmund Freud (a double one, no less). But it is difficult to see exactly how psychoanalysis entered into his scheme of public relations in which the tapping of desires
along intersecting vectors of multiple social identities is pretty much aboveboard.
While the agency of the PR adviser might be largely hidden (the source of information), it did not necessarily follow that this sort of publicity worked primarily on
the consumer's unconscious (how information is processed). Unconscious drives
and psychic processes of condensation and displacement for Freud were far more
complex matters than simply a condition of unawareness. Bernays was talking
about veiled (or not so veiled) appeals to women who might like silk for various
reasons, not women who buy silk because they want to sleep with their fathers.

Of course Bernays loved on occasion to play the Freud card, and he included
a long section in his autobiography detailing his promotional efforts on behalf
of his famous uncle Sig. (At one point in this chapter he stops to speculate how
much each of his uncle's letters would fetch in the open market.) Freud for his
part politely acknowledged receipt of the copy of *Crystallizing Public Opinion*
his nephew sent him, calling the book a "truly American production" and archly
leaving it at that (270). The same year Lippmann published *Public Opinion*,

Freud published *Group Psychology and the Analysis of the Ego*, and a compelling argument was made by Theodor Adorno in 1951 that Freud's analysis of authoritarianism in that book could help account for the rise of the Nazis and Nazi propaganda, which Adorno saw as a talking cure in reverse, inserting material into the unconscious instead of drawing it out.[30] Just as Adorno was making his case, moreover, reports were emerging from the conflict in Korea (1950–1953) that American prisoners of war had been subjected to a special kind of subliminal hypnosis or "brainwashing."[31]

But Bernays's pleasure-based special pleading would seem a far cry from nefarious Nazis or brainwashing Communists, tempting as it might be to retroactively read these sinister techniques into Bernays's writings from the 1920s. Aside from fleeting references to Freud here and there in these two polemical books, Bernays steered clear of his uncle, preferring instead to draw on Anglo-American authorities to bolster his views. In *Crystallizing Public Opinion*, for example, he cited at length William McDougall, a Progressive social psychologist noted for his 1908 theory of the primary instincts. Just as Bernays was no Lippmann, McDougall was no Freud. Going through these seven instincts and their attendant emotions one by one ("flight-fear," "repulsion-disgust," "pugnacity-anger," and so on), Bernays mechanically showed how the public relations counsel could exploit each instinct in particular ways, by staging dramatic contests, for instance (156–157). To be sure, this was a wider range of emotions than the feelings of pride, hatred, and fear that the Committee on Public Information harnessed during the war, but this categorizing of "instincts" does not seem an especially insightful or original account of group psychology.

It is surprising that Bernays seemed so wedded to Progressive models of social science since by the 1920s these paradigms were giving way to more empirical studies (including those of McDougall) that tracked voting behavior, measured IQs, and sought to apply psychology to politics in more precise, scholarly ways.[32] These academics might have supported Bernays's assumptions about the public's serious need for strong direction, but the public relations counsel throughout his career displayed little interest in quantitative methods of analysis. Given Bernays's efforts to portray PR as a new science, the absence of hard data or facts in his books is particularly conspicuous.

This relative inattentiveness to numbers is doubly disconcerting when it comes to Bernays's confident assessments regarding the tremendous success of his various publicity campaigns. After all, even a propagandist like George Creel—an equal if not superior to Bernays when it came to grandiose bluster—offered scads of statistics in telling his self-serving story about how the Committee on Public

Information "advertised" America during the war. If not actually gauging the effects of publicity, Creel's bureaucratic number crunching at least demonstrated the astonishing extent of its persuasive reach.

But in his two books published during the 1920s and his 1965 autobiography, Bernays gives us nothing of the sort, compelling us by the sheer force of his assertive rhetoric to take him at his word. Even at a nascent stage of the development of analytic metrics, surely corporations during this period with an eye on the bottom line were able to determine how many packages of bacon were sold before a particular publicity campaign as opposed to how many during and after. Yet the otherwise garrulous Bernays was pretty much silent on the subject. The most notable instance when he did try to evaluate success, interestingly, concerned publicity on behalf of the National Association for the Advancement of Colored People, an effort led by his wife, Doris Fleischman, that he was very proud of, even though it has been mostly overlooked by scholars.[33] Boasting how this campaign roused people to fight injustice, Bernays was left to surmise that the "weapons" his publicity afforded the NAACP "very probably" led to a decline in lynching, although "further results are hard to measure with a slide-rule" (*Propaganda*, 150).

As I previously suggested, most scholars have been willing to give Bernays a free pass on such assertions, because his claims help reinforce the notion of him as a publicity genius, evil or otherwise. If all his schemes actually amounted to little or nothing, then why bother to take him so seriously? To endorse his power is to endorse the (sinister) power of propaganda itself, which is waiting to be demystified and dismantled by academics intent on cutting through the spin. Just as he titled his autobiography an "idea," commentators seem taken with him precisely as an idea, a cautionary allegory about the manipulative force of consumer capitalism. Yet as his biographer ventured to observe, "his short tenure with client after client suggests he didn't always make the impact he claimed,"[34] which very well might be an understatement.

Even if we grant him this terrific power to sway the beliefs, values, and habits of compliant masses, what if anything does this have to do with democracy? To allow that his methods possessed "social value" (*CPO*, 138), as he insisted, in bringing communities of customers together still avoids the question of how these arranged clusters focused on theatrical PR events would or could constitute any sort of deliberative public sphere. While Bernays tried to address this question at some length in his second book, *Propaganda*, his first book hinted at the path his thinking would take. At one point in *Crystallizing Public Opinion* he openly took exception to Lippmann, instead of simply misrepresenting his ideas: "Mr. Lippmann

says propaganda is dependent upon censorship. From my point of view the precise reverse is more nearly true. Propaganda is a purposeful, directed effort to
overcome censorship—the censorship of the group mind and the herd reaction"
(133).

With perhaps George Creel and the CPI in mind, Lippmann in *Public Opinion* sensibly argued that censorship and propaganda were two sides of the same
coin, since to steer the public in one direction requires suppressing information
by which it might move elsewhere. But Bernays came up with the curious notion that propaganda deliberately works to counteract "censorship," by which he
seems to have meant conformist thinking. This line of reasoning suggests that
Bernays had bigger fish to fry than explaining and defending the new practice
of public relations. Later in the volume he returned to the matter of definitions:
"The only difference between 'propaganda' and 'education,' really is in the point
of view. The advocacy of what we believe in is education. The advocacy of what
we don't believe in is propaganda" (*CPO*, 200). It all depended on "the point of
view," as if all points of view were equally valid, or incapable of rational adjudication.

In his second book Bernays boldly developed this pragmatist approach to mass
persuasion, a relativism arguably borne out by the history of the term *propaganda*.
The simple title of the book was audacious in itself. Even though during the war
members of the CPI routinely used the word among themselves to refer to their
work, it quickly became a tainted and discredited category to signify all that was
"insidious, dishonest, underhand[ed], misleading," as Bernays put it in *Crystallizing Public Opinion* (200). To explicitly call public relations "propaganda" in 1928
was a provocation, a sign of real chutzpah, in other words. That nerviness was
apparent in the very first sentences of his book:

> The conscious and intelligent manipulation of the organized habits and
> opinions of the masses is an important element in democratic society. Those
> who manipulate this unseen mechanism of society constitute an invisible
> government which is the true ruling power of our country.
>
> We are governed, our minds molded, our tastes formed, our ideas suggested,
> largely by men we have never heard of. This is a logical result of the way in
> which our democratic society is organized. Vast numbers of human beings must
> cooperate in this manner if they are to live together as a smoothly functioning
> society. (*Propaganda*, 37)

What kind of strange parallel universe is this? Denounced in the 1912 Progressive Party platform as "the unholy alliance between corrupt business and corrupt

politics," the phrase *invisible government* was invoked to decry a pattern of hidden coercion that would also increasingly concern Lippmann, Dewey, and others both before and especially after the war (see chapter 4). Taking the bull by the horns, Bernays flipped the concept to convert it into the very centerpiece of (his) democracy. But why cannot social cooperation be self-regulating? Why should public relations counsels be in charge of this covert governing (as opposed to Lippmann's wider class of administrative experts), and on what higher grounds would these decisions be made? Throughout the rest of his book, Bernays danced around these key issues, usually by way of example rather than argument, which leads to another question: Why bring this secret power into the open, making the invisible all too visible, beyond seeking the gratitude of a public otherwise unaware of how it is being so intelligently manipulated for its own good? What magician reveals all his tricks?

Bernays's unrepentant attempt to recuperate and install propaganda as the social mechanism running democracy required him to collapse any distinction between the political and the economic. Although he followed these outrageous paragraphs with a brief reference to the Constitution, it quickly becomes clear that as in his previous book, what really energized and excited him were examples from his own public relations practice. "In theory," he remarked, "everybody buys the best and cheapest commodities offered him on the market." But there were so many products that "economic life" had become "hopeless[ly] jammed." And so "to avoid such confusion, society consents to have its choice[s] narrowed to ideas and objects brought to its attention through propaganda of all kinds. There is consequently a vast and continuous effort going on to capture our minds in the interest of some policy or commodity or idea" (39).

Even though "commodity" was slyly sandwiched between "policy" and "idea," Bernays explicitly made the capitalist market central to his social scheme and a model for explaining everything else: we choose to believe in the same way we choose to buy, which for Bernays was a more primary process, or at least one whose emotional currents he fully understood. As he bluntly put it, "politics was the first big business in America" (111), although it now lagged behind business in knowing how to reach its public. It was time for big business to remake politics in its own image. While Progressives agitated for the rights of citizens to safely consume, Bernays reversed this logic to suggest that consuming can effectively organize a citizenry, thanks to the guidance of public relations counsels such as himself. While he happily divulged the operations and methods of this "invisible" government, what remained deeply buried in his account were the pecuniary motives driving this corporate governance. The word "profit" showed up only four times in his book, for instance, and then it was linked to "the public's benefit" (67), as if the two automatically went together.

Yet Bernays appreciated that dictating what consumer-citizens bought or thought was an insufficient argument for propaganda, unless he arrived at some sound higher principles directing these choices. Building on his first book's claim that propaganda is opposed to censorship, Bernays came up with an even quirkier elaboration: "the new propaganda, having regard to the constitution of society as a whole, not infrequently serves to focus and realize the desires of the masses" (57). In other words, if people want to agitate on behalf of food-processing reform, they need propaganda to organize and articulate their demands. This was especially true for "active proselytizing minorities" intent on expressing important but un-fashionable views. Leaving aside his cagey language (which was marked by slip-pery qualifications and ambiguities), Bernays by a rhetorical sleight of hand rede-fined the word *minority*, which referred no longer simply to numbers but now to values and opinions that might be out of favor by the mainstream but needed to be heard for "the progress and development of America": "only through the active energy of the intelligent few can the public at large become aware of and act upon new ideas" (57). But this "intelligent few" represented the public relations elite, not marginalized groups searching for a voice. Why should these few "invisible wirepullers" (60), who called all the shots, necessarily endorse the politics of mi-norities, just because each group was not a statistical majority? Did Bernays really think this was how power worked? While rich, powerful people might have the re-sources to take up unpopular causes, and while there are clearly occasions when they would be drawn to help the disadvantaged and oppressed, such a model of "progress" seems a dubious foundation for a democratic public sphere.

Bernays's invocation of American "progress" indicated one motive behind such shaky reasoning. For all of his valorizing of big business as a basis for public politics, Bernays even in 1928 imagined himself as a Progressive, if a residual one, still committed to the liberal reconstruction and reform of the nation. That is why toward the end of his book, after two long chapters titled "Business and the Public" and "Propaganda and Political Leadership" (the centerpieces of his ar-gument), Bernays turned to a number of subgroups and subfields largely outside the domain of consumption and therefore more directly oriented toward civic virtue: women's activities, educational reform, social services, art, and science.[35] Again, he insisted that the "new propaganda" could help lead to the "acceptance of minority ideas" (131), here pertaining to women, but he was still hard-pressed to explain what made these ideas worth upholding, beyond the fact that they were "intelligent." Intelligence seems to be the single human trait Bernays most

admired, especially his own intelligence, which became the sufficient grounds
for consumers to put their trust in the public relations counsel. For Bernays, there
was no standard outside of himself.

In his previous book Bernays had closed with a brief section on ethics, albeit
a sketchier discussion than the more robust code of principles Ivy Lee had announced in 1906. Lee's efforts were partly designed to persuade his patrons to
support public service projects as noblesse oblige. Lee, after all, had a strong
commitment to protecting and preserving the reputation of his corporate clients,
whereas Bernays always seemed less interested in promoting his paymasters than
in entrancing the buying public. But in *Propaganda* Bernays largely avoided even
a cursory consideration of what a responsible counsel might owe that public. At
one point, he did offer a few familiar moral platitudes—avoid conflicts of interest,
avoid clients with unmarketable products (more practical than ethical!), always
be candid—but these self-policing strictures were pretty much undermined by
the passage that directly preceded them: "In law, the judge and jury hold the de-
ciding balance of power. In public opinion, the public relations counsel is judge
and jury, because through his pleading of a case the public may accede [to] his
opinion and judgment" (70). Acting as both judge and jury, the intelligence of
public relations practictioners left little room for consumer-citizens to do or say,
other than to consent and enjoy the show.

CHAPTER 6

Foreign Intelligence

In his autobiography Bernays tells an entertaining story about a box of cigars. In Paris right after the war Bernays had run into Carl Byoir at the Committee on Public Information headquarters. Byoir mentioned that he was on his way to visit the newly independent Czechoslovakia, and Bernays asked him to take some Coronas as a gift to his uncle Sigmund in Vienna. Sometimes a box of cigars is only a box of cigars, but not in this case. Freud returned the favor by handing Byoir a copy of his latest book to give to Bernays, who arranged to have it translated into English as *The General Introductory Lectures to Psychoanalysis.* And so "a box of cigars from an admiring nephew, delivered by a member of an American mission to Czechoslovakia, was helpful in introducing psychoanalysis in the United States."[1] But we can draw other lessons from this little anecdote by asking, What exactly were Byoir and Bernays doing in Paris? Why was Byoir going to Czechoslovakia? And how did this interaction with Byoir help launch Bernays in his career as a public relations specialist? The answers to these questions can help us to appreciate the transnational dimension to public relations, which emerged directly out of the wartime experience of the CPI propagandists. The war taught them the importance of molding opinions about America abroad and gave them an understanding of how foreign countries would draw on their (paid) expertise to help shape American attitudes toward these nations.

As I previously indicated, next to the chair, George Creel, Carl Byoir was the most important administrator in the Committee on Public Information, to a large extent running the daily affairs of the wartime agency. Bernays too was employed by the CPI but in a far smaller capacity, working in the Foreign Press Bureau and exporting "articles, photographs . . . on American agriculture, labor, religion, medicine and education to overseas posts for placement." Bernays noted in his autobiography that he "staged events" and "planned and carried out a campaign directed at Latin American businessmen" (155–157). The transition from antebellum theatrical promoter to state propagandist during the war seems to have been a seamless one for Bernays, enabling him to expand his repertoire and broaden his outlook. In his detailed recounting of the CPI, *How We Advertised America*, George Creel mentions Bernays by name only once in passing,[2] suggesting that Bernays was a small cog in this "enormous propaganda machine" (155), as Bernays called it. The young man was one of dozens of operatives tasked with spreading the gospel of democracy from the agency's Foreign Press Bureau, part of a broader Foreign Services Section, whose activities Creel devoted fifteen full chapters to describing, from Mexico to Spain to Russia. As Creel fervently attested, during the war it was just as important, if not more so, to capture the hearts and minds of people abroad as those of the citizens of the United States. Sometimes the CPI used the same films and pamphlets that were directed to Americans, but often the material was designed to target particular countries and cultures. For such propaganda to be effective, Creel realized, it needed to be geared to specific audiences.

Bernays ended up in Paris soon after the armistice as part of the official US press mission to the peace conference. Here is where things got interesting, as they tended to do with Bernays. Before departing for Europe, he issued a press release that was picked up and reported on November 21, 1918, by the *New York World* as follows: "The announced object of the expedition [the CPI mission] is 'to interpret the work of the Peace Conference by keeping up a worldwide propaganda to disseminate American accomplishments and ideals'" (quoted in *Biography of an Idea*, 161). As we have seen, Bernays was not shy about using the *p*-word. But when the story came out, Creel immediately took flack from members of Congress, who interpreted Bernays's words to mean that the CPI would be exerting censorship and control of the peace conference's publicity. Creel vehemently denied this charge, insisting that now that the war was ended, the role of the CPI "will be to open every means of communication to the press of America without dictation, without supervision, and with no other desire than to facilitate in every manner the fullest and freest flow of news" (quoted on 164).[3]

Never one to apologize for a blunder, Bernays in his autobiography implied that Creel's statement was disingenuous, that the mission was in fact not purely clerical, as Creel asserted, but indeed intended to manage publicity. In a gesture of audacity, Bernays then chided Creel and the CPI for not following through with their original intentions, suggesting that the inability of the press mission to properly propagandize actually contributed to the American failure during the conference. In typical fashion, from his perspective as a relatively minor func-tionary for the CPI, Bernays self-importantly weighed in on a sensitive matter of great historical significance. What his retrospective analysis failed to consider, but Creel fully understood, was that as soon as the war was over, the CPI was essentially finished too, since Americans would simply not tolerate a peacetime propaganda agency run by the government.

Stranded in Paris, what were these CPI press operatives left to do, if not advo-cate for America? Byoir found his answer in traveling to Czechoslovakia, whose postwar status suddenly made it imperative for the newly independent country to gain some footing on the world stage. During the war Byoir had worked with many Americans of foreign extraction to support the military effort. Back in the United States, the well-connected former associate chair of the CPI would publicize on behalf of Czechoslovakia, as well as Lithuania, which had not yet achieved independence. Since the CPI had essentially served as a publicity bu-reau for the United States, why not begin an enterprise to represent the interests of other nations, an endeavor that might be just as lucrative as representing cor-porations? Having marketed American ideals (especially Wilsonian democracy) abroad during the war, these publicists would continue to sell advice and promote goods and opinions around the globe, essentially turning public relations into an import-export business.[4]

As the map of Europe was being redrawn during the peace conference, the emergent geopolitical territories, now suddenly achieving nationhood, realized that when it came to publicity, they needed a level of expertise and sophistication that only shrewd Americans schooled by the culturally savvy CPI could bring. Public relations counsels like Byoir, Lee, and Bernays were fond of talking about their profession as a "two-way street," both shaping a public and responding to this public's needs. It is easy to be skeptical about such a self-serving conceit. But as a fertile training ground for PR pioneers, the CPI did serve as an international two-way street, allowing Americans to exert influence in other countries, but also helping those countries influence opinion in the United States about their own agendas. In a highly resonant essay published in the American Manufacturing Export Association Newsletter in 1920, just as his business was taking off, Ber-nays noted that by "careful control over incoming and outgoing news routes," the US government during the war was able to sway public opinion abroad, thereby creating positive feelings about America: goodwill that exporters could exploit to develop new markets and customers. According to Bernays, the CPI was thus instrumental in paving the way for "the close connection between political prop-aganda and its commercial significance."[5] This is a crucial insight.

As Byoir and Bernays in 1919 were discussing their uncertain futures over lunch after returning from Paris, Byoir suddenly popped the question: "Would you, Ed, like to do publicity on a free-lance basis for the [Lithuanian National] Council, trying to win the support of the American people for Lithuanian recognition?" (*Biography of an Idea*, 188). Framing this prospect as an affirmation of Wilson's Fourteen Points ("self-determination for ethnic entities"), Bernays used this opportunity to start his PR career, with Lithuania his first official client. In his various books, Bernays described the campaign in loving detail, emphasizing once again that his approach was not political but rather cultural and emotional: getting Americans to appreciate the richness and appeal of Lithuanian music, drama, food, folk traditions, and so on. In a reversal of the CPI logic during the war, Bernays was now advertising Lithuania in the United States, rather than advertising America abroad. In a similar reversal, Bernays's second client was the War Department, which retained him to drum up public support for hiring returning soldiers: just as conscription had required CPI publicity, so too demobilization, although it was now in the capable hands of unregulated private entrepreneurs like Bernays, who had honed their craft while serving the government.

But for PR counsels Byoir and Lee, representing foreign interests would lead to highly problematic political entanglements, as we shall see. Even during the war, the CPI's Foreign Services Section ran into similar difficulties when it came to promoting America on a massive scale, nation by nation. The professed credo of the CPI was not to interfere in the internal affairs of other countries. But this was easier said than done. At the same lunchtime "bull session" that launched Bernays in public relations, another powerful former associate chair of the CPI, Edgar G. Sisson (a magazine editor before the war), also happened to be in attendance. Sisson had figured prominently in what was arguably the CPI's most embarrassing episode. In November 1917 this key member of the News Division had traveled to Russia to bolster the "educational work," as Creel put it (*HWAA*, 275), of Arthur Bullard, who prior to the US entry into the war had helped come up with the idea for the Committee on Public Information (see chapter 2). That the American government would station two of its very best men in Russia speaks to the crucial significance of the country, which after all was a vital if shaky ally occupying the eastern front against Germany.[6] To specifically inform the Russians about Wilsonian democratic ideals, presumably more unfamiliar to them than to the French or British allies, Bullard had written the pamphlet *Letters to a Russian Friend*, of which 150,000 copies (in Russian) were distributed throughout the country, Creel reported (*HWAA*, 394).

The problem, of course, was that Sisson arrived in Russia at the tail end of the revolution, when Alexander Kerensky's more moderate government had just fallen to V. I. Lenin's Bolsheviks. Whether the new Soviet leadership would continue to support the Allied effort, or withdraw from the war, as Lenin promised, was naturally of utmost concern to Wilson and his State Department. How the United States sought to keep the Soviets on the side of the Allies while simultaneously trying to undermine and discredit the legitimacy of the Bolsheviks is a complex issue still debated by historians.[7] But that was centrally a matter of diplomacy and military intervention, not under the purview of the CPI, which was not intended to make or execute any foreign policy decisions. The agency's educational work was somewhat hindered by the new Soviet government, as Sisson reported back to Creel, but not entirely curtailed, as long as the committee's "Russian campaign" to disseminate pamphlets, posters, and films "making Russian[s] understand America" (*HWAA*, 374) did not meddle in the political chaos of the revolution and the ongoing civil war.

Yet Sisson quickly began to betray his hostility toward the new regime, despite Creel's assurance that "it had been decided not to attack Bolshevism or discuss political questions in Russia directly" (*HWAA*, 385).[8] Sisson in Petrograd soon came indirectly into contact with a group of anti-Bolsheviks, who fed him undercover information, effectively turning the CPI representative into an intelligence agent. When he left the country in early March 1918, Sisson smuggled out sixty-eight documents purporting to prove that Lenin and Leon Trotsky were paid agents of the German general staff, which had hired them to overthrow the czar and stop fighting Germany. The US State Department not only sanctioned Sisson's acquisition of these documents, but via the American ambassador, David R. Francis, paid a steep price for them, with Wilson's personal approval.[9]

Many of these incendiary Sisson Papers, as they became known, had already circulated in Europe, where they had been studied and regarded with some suspicion as fairly crude fabrications concocted by counterrevolutionaries.[10] These facts were directly conveyed to Creel, including the assessment of Walter Hines Page, the US ambassador to Britain, that those documents that appeared "genuine were old and not of particular value, and those which had propaganda value were of a doubtful character."[11] Despite this warning, Creel arranged for a pair of historians (one of whom knew no Russian) to authenticate the documents, which if published, Colonel House in the meantime warned President Wilson, would constitute "a virtual declaration of war upon the Bolshevik Government."[12] With Wilson's blessing, Creel in mid-September 1918 released them to the press, followed by an official CPI pamphlet, *The German-Bolshevik Conspiracy*, in an edition of 137,000.[13]

Here was the most dramatic and important instance of the CPI knowingly promulgating likely (if not certain) falsehood, although in his Cold War auto-biography (1947) Creel unrepentantly still insisted that the documents were not forgeries; yet they were conclusively shown to be fabrications in 1956.[14] Published so close to the end of the war, after months of delay, *The German-Bolshevik Conspiracy* pamphlet possessed anti-Soviet "propaganda value" that had little or nothing to do with defeating Germany or promoting American democracy. In this regard, as a piece of covert (and phony) foreign intelligence, the Sisson Papers were clearly out of bounds for the CPI. But that did not stop Creel and Wilson.[15]

After the war, public relations counsels trained in CPI operations abroad continued to blur the line between information (advocacy) and action (policy), anticipating the Cold War development of "public diplomacy," a euphemism for propaganda coined in the 1960s, which sought to supplement or reinforce American national and commercial interests around the world.[16] If propaganda in general represents politics pursued by other means, then this sort of public relations functioned as surrogate diplomacy, often highly coercive and pursed by unofficial means. Working for the United Fruit Company during the 1950s, for example, Bernays infamously generated alarmist publicity that helped topple leftist Jacobo Arbenz, the president of the "banana republic" Guatemala. But Bernays might have been less motivated by ideological hostility against the "red menace" than by a more pragmatic concern that his client's profits would take a big hit if Arbenz stayed in power.[17]

If Communism was bad for business, as Bernays realized, then perhaps business could be bad for Communism, a more interesting and unusual prospect advanced by Ivy Lee in the 1920s. Of all the PR counsels in the first three decades of the century, Lee was the most internationalist in outlook, constantly pursuing business opportunities abroad while vigorously arguing against the narrow-minded isolationist and nationalist attitudes shared by many of his colleagues. From the very beginning of his career, he had always followed the global flow of money, touring Europe and Russia in 1905 and traveling to Panama in 1906, the year he issued his "Declaration of Principles." In Panama he worked on a stock fraud case while studying the potential for railroad publicity linked to the construction of the Panama Canal. Three years later he left his lucrative position representing the Pennsylvania Railroad to manage the London branch of a banking firm, explaining to his son, "I think international investment banking and finance will play an increasingly major role in world affairs in the years ahead."[18]

Given his experience in international finance and his expertise in corporate public relations, Lee was a logical choice during the war to direct publicity for the American Red Cross, an agency that in many ways resembled the CPI, if not quite so extensive in scope and more narrowly humanitarian in focus. As Lee defined its mission (sounding a lot like Creel), the Red Cross was "not only a great relief organization but a great social and moral force, including the gospel of service and sacrifice."[19] Beyond his acumen at fundraising (he was no slouch there), Lee also appreciated how the Red Cross could function as yet another kind of publicity bureau for the United States, giving "the world an entirely new vision of the essential meaning of American life and character," not as "a nation interested primarily and largely in money-making" but one "of ideals and sympathy and love of peace."[20]

It would be easy to dismiss such sentiments as cynical claptrap, especially coming from Rockefeller's hired gun, but Lee did earnestly believe that the Red Cross was crucial for "promoting better understanding between ourselves and all the Allied nations."[21] After the war, he continued to preach in this vein, chiding his fellow Americans, especially businessmen, for turning their backs on their global responsibilities. In an address to members of the American Institute of Banking titled *The Vacant Chair at the Council Table of the World* (1922), he decried the absence of the United States in the League of Nations. Like Bernays and many others after the war, Lee regarded politics as basically a subspecies of capitalist enterprise, which was now the dominant force across the globe. Like Bernays, after the war Lee took on various foreign clients, publicizing the activities of and securing loans for the governments of France, Poland, and Romania. But more so than for Bernays, international PR work for Lee had a strong ideological basis, and he sought to convince Americans that they could not afford to ignore the politics and economic hardships of other nations, such as Germany, whose "prosperity involves the prosperity of our own people," as he argued in his talk to the bankers.[22] If "the world is today profoundly an economic unit" (10), Lee observed, if "the money markets of the world today are substantially one" (22) thanks to advanced communications such as the telephone, telegraph, and radio, then that understanding demanded a full engagement with other countries, including not just US trading partners, but presumed adversaries of the United States as well.

Having first visited Russia during a moment of turmoil, the failed 1905 revolution, Lee decided in 1927 to return in order to see for himself what the post-revolution Communist state had become.[23] His account of the journey, *USSR: A World Enigma*, ostensibly undertaken as a private citizen, is quite absorbing and yet not exactly the musings of an innocent tourist, given Lee's impressive corporate resume and quasi-diplomatic stature, which enabled him to meet with high-ranking Soviet officials. Again, a cynic might say that Lee was simply being opportunistic, sizing up the chances for an emerging new world market to become available for American commercial interests. But such a view ignores the genuine intellectual curiosity that Lee displayed throughout his book about Russian culture more broadly, as well as his surprisingly open-minded attitude toward Communism. Although he was a "man distinctly allied with capitalism," he nonetheless took pains not to demonize "the enemy's camp," as he called the USSR.[24]

This was no ordinary travelogue, given Lee's professed motives in writing the book, as he explained in his introduction: "We hear a great deal in the United States about 'Bolshevik Propaganda' and the Russian menace. I wanted [to] find out just how that propaganda is carried on, what the nature of it is, what the story is that is being told through such propaganda, and just how it is being told" (6). This distinct focus invites us to regard the book as a companion piece to Bernays's *Propaganda* (published the following year), although Lee was less inclined to make unsubstantiated generalizations and more interested in examining how propaganda worked in a particular, perhaps unique, context. What most impressed him, right off the bat, was the Soviet government's ability to "saturate" its citizens with beliefs and values via names, mottoes, signs, posters, and slogans that all served to reinforce "the new social conditions under which they live" (26). It might be going too far to say that Lee expressed nostalgia for the patriotic saturation that had similarly been accomplished in the United States by the CPI and the Red Cross during the war. But he did seem to admire, without too much begrudging, the state's capacity to centralize and disseminate information, or "to combine political propaganda with cultural education" (35), as he quoted one of many passages from the government's official English-language guidebook. The result, he implied (but did not come out and say), was a new Soviet subject, at once enlightened and forged by revolutionary ideology, which suggested that people, not just opinions, might be manufactured by mass persuasion, far beyond what the most militant Progressive might have imagined.[25]

In addition to citing the guidebook, Lee witnessed this process firsthand, visiting the offices of TASS, the Soviet news agency, where he saw how "the distribution of news is, like everything else in Russia, concentrated in one organization under direct control of the Government" (51). As he detailed the various media and methods at the disposal of state journalism, such as radio broadcasting, he encountered something new, "wall-newspapers," a "kind of forum where the workers critically discuss all the more or less important matters and events at the plant. Not only are the trade union organizations at the factory or establishment criticized and satirized, but even the plant administration is not spared"

(55). If this was not a sort of democracy, it sure looked like it. Although Lee was obviously not about to endorse this practice for American labor-management relations, he clearly was impressed by it, despite the fact that his honest observation did not square with his other more predictable conclusions deploring the tendencies of Soviet "censorship" to deaden "human expression" (58).

Lee ran into the same sort of enigma when he quoted a worker he met in Moscow who told him, in a seemingly unscripted speech, "The people are THINKING— even the farmers are being allowed to think, and to hold meetings. It doesn't matter what he says at such meetings or what he thinks at the moment; the fact that he is being allowed to talk and meet is arousing his political conscience and in the long run he can be relied upon to think soundly" (72). Lee simply let stand this comment, which therefore carried as much weight as the remarks offered by elite Communist officials and intellectuals, like Prime Minister Alexei Rykov and Karl Radek, whom he visited and interviewed. Although it seemed contradictory, propaganda aimed at the proletariat might actually enhance participatory democracy, not stifle it.

Despite these utopian possibilities, Lee was confident that when it came to Russia's political economy, the Communist experiment was bound to fail because of the relentless global reach of capital. Here he marshaled for support two authorities who would otherwise seem to have little in common: Wilson and Trotsky. Just after the war, Wilson famously remarked (as quoted by Lee): "The men who do the business of the world now shape the destinies of the world" (155). Trotsky seemed to have recognized the same thing, warning (as paraphrased by Lee) that the Soviet state "MUST PRODUCE MORE CHEAPLY OR GO DOWN" (154, emphasis in original). Lee summarized the logic behind Germany's active dealings with the USSR by claiming that the "best way to kill Bolshevism is to trade with the Russians" (130). International competition, "an influx of capitalist goods, INCOMPARABLY BETTER AND CHEAPER THAN OURS" (95, quoting Trotsky again, emphasis in original), would be the weapon to defeat Communism. That was the reason Lee counseled a policy of recognition and engagement, not containment, anticipating the advice of Lippmann during the Cold War, although Lee's version of diplomacy was economic, not political, a "propaganda of deeds rather than words" (155), or what he called "the business statesmanship of the world" (156). For advocating such an unpopular approach, Lee was deemed a Soviet agent by some of his fellow Americans, especially those in the business community—a rather odd charge considering Lee's intimate ties to the Rockefellers.[26]

Lee never made any headway in securing the Bolsheviks as business clients, but a couple of years after his trip to Russia he did succeed with a major German

corporation, landing a public relations contract in 1929 with the American holding company of the huge industrial firm IG Farben, known as the "dye trust." On
the eve of the Great Depression, snagging an account affiliated with the largest
chemical manufacturing enterprise in the world was quite a coup. For a retainer
of $3,000 a year, Lee offered public relations advice for the US operations of
Farben subsidiaries such as Agfa Photo and Bayer, run by a board of directors that
included Edsel Ford, Walter Teagle (the president of Standard Oil of New Jersey), and various Wall Street bankers and influential German financiers. When
Hitler came to power in 1933, Lee's ties with IG Farben suddenly expanded; an
executive of the parent company, Max Ilgner, hired him for an additional $25,000
a year (the hefty salary increase speaks for itself) to advise Farben about how to improve its reputation in the United States and, well beyond that, how to enhance
the image of the new regime more generally. Given the bad press surrounding
the rise of the Nazis, relations between Germany and America, particularly business relations, were suffering. In the spring of 1933, for instance, American Jews
organized a worldwide boycott of German goods.

Two important points about this new arrangement between Lee and Farben
need to be emphasized before I move on to some of the more disturbing and
sordid details. First, the lines between the German enterprise and its American
subsidiaries were porous and fluid; the world was now driven by global markets
after all, as Lee had stressed during his trip to the USSR. Trying to keep the US
side of the international conglomerate's operations neatly separated from the German side would be impossible. Second, the boundaries between private business
and public politics, in both America and Germany, had also become porous and
fluid, thanks in large part to the profession of public relations as practiced by the
likes of Lee, Bernays, and Byoir.

Lee's corporate counterpart Max Ilgner, for instance, was an ambitious,
self-promoting former salesman, like Lee a master of publicity, who by 1934 had
attained significant authority within Farben, overseeing market research, press
relations, financial administration, overseas accounts, and, most significant, the
company's contacts with the new German government.[27] Not only was Ilgner
personally committed to the new Nazi regime, but so was the entire corporation,
which had given a sizable donation to the Nazi Party after some direct intimidation by Hitler weeks before its March 1933 election victory. This subsidy was followed later that year by a "deal of truly Faustian proportions," largely engineered
by Ilgner, which put Farben's synthetic fuel program (crucial for waging war) at
the disposal of the government, so that "from now on the IG's fate and fortunes
would be inextricably tied to those of the Third Reich."[28] As in the case of mo-

nopoly trusts in the United States around the turn of the twentieth century, and
as in the case of the Soviet Union's centralized, state-run economy, with the Nazis
effectively dictating Farben's financial course, commerce and politics became
fused in a way that afforded great opportunities for the craft of public relations.

Given his contacts, at once personal and business, Ilgner arranged for Lee,
who was visiting Berlin in January 1934, to confer with Joseph Goebbels and other
cabinet ministers and party leaders about how the United States could be induced
to better understand the new Germany. The previous spring, in advance of these
discussions, he had already been cordially introduced to Chancellor Hitler. Before the January meetings, the publicist and his son James, Lee's PR partner,
made a courtesy call to American ambassador William Dodd, who recorded his
damning first impression in his diary: "Ivy Lee showed himself at once a capitalist
and an advocate for Fascism. He told stories of his fight for Russian recognition
and was disposed to claim credit for it. His sole aim was to increase American
business profits."[29] A week later Lee returned to the American embassy to report
on his face-to-race discussions in Germany, telling Dodd that "he had warned
Goebbels to cease propaganda in the United States, urged him to see the foreign
press people often and learn how to get along with them." After having witnessed
Goebbels give a speech to the foreign press corps, Dodd later noted in his diary
that "it was plain that he [Goebbels] was trying to apply the advice which Ivy Lee
urged upon him a month ago" (83). After running into James Lee, who had stayed
in Germany to continue the PR advising, Dodd in his diary bluntly summed
up the elder Lee as "the clever big business propagandist who has been trying
for a year or more to sell the Nazi regime to the American public" (131). This
assessment accorded with Dodd's earlier description of Lee's publicity activity as
"strange work" (76).

Strange, indeed. Schmoozing with the Nazi chancellor and his minister of
propaganda was probably not such a good idea, most Americans would have
agreed.[30] When members of Congress got wind of the publicist's meetings in Germany, they hauled him before the McCormack-Dickstein Committee, an early
iteration of the House Un-American Activities Committee (HUAC), which had
been authorized in March 1934 to investigate Nazi propaganda activities in the
United States. Lee's testimony before the committee on May 19, 1934, was fascinating, not only for shedding light on what Lee was doing or thought he was doing
(or how he spun it), but also for raising crucial questions about the definitions of
propaganda, the relation between the public and private domains and between
politics and business, and the limits and ethical implications of manufacturing
consent, as Lippmann had called it, now set in a volatile transnational context. In

his responses Lee echoed some of the very same statements about the importance of honest disclosure he had made a full twenty years earlier, when grilled by the Industrial Relations commissioner, Frank Walsh, about his PR role in representing John D. Rockefeller Jr. after the Ludlow Massacre of 1914 (see chapter 2).

Perhaps because of the restricted scope of their mandate, the three men interviewing Lee (Representatives John McCormack and Samuel Dickstein and committee counsel Thomas W. Hardwick) tended to focus on his suspected dissemination of Nazi propaganda inside the United States. Here Lee was on pretty safe ground; he could simply deny such activity without needing much spin. Although IG Farben and Lee's son might have sent him loads of pro-Nazi literature from both "official and unofficial sources," this was mainly for his own edification and not to pass on to others.[31] Lee was too prominent to be serving merely as a low-level conduit or agent provocateur. Dickstein and Lee went back and forth about whether this printed material—"books and pamphlets, and newspaper clippings and documents, world without end," as Lee described it—was "propaganda" (potentially subversive) or "literature" (protected free speech), with Dickstein testily replying to Lee at one point that "you may call it anything you like" (256). But there was certainly nothing illegal about reading how Germany sought to represent itself to the world. Committee chair McCormack also spent a fair amount of time chasing the money trail and tracking Farben's payments to Lee, although this was pretty much by the book, beyond the startling jump in salary once he was retained by the parent company. Far more interesting and problematic was pinning Lee down on what he exactly did for IG Farben to command such a hefty fee.

For such a confident, savvy, and experienced PR man, Lee had a surprisingly hard time explaining his profession, opening his testimony by saying that his work was "very difficult to describe" and closing it with a similar bumbling admission: "I am not an advertising agency. My business—I do not know how to describe it" (269). Whether strategically evasive or not, Lee did offer that as soon as the Nazis took over Germany he was paid by Farben "for advisory services in connection with political relationships" (262). Dickstein then asked, "[S]omething more personal or private?" to which Lee responded, "No. It was in connection with their business." An American citizen hired by a huge German corporation to advise its management about public opinion as it pertained to Nazi politics—this was a highly unusual arrangement, to say the least.

Although Dickstein did not seem to pick up on the implications of this exchange, the committee's counsel, Hardwick, did, asking a series of probing questions that arrived at the heart of the matter. Hardwick got Lee to admit that in advising Farben about "political relationships," as he vaguely called it, the distinction between commerce and government would grow fuzzy, since Farben wanted Lee to tell the company how to directly exert influence on American opinions about Nazis in order to improve business relations between the two nations. Hardwick additionally prodded Lee to acknowledge that "since Hitler came into power, the German Government has assumed a pretty thorough control of private business" (267), although Lee still refused to see that Farben might therefore have been acting on behalf of the Nazis.

When he came to describing his actual conversations with Nazi officials arranged by Farben, Lee clung to the distinctions between private and public affairs, at times to ludicrous effect. Volunteering that he had met Hitler in 1933, a fact seemingly unknown to the committee, Lee insisted that he did so "just as any foreign traveler might meet him," as if the new chancellor would be welcoming random American tourists curious for a chat. But he was no casual visitor. He explained that "they" (presumably, Farben executives such as Ilgner) introduced him to Hitler "as a personal matter, to size him up" (264). Lee divulged little about what he discussed with Hitler, but he did go into some detail about his conversation with Goebbels. He reported (as he did to Ambassador Dodd) that he discouraged the minister from disseminating propaganda in the United States. Lee deemed such activity counterproductive and "very bad business," urging Goebbels instead to cultivate foreign correspondents in order to use publicity "in the normal way" (249). As Lee suddenly remembered late in his testimony, Goebbels agreed not to "interfere in anything in the United States" (265).

Lee also explained how he cautioned Goebbels that the Nazis' treatment of Jews "could never be justified in the American public opinion, and there was no use trying" (249). He repeatedly presented the issue primarily as practical, not moral, and the thought of Lee advising Goebbels to dial back Nazi anti-Semitism is like—well, it is difficult to know how to complete such a comparison. He said he had "a very interesting talk" with Goebbels about his title, "[Minister of] Propaganda and Enlightenment," but unfortunately the committee did not pursue this subject, so we are left to surmise what common ground America's most accomplished publicist for hire and the master of Nazi mass persuasion might have found.

When the committee's hearings were made public in July 1934, the American press was relentless in its excoriation of Lee, who was suffering from a brain tumor and would die in November. In his father's defense James claimed that Lee was simply supremely naïve, yet another American innocent who thought he could change the world, in this case by giving sage, paid advice to the Nazis and Farben about how to run their "business."[32] (Everything was pretty much "business" for Lee.) Precisely when Americans began to understand what was happening in Germany has been thoroughly debated by scholars, but there is little question that by 1934 a well-informed citizen who carefully read the news, as PR counsel Lee certainly needed to do, would have known better.[33] The Nazis had early on made apparent their intense hostility to democracy and any sort of democratic process; Goebbels, for instance, in his newspaper the *Attack* (*Der Angriff*) openly declared on April 30, 1928, while running for office, "We are entering the Reichstag in order that we may arm ourselves with the weapons of democracy from its own arsenal."[34] On the eve of his election in 1933, Hitler echoed Goebbels, vowing to use the "weapons of democracy" to destroy democracy.[35] These were grotesque twists on George Creel's phrase *weapons of democracy* that the Progressive muckraker in 1914 could never have foreseen. As for Lee, days before his testimony made news, he published his last pamphlet, with the unnerving title *The Problem of International Propaganda: A New Technique in Developing Understanding Between Nations.*

Lee was not the only American public relations counsel to interact with the Nazis. Bernays, as we might expect, had his own disturbing Goebbels story, if not quite as dramatic as Lee's. In his autobiography Bernays recounted running into a Hearst foreign correspondent, Karl von Wiegand, in the summer of 1933. Wiegand had recently returned from Germany, where he had met Goebbels, who had proudly showed the reporter his "propaganda library," including of course *Crystallizing Public Opinion*. According to Wiegand, this book by Bernays was serving as a basis for the "destructive campaign against the Jews in Germany," although neither Wiegand nor Bernays bothered to spell out exactly how Goebbels was putting the book to use. First expressing shock, Bernays then more blandly went on to chalk up this abuse of his ideas to the fact that "any human activity can be used for social purposes or misused for antisocial ones" (*Biography of an Idea*, 652). Stuart Ewen accurately deemed this anecdote a piece of "public relations folklore," because being strictly hearsay, the story's truth is difficult, if not impossible, to independently confirm.[36]

During his testimony before the McCormack-Dickstein Committee, Lee was asked briefly about Carl Byoir, whose publicity firm was also under investigation for Nazi propaganda activity. After he helped to propel Bernays's legendary vocation in public relations with that Lithuania account right after the war, Byoir's own career had settled into a fallow period during the 1920s. Having spent some years pushing products of dubious merit, such as patent medicines and hair tonics, Byoir for health reasons in 1928 moved to Cuba, where he began working with the government of Gerardo Machado to promote American tourism on the island. His great success in Cuba led to his 1930 founding of the PR firm Carl Byoir and Associates, which among other clients secured a contract in October 1933 with the German Railroads Tourist Bureau to repeat his Cuban accomplishments, this time in Nazi Germany.[37]

Ironies abound in this strange episode. Grilling Byoir's junior partner, Carl Dickey, the McCormack-Dickstein Committee's investigators pursued the same line of inquiry as they had with Lee concerning his Farben connections, pointing out to Dickey that the German railroad system was directly owned and operated by the government.[38] Dealing with the railroads would therefore be equivalent to dealing with the Nazis. Here the evidence was stronger and clearer than in the case of Farben, which ostensibly was a private enterprise, because soon after assuming power, Hitler had nationalized the railroads. Irony 1: The state control of utilities, transportation, and communications industries, which many American Progressives had yearned for since the turn of the twentieth century, had actually been accomplished by the totalitarian regimes of the Russian Bolsheviks and the Nazi Party.

The core tenet of Hitler's party was the virulent, relentless demonization of Jews, so that the main goal of Byoir's publicity for the German railroads, as Dickey testified, was to mitigate and readjust negative American attitudes toward Nazis and Nazi anti-Semitism in order to improve the tourist business. So, irony number 2: Byoir, like Bernays, was Jewish, and here he was, openly aiding the professed mortal enemy of all things Jewish.

The third irony was the heaviest. To help with this tourist campaign, Dickey and Byoir had hired George Sylvester Viereck. Born in Munich but moving to New York City at age twelve (in 1896), Viereck was a well-known man of letters who became during World War I a key propagandist for Germany while still living in the United States. During the war, as the committee members reminded Dickey, Viereck had from 1914 published the newspaper the *Fatherland* (*Vaderland*), seeking to give Americans (including German-Americans) the official German perspective on the war. Before the United States entered the fray, he routinely met with the German propaganda cabinet back in Germany.[39] After the Allied victory, Viereck continued his career in journalism, interviewing various luminaries, including Freud in 1923. That same year he became one of the first American reporters (soon after Wiegand in 1922) to interview Hitler, and he predicted great things from the charismatic leader. Later in the decade he befriended Edward House and went on to publish a book about the close companionship between House and President Wilson. Encountering the journalist in Berlin in the summer of 1933, Ambassador Dodd recorded in his diary: "At 12 o'clock George Sylvester Viereck came with a letter from Colonel House. Viereck impressed me as unstable, a real pro-Nazi, here to see officials of the government" (28).

It was odd enough that House would enjoy Viereck's company, but the fact that Byoir's firm would pay him a sizable sum, nearly $2,000 a month, to work with the German railroads seems hard to fathom, even taking into account his intimate knowledge of the country and its people. Byoir, recall, learned the craft of publicity while employed by the CPI, where he was no bit player but the single most important and influential administrator besides Creel. For a key American wartime propagandist fifteen years later to hire the very propagandist who had so vigorously advocated on behalf of the evil "Hun" and Prussian autocracy for a campaign to promote tourism in the land of the defeated enemy was curious indeed. Perhaps this was simply an instance of business concerns overriding all others. But a stranger impulse might have been operating here, encouraging Byoir to gravitate to a fellow publicist, apparently with no hard feelings, although one was a Jew and the other a Nazi true believer.

Odd too that the committee's inquiry did little lasting harm to Byoir, although Viereck was imprisoned by the United States as a German agent in 1942. Carl Byoir and Associates went on in the next two decades to become one of the most successful and admired public relations outfits in America, raising funds for the eradication of polio and the Democratic National Committee, and conducting publicity for the great supermarket chain A&P, among many other notable clients. Byoir died in 1957, but in 1988 the PR firm Hill and Knowlton absorbed the firm he had founded, now under the leadership of one of his trusted executives. Two years later, in 1990, Hill and Knowlton was hired by the government of Kuwait for $12 million to help promote a US-led invasion of Iraq.[40]

Conclusion

When an American public relations counsel is hired to give advice to another country's minister of propaganda, certain implications follow. In his final publication (based on a speech given in London on July 3, 1934) before dying of cancer, Ivy Lee offered an affirmative take on the global reach of his business practice. He turned his attention to "international propaganda," which he described as a "new technique." But it is hard to see exactly what was new in Lee's argument, other than an uncharacteristically sugary tone of optimism. Perhaps he was trying to make amends for his association with Nazis, but Lee's suggestions for promoting world peace and mutual understanding between nations sounded more utopian than even Dewey. He repeated his familiar refrain about the efficacy of honest disclosure. Propaganda is only evil when it is "secret, underground, and indirect," but when the source of information is known, then ultimately truth will endure against the machinations of "unseen assassins."[1] Of course truth is relative, depending on one's own interpretation of facts, as Lee had emphasized throughout his career. But sincerity and fidelity can be accurately gauged by the masses, Lee contended, as long as publicity remained out in the open. Yet mere disclosure seems a shaky moral foundation upon which to justify propaganda once we consider the mass spectacles and rallies choreographed by Goebbels and his fellow Nazis, who broadcast their terrorizing messages of venomous hate with impunity. Assassins are assassins, whether unseen or not.

Lee's faith in transparency rested on a broader faith in the democratic public itself, which Lee no longer disparaged as an unruly "crowd." This faith extended beyond the United States to include totalitarian regimes like Russia and Germany, because for Lee "dictatorships are, in the last resort, but an expression of mass emotion and power" (19), and even dictators must abide by the "sovereignty of the masses." So where did propaganda fit in? While he insisted that it was the appeal to reason that drove his international work, his reference to "emotion and power" suggested a darker side to large-scale persuasion. In a curious turn in his argument, Lee acknowledged that new research in mass psychology "tended to perfect methods by which the emotions of the collective man can be touched and stirred" (23). But this patriotic arousal of "subconscious reflexes" by banners, marches, and slogans, he reasoned, would lose its "psychological power" beyond the frontiers of the nation, and therefore another sort of international propaganda, diplomatic in nature, was required. While his concluding analysis of print, cinema, and radio was shrewd and occasionally unconventional—he suggested that leaders like Joseph Stalin (but no mention of Hitler) buy advertising space in American newspapers to articulate their government's positions on world affairs—the virtues of these various media he celebrated seem little match for the negative "devices and incantations of professional propagandists" (23) that he sought with his new diplomatic brand to render obsolete, along with war itself.

Lee's pamphlet was one of the last instances (at least in English) invoking the p-word in an affirmative sense and with a straight face. Despite his efforts and those of Edward Bernays (in his 1928 book), even the best public relations specialists could not put a positive spin on propaganda, especially after the likes of Goebbels embraced the concept and practice as a vital means of indoctrination. "Invisible government," as Bernays had audaciously applauded it, had during the 1930s increasingly become suspect, especially in the political realm, which led to institutionalized modes of combat: not only the hearings of the McCormack-Dickstein Committee, which were designed to stop the spread of Nazi ideology in the United States, but also academic enterprises like the Institute for Propaganda Analysis (IPA), founded in 1936 to study and warn American citizens about the harmful effects of mass persuasion.[2] With the rise of totalitarian regimes, propaganda could no longer be innocently taken as a kind of education, shaping and organizing the intelligence of the American public; now, education was enlisted precisely to counter the power of print, radio, and cinema, all perceived as potentially threatening forms of coercion and pacification.

Where did that leave public opinion? James Bryce in 1888 had celebrated voting, press, and vigorous public debate as the foundations undergirding the "American Commonwealth," the crucial means by which the consenting governed actively weighed in on their democratic government. But in the most authoritative account of this bourgeois sphere, publicness began to collapse near the end of the nineteenth century because of two related pressures or historical tendencies:

the increasing intervention of the state in matters traditionally overseen and man-aged by the family or civil society; and the growing interference of commercial and corporate interests in the shaping of rational political deliberation.[3] The case of Ivy Lee consulting with Goebbels seemed to merge these two tendencies, in addition to dramatizing an additional one that Lee foresaw—the rise in interna-tional propaganda, which Lee regarded as a new kind of public diplomacy. But once spheres of influence cross borders, as for instance when Kuwait in 1990 hired an American firm to sway American opinion in favor of invading Kuwait's enemy, Iraq, then what sort of "public" does this constitute?

Perhaps we should be wary of this teleological scheme that inexorably leads to the destruction of publicness thanks to a blurring of boundaries between state and civil society, between commercial interests and politics, and between na-tions. After all, the global spread of indoctrination was nothing new; it started in the seventeenth century with the Catholic Church's Congregatione de Prop-aganda Fide and continued during the French Revolution. If the emergence of the public sphere in the eighteenth century can be understood as a "structural transformation," so too the increasing emphasis on mass publicity during the early twentieth century can be considered a transitional moment rather than a mere erosion and disappearance, especially in the United States. This process of transformation is particularly evident when we trace the contending forces in play before America entered the Great War. To summarize, around the start of the twentieth century, muckrakers, politicians, and corporations in the very midst of Progressive reform all vied to direct public opinion to further their agendas. Walter Lippmann's subsequent gloomy assessment was that this incessant whirl-wind of information simply befuddled citizens who lacked the competence to intelligently assess and organize the propaganda blown their way.

But this robust competition of interests (special or otherwise) pointed to a segmenting, separating, and sharing of power that, at least, prevented any single domain from dominating the public. Of course as soon as the United States en-tered the war, then these divided powers were quickly consolidated and reverted back to the state, thanks in large measure to Creel's Committee on Public Infor-mation. Once the war ended, just as rapidly mass persuasion largely became a matter of "unregulated private enterprise," to invoke Lippmann again, resulting in a "phantom public." What Lippmann saw as a grave threat to democracy, public relations counsels seized as an opportunity, although all shared a strong residual Progressive faith in administrative efficiency and expertise that persisted well into the 1920s.

It is important in reviewing this history to avoid the temptation to identify one sort of propaganda practice as benign or "good" in contrast to "bad" or evil propaganda, based strictly on the politics we might prefer. Take what might seem to be an obvious point of contrast: the Children's Bureau, as run by Julia Lathrop, compared to the Torches of Freedom mock suffrage parade staged by Bernays on behalf of the American Tobacco Company. What has more social value, saving babies or selling cigarettes? Lippmann cautioned over and over again that matters of "the common good" are rarely if ever so clear-cut. But even in this extreme comparison, complexities abound. In a quintessential gesture of Progressive reform, the CB sought to safeguard the country's youngest and most vulnerable citizens by treating them as national resources in need of protection. Yet recall that Lathrop's efforts initially met with some resistance, including from potential beneficiaries who did not want the state to interfere in their family affairs. Only by quickly making the central mission of the bureau to be decreasing infant mortality rather than restricting child labor was Lathrop able to gain the support she needed to effectively operate her agency. On the other hand, while Bernays was primarily concerned with getting women to smoke Lucky Strikes, his publicity stunt clearly stirred up newspaper editorials and discussions across the country about the role of women in American society more broadly.

Leaving particular outcomes aside, the key difference between Lathrop and Bernays was in the way each of them went about the business of propagandizing. Lathrop was remarkably responsive to her constituents, personally replying to letter after letter, listening to poor women's concerns, and adjusting the bureau's policies and mass publicity campaigns to meet those concerns, while still maintaining a firm sense of what she thought was in their best interests. In Dewey's terms, this was a conversation. Bernays, on the other hand, engineered a unilateral letter-writing campaign to the press about his parade in order to steer opinion in favor of women smoking; there is no indication that he bothered to listen to other voices or modify his own views, which conveniently happened to coincide with the views of his corporate client. There was nothing reciprocal about his relation to his targeted audience. Although near the end of his book *Propaganda* he took pains to show how his public relations strategies could be harnessed for useful social service and educational projects, it is clear that what interested him most were "the mechanics" of propaganda, as he titled the final chapter in the volume.

Another word for *mechanics* is *technique*, which is the term Randolph Bourne used over and over to describe the pursuit of war as well as the means by which American citizens were persuaded en masse to support that war effort. Bourne understood that modernity's growing fixation on autonomous techne, or technological mastery for its own sake, would tend to transform the means to a given end into ends themselves. As soon as the state calls for war, the reasons (and reason in general) fall by the wayside. In the figure of his increasingly monomaniacal Connecticut Yankee, Twain too anticipated this inclination toward purposeless administering in the name of "progress," an attitude that is epitomized in the novel by Sir Boss's cavalier making and equally cavalier destroying of his "man-factories." Public relations experts like Lee and Bernays similarly molded people's thoughts and behavior simply because they could, a fact that Lee was reluctant to disclose but Bernays took pleasure in celebrating.

Yet this administrative and technological tendency for means to turn into ends need not be inevitable. Consider the Four Minute Men speakers program. Part of the massive, overarching Committee on Public Information's propaganda apparatus developed by George Creel, the 4MM would seem at first glance to confirm Bourne's worst fears. What could be more coercive than an "army" of 75,000 volunteers spreading out across the country night after night to inundate millions of captive moviegoers seeking some innocent entertainment with brief but urgent patriotic war appeals? But these were not robotic emissaries of the state reading mechanically from predetermined scripts. The men (and there were also women) were respected members of local communities who talked earnestly "from the heart" to their fellow citizens, speaking in the vernacular of their neighbors (in Yiddish or Italian, for example) and trading rhetorical tips with other speakers. Although not a genuine dialogue in Dewey's sense, for the speakers at least this grassroots propagandizing represented an intense, earnest civic engagement quite in keeping with Progressive ideals.

After the war, those ideals that hinged on the fate of democratic public opinion became a source of struggle and perplexity for Lippmann and Dewey, a legacy that remains for us a century later. Is the Internet some version of the "Great Community" that Dewey envisioned and cherished, filled with a multiplicity of voices and encouraging interlocutors to share ideas? Or does such multiplicity create a media environment that can only lead to greater misinformation and confusion, preventing the "omnicompetent" citizen, as Lippmann dubbed this mythic creature, from making coherent sense of the world? Or perhaps worse still, does the Internet primarily function as a colossal machine for manufacturing consent (Lippmann again), a vast echo chamber in which people seek simply to confirm beliefs that they already hold, rather than allow themselves to be convinced by other points of view?

How do we explain the mechanisms of persuasion and the dismal state of public opinion before and during the 2003 US-led invasion of Iraq? Was President George W. Bush's "with us or against us" approach, along the lines of

Creel's friend-foe mentality during World War I (subsequently theorized by Carl Schmitt), so corrosive as to dissolve any sustained critical deliberation? While there were certainly pockets of resistance and dissent, which were arguably stronger than during World War I, the vast majority of American citizens and the mainstream press compliantly went along with the Bush administration, and once the war began, those opposed mostly fell into a sullen silence—precisely the kind of resignation or acquiescence that the self-proclaimed malcontent Bourne valiantly contested in article after article until the very end of the Great War, which also marked his own untimely end by influenza. In an ostensibly open democracy such as the United States, in which information would seem to flow freely, how could the coverage of the Iraq invasion be so one-sided and shoddy as to compel the *New York Times* (the same newspaper that Lippmann tested and found wanting in 1920) to publish an editorial in May 2004 apologizing for its lack of rigor and its reliance on faulty sources?[4] This clearly was a "failure of intelligence," not the sort that the Bush administration offered as an excuse (being misled by foreign informants), but rather a failure of the domestic *social* intelligence that Progressives championed as necessary for a vibrant democracy to thrive and flourish.

Focusing on the strong cast of characters who both analyzed and practiced mass publicity during the Progressive Era, from Wilson, Lathrop, and Creel, to Dewey and Lippmann, to Lee and Bernays, in this book I have concentrated on methods and motives, which are largely matters of production and dissemination. But propaganda also entails reception, how information is received by persons and groups who constitute a public or publics by participating in such acts of communication. If incapable of total comprehension (as Lippmann might have it), individuals are more than passive victims or dupes; if infinitely malleable (as Progressive social scientists posited), they also have the capacity to shape themselves, especially in relation to others. Citizens continue to bear some responsibility for trying to occupy and hold the grounds of belief in order to avoid being complicit in the ceaseless efforts by those in power to direct them in how to act, think, and feel. Such efforts to influence and coerce opinion might be endless, but the manufacturing of consent is never a foregone conclusion, as Lippmann even at his bleakest intuited. Looking closely at how Progressives such as Lippmann and Dewey grappled with the public and its problems—problems clearly still with us today—reminds us that beyond the state, public relations experts, and sundry masters of spin, our weapons of democracy might have many other users and many other uses.

Notes

INTRODUCTION

1. Walter Lippmann, *Liberty and the News* (New York: Harcourt, Brace and Howe, 1920), 5; Walter Lippmann, *The Phantom Public* (New York: Macmillan, 1925).

2. James quoted in Robert B. Westbrook, *John Dewey and American Democracy* (Ithaca, NY: Cornell University Press, 1991), 14. This paragraph and the following are drawn from the introduction in Jonathan Auerbach and Russ Castronovo, eds., *The Oxford Handbook of Propaganda Studies* (New York: Oxford University Press, 2013).

3. John Durham Peters, *Courting the Abyss: Free Speech and the Liberal Tradition* (Chicago: University of Chicago Press, 2005), 112.

4. The closest approach to my own can be found in Eldon J. Eisenach, *The Lost Promise of Progressivism* (Lawrence: University Press of Kansas, 1994), esp. 74–103, although in discussing various efforts to nationalize public opinion, he did not engage some of the darker implications of the administrative retooling of citizens, as I do. For a concise overview examining Progressive worries over the rise of publicity, see Michael Schudson, *The Good Citizen: A History of American Civic Life* (New York: Free Press, 1998), 192–202. Schudson wryly noted that during this period "too many thinkers took the existence of propaganda as proof of its efficacy" (201).

5. Scott L. Althaus and Devon M. Largio, "When Osama Became Saddam: Origins and Consequences of the Change in America's Public Enemy #1," *PS: Political Science and Politics* (October 2004): 795–799. The authors showed how this misperception was partly due to the format and wording of the poll questions themselves.

6. Robert C. Binkley, "The Concept of Public Opinion in the Social Sciences," *Social Forces* 6 (1928): 389–396. Binkley was a fascinating figure, one of the first historians of media who wrote on the preservation of records, including newer technologies of storage such as microfilm.

7. See also Jeremiah W. Jenks, "The Guidance of Public Opinion," *American Journal of Sociology* 1, no. 2 (September 1895): 158–169, for a discussion singling out schools and newspapers as two flawed institutions that distort and coerce public opinion.

8. Woodrow Wilson, "The Study of Administration," *Political Science Quarterly* 2, no. 2 (June 1887): 197–222 (subsequent references cited parenthetically in text). For a valuable discussion of Wilson's essay, see Ronald J. Pestritto, *Woodrow Wilson and the Roots of Modern Liberalism* (Lanham, MD: Rowman and Littlefield, 2005), 221–246. For an earlier look at Wilson in relation to German theories of bureaucracy, see Robert D.

Cuff, "Wilson and Weber: Bourgeois Critics in an Organized Age," *Public Administration Review* 38, no. 3 (June 1978): 240–244.

9. John Dewey, "The Ethics of Democracy," in *The Early Works of John Dewey*, vol. 1 (Carbondale: Southern Illinois University Press, 1969), 227–249 (subsequent references, including Dewey's quotations from Maine, cited parenthetically in text).

10. On the *Thought News* project, see Neil Coughlan, *Young John Dewey* (Chicago: University of Chicago Press, 1975), 100–109; Westbrook, *John Dewey and American Democracy*, 52–58; Andrej Pinter, "*Thought News*: A Quest for Democratic Communication Technology," *Public Opinion Quarterly* 10, no. 2 (2003): 93–104. There was a precursor to *Thought News*, an American magazine established in 1886 named *Public Opinion* (what else?) that reprinted snippets from other publications in order "to impartially reflect public opinion" by "focalizing many and divergent views and opinions." But this journal did not have the grander philosophical ambitions of *Thought News*.

11. All quotations in Coughlan, *Young John Dewey*, 102, 105. It is uncertain whether the April 1892 notice was written by Ford or Dewey.

12. George H. Mead, "The Working Hypothesis in Social Reform," *American Journal of Sociology* 5, no. 3 (November 1899): 367–371 (subsequent references cited parenthetically in text).

13. On the implications of this late nineteenth-century erosion of a self-contained public sphere, see Jürgen Habermas, *The Structural Transformation of the Public Sphere: An Inquiry into a Category of Bourgeois Society*, trans. Thomas Burger (1962; rpt., Cambridge, MA: MIT Press, 1989). For an extended discussion of Habermas, see my "Essay on Sources."

14. Dorothy Ross, *The Origins of American Social Science* (Cambridge: Cambridge University Press, 1991).

15. Charles Horton Cooley, *Social Organization: A Study of the Larger Mind* (New York: Scribner's, 1909), 121.

16. Edward Alsworth Ross, *Social Control: A Survey of the Foundations of Order* (New York: Macmillan, 1901).

17. See Morris Janowitz, *The Last Half-Century: Societal Change and Politics in America* (Chicago: University of Chicago Press, 1978), 27–39. Dorothy Ross deemed Janowitz's account overly sanguine, ignoring "the fatal conceptual and ideological ambiguities imbedded [*sic*] in the term" (*Origins of American Social Science*, 248n74). But it is useful to emphasize the idealistic implications of Edward Ross's wide-ranging analysis (inflected by anthropology), which argued for the necessity and vitality of social control, since these positive aspects have been subsequently overshadowed and overtaken by darker interpretations of the term. For one analysis that stressed Progressive reform and education as manipulative, if not downright sinister, see Christopher Lasch, *The New Radicalism in America: The Intellectual as a Social Type* (New York: Knopf, 1966). For a more balanced discussion of social control as a mode of Progressive administration, see R. Jeffrey Lustig, *Corporate Liberalism: The Origins of American Political Theory, 1890–1920* (Berkeley: University of California Press, 1982).

18. Ross, *Origins of American Social Science*, 53–140.

19. Robert E. Park, *The Crowd and the Public and Other Essays*, ed. Henry Elsner Jr. (Chicago: University of Chicago Press, 1972); Daria Frezza, *The Leader and the Crowd: Democracy in American Public Discourse, 1880–1941*, trans. Martha King (Athens: Uni-

versity of Georgia Press, 2007); Christian Borch, *The Politics of Crowds: An Alternative History of Sociology* (Cambridge: Cambridge University Press, 2012). Frezza cited a variety of American intellectuals, such as William James, who anxiously felt obliged to criticize Le Bon's theories, particularly in relation to American democracy.

20. Mary O. Furner, *Advocacy and Objectivity: The Crisis in the Professionalization of American Social Science, 1865–1905* (Lexington: University of Kentucky Press, 1975); Mary O. Furner, "Social Scientists and the State: Constructing the Knowledge Base for Public Policy," in *Intellectuals and Public Life: Between Radicalism and Reform*, ed. Leon Fink, Stephen T. Leonard, and Donald M. Reid (Ithaca, NY: Cornell University Press, 1996). See also Leon Fink, *Progressive Intellectuals and the Dilemmas of Democratic Commitment* (Cambridge, MA: Harvard University Press, 1997).

CHAPTER 1:   Giving Direction to Opinion

1. James Bryce, *The American Commonwealth*, vol. 3 (London: Macmillan, 1888), 3 (subsequent references cited parenthetically in text).

2. For a rich analysis that teased out the less sanguine, more paradoxical aspects of Bryce's thinking, see Adrian Vermeule, "'Government by Public Opinion': Bryce's Theory of the Constitution" (Harvard Public Law Working Paper, 2011), http://ssrn.com/abstract=1809794.

3. For a classic account of the relation between ideology and utopia, see Fredric Jameson, "Reification and Utopia in Mass Culture," *Social Text* 1 (Winter 1979): 130–148.

4. Edward Bellamy, *Looking Backward, 2000–1887*, ed. Cecelia Tichi (New York: Penguin, 1982), 66 (subsequent references cited parenthetically in text).

5. Jonathan Auerbach, "'The Nation Organized': Utopian Impotence in Edward Bellamy's *Looking Backward*," *American Literary History* 6, no. 1 (1994): 24–47.

6. Walter Lippmann, *The Phantom Public* (New York: Macmillan, 1925).

7. For another dystopian response to Bellamy, originally published in 1888, see Ambrose Bierce, *The Fall of the Republic and Other Political Satires* (Knoxville: University of Tennessee Press, 2000), 101–113. Bierce in this futuristic satire was even more cynical than Twain in refusing to allow for any grounds for political authority beyond self-interest, dismissing "freedom of speech," "rule of the majority," and "public opinion" as completely empty, bankrupt concepts.

8. Mark Twain, *A Connecticut Yankee in King Arthur's Court*, ed. Justin Kaplan (New York: Penguin, 1971), 53 (subsequent references cited parenthetically in text).

9. See, for instance, John F. McClymer, *War and Welfare: Social Engineering in America, 1890–1925* (Westport, CT: Greenwood, 1980); John M. Jordan, *Machine-Age Ideology: Social Engineering and American Liberalism, 1911–1939* (Chapel Hill: University of North Carolina Press, 1994).

10. Andrew Carnegie, *Triumphant Democracy; or, Fifty Years' March of the Republic* (New York: Scribner's, 1886), 101. Consider also Lester Frank Ward's remarks (circa 1872): "Every child born into the world should be looked upon by society as so much raw material to be manufactured." Quoted in Samuel Bowles and Herbert Gintis, *Schooling in Capitalist America: Educational Reform and the Contradictions of Economic Life* (New York: Basic, 1976), 125. There are crucial distinctions to be made between training and education, as I discuss in chapter 4.

11. For a discussion of Twain's novel that resembles my own, but with more of a

focus on automatism rather than the theatrics of persuasion, see Walter Benn Michaels, "Promises of American Life," in *The Cambridge History of American Literature*, vol. 3, ed. Sacvan Bercovitch (Cambridge: Cambridge University Press, 2005), 291–298. See also William V. Spanos, *Shock and Awe: American Exceptionalism and the Imperatives of the Spectacle in Mark Twain's A Connecticut Yankee in King Arthur's Court* (Hanover, NH: Dartmouth College Press, 2013). Spanos emphasized that Twain is complicit in Morgan's genocidal project.

12. For an analysis of how first-person narration tends to collapse distinctions between author and character, see Jonathan Auerbach, *The Romance of Failure: First-Person Fictions of Poe, Hawthorne, and James* (New York: Oxford University Press, 1989).

13. For a discussion of how the oligarchs in London's dystopia maintained hegemonic control of public opinion, see my introduction to Jack London, *The Iron Heel*, ed. Jonathan Auerbach (1908; rpt., New York: Penguin, 2006), vii–xxi.

14. Edward M. House, *Philip Dru: Administrator, a Story of Tomorrow, 1920–1935* (1912; rpt., Upper Saddle River, NJ: Literature House/Gregg Press, 1969), 51 (subsequent references cited parenthetically in text).

15. For a brief discussion of the novel situating it in relation to Progressive jurisprudence and questioning the sacrosanct status of the Constitution, see Maxwell Bloomfield, "Constitutional Ideology and Progressive Fiction," *Journal of American Culture* 18, no. 1 (Spring 1995): 77–85. For a discussion of why Progressives attacked judicial review as anti-democratic, see Marc Stears, *Progressives, Pluralists, and the Problems of the State: Ideologies of Reform in the United States and Britain, 1909–1926* (New York: Oxford University Press, 2002).

16. On House, see Godfrey Hodgson, *Woodrow Wilson's Right Hand: The Life of Colonel Edward M. House* (New Haven, CT: Yale University Press, 2006). For a discussion of Wilson's early essay on the study of administration, see my introduction.

17. For a discussion of this campaign in relation to the public sphere and the new technology of cinema, see Jonathan Auerbach, *Body Shots: Early Cinema's Incarnations* (Berkeley: University of California Press, 2007), 15–30, esp. Theodore Roosevelt's grudging praise of Hanna: "he has advertised McKinley as if he were a patent medicine" (19). For a discussion of the 1912 presidential campaign emphasizing its differences from the 1896 one, see George Kibbe Turner, "Manufacturing Public Opinion: The New Art of Making Presidents by Press Bureau," *McClure's Magazine* 39 (July 1912): 316–327. Turner assumed that by 1912 party politics had given way to election by "direct popular choice" (318) shaped by publicity bureaus manufacturing competing opinions for the electorate.

18. For one early exception intelligently assessing the novel, see Christopher Lasch, *The New Radicalism in America: The Intellectual as a Social Type* (New York: Knopf, 1966). Lasch was interested in understanding how "a man of such completely conventional opinion as House should nevertheless have imagined himself as a revolutionary despot" (233).

19. In his *Forum* magazine article "A Calendar of Great Americans" (February 1894), Wilson went on to disparage Jefferson as "abstract, sentimental, rationalistic, rather than practical." Quoted in John Milton Cooper, *Woodrow Wilson* (New York: Knopf, 2009), 74.

20. On Wilson's Hegelianism, see Will Morrisey, *The Dilemma of Progressivism* (Lanham, MD: Rowman and Littlefield, 2009); Ronald J. Pestritto, *Woodrow Wilson and the Roots of Modern Liberalism* (Lanham, MD: Rowman and Littlefield, 2005). In general

Pestritto and Morrisey tended to overestimate the ideological impact of Hegel on American Progressivist conceptions of the state, while underestimating the less theoretical, more pragmatic, and flexible attitudes of practicing politicians like Wilson and Roosevelt.

21. Daniel T. Rodgers, *Contested Truths: Keywords in American Politics Since Independence* (New York: Basic, 1987), 160.

22. Friedrich Schiller, *On the Aesthetic Education of Man*, ed. and trans. Elizabeth M. Wilkinson and Leonard A. Willoughby (1794; Oxford: Clarendon, 1967), 19–21.

23. Gustave Le Bon, *The Crowd: A Study of the Popular Mind* (1895; English translation, New York: Macmillan, 1896). For contemporaneous reviews of Le Bon by William James and others, see Daria Frezza, *The Leader and the Crowd: Democracy in American Public Discourse, 1880–1941*, trans. Martha King (Athens: University of Georgia Press, 2007).

24. Gabriel Tarde, "Opinion and Conversation," in *On Communication and Social Influence*, ed. Terry N. Clark (Chicago: University of Chicago Press, 1969), 297–318 (subsequent references cited parenthetically in text). See also Robert E. Park, *The Crowd and the Public and Other Essays*, ed. Henry Elsner Jr. (Chicago: University of Chicago Press, 1972), the 1903 doctoral dissertation of this influential Chicago School sociologist (trained earlier in journalism), originally published in German.

25. Tarde's metaphor of the "groove" suggestively resonates beyond writing and print to engage the newer technologies of sound recording and playback introduced near the end of the nineteenth century, which allowed for unerring inscription, reproduction, and (endless) repetition.

26. For two impressive accounts of these transnational relations, see James T. Kloppenberg, *Uncertain Victory: Social Democracy and Progressivism in European and American Thought, 1870–1920* (New York: Oxford University Press, 1986); and Daniel T. Rodgers, *Atlantic Crossings: Social Politics in a Progressive Age* (Cambridge, MA: Harvard University Press, 1998). But Kloppenberg failed to even mention Tarde or Le Bon (both influential thinkers), preferring to dwell on those Europeans closest to American Progressives in temperament and mission. On American foreign relations more generally during this period, see Alan Dawley, *Changing the World: American Progressives in War and Revolution* (Princeton, NJ: Princeton University Press, 2003).

27. Herbert Croly, *The Promise of American Life* (New York: Macmillan, 1909), 284. To be fair to Croly, his next book did not display the paternalism that undergirds this passage, which is filled with the modal "must." See Herbert Croly, *Progressive Democracy* (New York: Macmillan, 1914).

28. Wilson's religiosity was sufficiently fascinating to induce Freud to lend his name, if little else, to a psychoanalytic study of the president, a line of inquiry clearly outside my present concerns. See Sigmund Freud and William C. Bullitt, *Thomas Woodrow Wilson: A Psychological Study* (Boston: Houghton Mifflin, 1967).

29. Woodrow Wilson, *Congressional Government* (1885; rpt., New York: Meridian, 1956), 71. For Wilson's account of how key sections of this book were borrowed by Bryce, see Cooper, *Woodrow Wilson*, 63.

30. Woodrow Wilson, *The State* (Boston: Heath, 1889), 594, 20, 597.

31. Woodrow Wilson, *Constitutional Government in the United States* (1908; rpt., New York: Columbia University Press, 1921), 21, 68 (subsequent references cited parenthetically in text).

32. Croly, *Progressive Democracy*, 304. Croly offered an oddly naïve account of the passive role of the press in this executive guiding of public opinion, arguing counterintuitively that "direct government" is easier in a modern industrial state than in the past because active citizens have no need to actually meet, given the "complicated agencies of publicity and intercourse which are afforded by the magazines, the press and the like," with "the newspaper" serving as "an impersonal interlocutor" that allows Americans to obtain "information" and "effective expression" (264).

33. Henry A. Turner, "Woodrow Wilson and Public Opinion," *Public Opinion Quarterly* 21, no. 4 (Winter 1957–1958): 505–520; Elmer E. Cornwell Jr., *Presidential Leadership of Public Opinion* (Bloomington: Indiana University Press, 1966); James D. Startt, *Woodrow Wilson and the Press* (New York: Palgrave Macmillan, 2004).

34. Quoted in Turner, "Woodrow Wilson and Public Opinion," 513.

35. Startt, *Woodrow Wilson and the Press*, 56–57.

36. Rodgers, *Contested Truths*, 176–211.

37. Woodrow Wilson, *The Papers of Woodrow Wilson*, vol. 24, ed. Arthur S. Link (Princeton, NJ: Princeton University Press, 1977), 204. This is from an address in Nashville delivered on February 24, 1912, which was largely devoted to decrying corporate greed and the power of monopolies.

38. Arthur F. Bentley, *The Process of Government*, ed. Peter H. Odegard (1908; rpt., Cambridge, MA: Harvard University Press, 1967), 223, 240. On Bentley, see Dorothy Ross, *The Origins of American Social Science* (Cambridge: Cambridge University Press, 1991), 330–339.

39. See also Ambrose Bierce's definition of *politics* in his *Devil's Dictionary*: "[a] strife of interests masquerading as a contest of principles. The conduct of public affairs for private advantage." Quoted in Jan Stievermann, "'A Blackguard's Faulty Vision': Ambrose Bierce's Modern Cynicism and Its Claim for Intellectual Authority," in *Intellectual Authority and Literary Culture in the US, 1790–1900*, ed. Gunter Leypoldt (Heidelberg: Univeristatsverlag, 2012), 259–287. Unlike Bentley, Bierce did not even seem to allow for group interests or affiliations.

40. Charles A. Beard, *An Economic Interpretation of the Constitution of the United States* (New York: Macmillan, 1913), 17.

41. The term *publicity* in the early nineteenth century referred to transparent communication, as in Jeremy Bentham's remarks championing open judicial review: "publicity is the very soul of justice." Quoted in Gerald J. Postema, "The Soul of Justice: Bentham on Publicity, Law, and the Rule of Law," in *Bentham's Theory of Law and Public Opinion*, ed. Xiaobo Zhai and Michael Quinn (Cambridge: Cambridge University Press, 2014), 40.

42. Quoted in Scott M. Cutlip, *The Unseen Power: A History of Public Relations* (Hillsdale, NJ: Erlbaum, 1994), 24–25. On the bureau, see Stuart Ewen, *PR! A Social History of Spin* (New York: Basic, 1996), 86–89; Karla Gower, "US Corporate Public Relations in the Progressive Era," *Journal of Communication Management* 12, no. 4 (2008): 305–318; Ronald R. Rodgers, "The Press and Public Relations Through the Lens of the Periodicals, 1890–1930," *Public Relations Review* 36 (2010): 50–55.

43. Cutlip, *Unseen Power*, 12.

44. Stephen Ponder, "Progressive Drive to Shape Public Opinion, 1898–1913," *Public Relations Review* 16, no. 3 (Fall 1990): 94–104; Katherine H. Adams, *Progressive Politics*

and the Training of America's Persuaders (Mahwah, NJ: Erlbaum, 1999), 96–100. Stephen Skowronek called this episode "one of the pivotal administrative controversies of modern American state development." Skowronek, *Building a New American State: The Expansion of National Administrative Capacities, 1877–1920* (Cambridge: Cambridge University Press, 1982), 190.

45. Pinchot and Roosevelt in 1909 founded the National Conservation Association to serve as the "center of a great propaganda for conservation." Quoted in Adams, *Progressive Politics and the Training of America's Persuaders*, 99. On the 1913 conversion of part of Yosemite Valley into the Hetch Hetchy reservoir, a controversy that saw Pinchot's views prevail over Muir's, see Roderick Nash, *Wilderness and the American Mind* (New Haven, CT: Yale University Press, 1973), 161–181.

46. On Lathrop at Hull House, see Cecelia Tichi, *Civic Passions: Seven Who Launched Progressive America (and What They Teach Us)* (Chapel Hill: University of North Carolina Press, 2009), 89–122.

47. Quoted in Kriste Lindenmeyer, *"A Right to Childhood": The U.S. Children's Bureau and Child Welfare, 1912–46* (Urbana: University of Illinois Press, 1997), 26.

48. George Creel, Edwin Markham, and Benjamin B. Lindsey, *Children in Bondage* (New York: Hearst International Library, 1914; rpt., New York: Arno and New York Times, 1969), 397.

49. The source of this analogy was apparently a conversation in 1903 between Florence Kelley and Lillian Wald, who asked, "If the Government can have a department to look after the Nation's farm crops, why can't it have a bureau to look after the Nation's child crop?" See Lindenmeyer, *"A Right to Childhood": The U.S. Children's Bureau and Child Welfare*, 10.

50. Julia Lathrop, "The Children's Bureau," *American Journal of Sociology* 18, no. 3 (November 1912): 318–330, quotation on 318. Lathrop explicitly disavowed the connection between birth registration and military conscription (324).

51. Robyn Muncy, *Creating a Female Dominion in American Reform, 1890–1935* (New York: Oxford University Press, 1991), 38–65; Molly Ladd-Taylor, *Mother-Work: Women, Child Welfare, and the State, 1890–1930* (Urbana: University of Illinois Press, 1994), 74–103; Alice Boardman Smuts, *Science in the Service of Children, 1893–1935* (New Haven, CT: Yale University Press, 2006), 81–116.

52. Lindenmeyer, *"A Right to Childhood": The U.S. Children's Bureau and Child Welfare*, 49, 71.

53. Jacqueline K. Parker and Edward M. Carpenter, "Julia Lathrop and the Children's Bureau: The Emergence of an Institution," *Social Science Review* 55, no. 1 (March 1981): 60–77.

54. Molly Ladd-Taylor, *Raising a Baby the Government Way: Mothers' Letters to the Children's Bureau, 1915–1932* (New Brunswick, NJ: Rutgers University Press, 1986).

55. Ellen F. Fitzpatrick, ed., *Muckraking: Three Landmark Articles* (Boston: Bedford, 1994), 10. Unfortunately Fitzpatrick did not examine if and how categories of news, entertainment, and information were kept distinct from one another, a central and ongoing issue for the press and readers since the eighteenth century. On muckraking, see also Harold S. Wilson, *McClure's Magazine and the Muckrakers* (Princeton, NJ: Princeton University Press, 1970); Cecelia Tichi, *Exposés and Excess: Muckraking in America, 1900–2000* (Philadelphia: University of Pennsylvania Press, 2004); Leonard Ray Teel,

The Public Press, 1900–1945, vol. 5 of *The History of American Journalism* (Westport, CT: Praeger, 2006); Louis Filler, *Muckraking and Progressivism in the American Tradition* (New Brunswick, NJ: Transaction, 1996).

56. Theodore Roosevelt, "The Man with the Muck-Rake," April 14, 1906, www.ameri canrhetoric.com/speeches/teddyrooseveltmuckrake.htm.

57. One of those books was Upton Sinclair's influential novel *The Jungle* (1906), published to great public fanfare only a few weeks before Roosevelt's Gridiron speech.

58. Doris Kearns Goodwin, *The Bully Pulpit: Theodore Roosevelt, William Howard Taft, and the Golden Age of Journalism* (New York: Simon and Schuster, 2013), 179–184. Goodwin emphasized the close relations between Baker and Roosevelt, not their falling out.

59. Ray Stannard Baker, *Following the Color Line* (New York: Doubleday, Page, 1908).

60. All letter excerpts are from Ray Stannard Baker, *American Chronicle: The Autobiography of Ray Stannard Baker* (New York: Scribner's, 1945); Robert C. Bannister Jr., *Ray Stannard Baker: The Mind and Thought of a Progressive* (New Haven, CT: Yale University Press, 1966); John E. Semonche, *Ray Stannard Baker: A Quest for Democracy in Modern America, 1870–1918* (Chapel Hill: University of North Carolina Press, 1969). For the Hepburn Act and Roosevelt's dealings with the ICC, see Martin Sklar, *The Corporate Reconstruction of American Capitalism, 1890–1916* (Cambridge: Cambridge University Press, 1988), 228–285; and Skowronek, *Building a New American State*, 255–259. In general Skowronek saw the establishment of national railroad regulation, civil service reform, and the reorganization of the army as the three major focal points or institutions for state building during this period.

61. Quoted in Semonche, *Ray Stannard Baker*, 148.

62. See Robert H. Wiebe, *Self-Rule* (Chicago: University of Chicago Press, 1995). Wiebe noted that "no word carried more progressive freight than *publicity*" (163), but did not consider how the practice of publicity became such contested terrain during this period.

63. H. W. Brands, ed., *The Selected Letters of Theodore Roosevelt* (New York: Cooper Square Press, 2001), 422.

64. Baker, *American Chronicle*, 199.

65. "Editorial Announcement of a New Series of Articles by Ray Stannard Baker," *McClure's Magazine* 25, no. 6 (October 1905): 672.

66. "Manufacturing Public Opinion," *McClure's Magazine* 26 (February 1906): 451. For a thorough discussion of this article and dozens of similar ones from this period, see Kevin Stoker and Brad L. Rawlins, "The 'Light' of Publicity in the Progressive Era: From Searchlight to Flashlight," *Journalism History* 30, no. 4 (Winter 2005): 177–188. Their analysis is weakened by a reductive binary between positive publicity (the broad, altruistic searchlight of the muckrakers) and harmful publicity (the narrower, self-serving flashlight beam of the corporations), which, they argued, subsequently wrested control of public opinion from the press. But clearly by 1900 publicity had already become an ongoing contest between press and corporations, one further complicated by the role of government publicity experts, including presidents, whom they did not discuss.

67. Ray Stannard Baker, "How Railroads Make Public Opinion," *McClure's Magazine* 26 (March 1906): 535–549, quotation on 535 (subsequent references cited parenthet-

ically in text). For a brief discussion of the article, see J. Michael Sproule, *Propaganda and Democracy* (New York: Cambridge University Press, 1997), 23.

68. Like the word *propaganda*, which originated in horticulture (the propagation of plants), *broadcast* too is rooted in agricultural practice, the sowing of seeds across a wide area, but by the twentieth century the term had come to be associated with technologies of transmission.

69. "Editorial Announcement of a New Series of Articles by Ray Stannard Baker," 672.

70. See Henry C. Adams, "What Is Publicity?," *North American Review* 175, no. 553 (December 1902): 895–904. A professor of political economy and a statistician for the ICC, Adams took *publicity* to mean transparency mandated by law when he argued that the full disclosure of business practices was an "essential agency for the control of trusts," which he described as "highly centralized commercial powers[s]" that "can no longer be regarded as . . . private power[s]." For a discussion of Adams's argument that the railroads and municipal utilities constituted "natural monopolies" that called for public control, see Daniel T. Rodgers, *Atlantic Crossings: Social Politics in a Progressive Age* (Cambridge, MA: Harvard University Press, 1998), 107–108.

71. Walter Lippmann, *Drift and Mastery* (New York: Mitchell Kennerley, 1914), 5 (subsequent references cited parenthetically in text).

72. In the same chapter (13) as his reference to a "man-factory," the Connecticut Yankee Morgan likens feudal England to a "corporation" in which six board directors take all the profit, while the other 994 "dupes" in the corporation put up all the money and do all the work. For this swindled 99.4%, Sir Boss promises a "new deal," a resonant phrase subsequently echoed by both Theodore Roosevelt (Square Deal) and Franklin D. Roosevelt (New Deal).

CHAPTER 2: Friend or Foe

1. Although executive order 2594 bears the date April 13, 1917, this seems to be a case of backdating by the president, since every subsequent executive order pertaining to the CPI gave April 14, 1917, as the date of its establishment, as did the first press release announcing the committee's creation. See Woodrow Wilson, *The Papers of Woodrow Wilson*, vol. 42, ed. Arthur S. Link (Princeton, NJ: Princeton University Press, 1983), 59.

2. For studies of World War I propaganda, see George G. Bruntz, *Allied Propaganda and the Collapse of the German Empire in 1918* (Stanford, CA: Stanford University Press, 1938); Peter Buitenhuis, *The Great War of Words: British, American, and Canadian Propaganda and Fiction, 1914–1933* (Vancouver: University of British Columbia Press, 1987); H. C. Peterson, *Propaganda for War: The Campaign Against American Neutrality, 1914–1917* (Port Washington, NY: Kennikat, 1939); Cate Haste, *Keeping the Home Fires Burning: Propaganda in the First World War* (London: Allen Lane, 1977); Brett Gary, *The Nervous Liberals: Propaganda Anxieties from World War I to the Cold War* (New York: Columbia University Press, 1999); Jeffrey Verhey, *The Spirit of 1914: Militarism, Myth and Mobilization in Germany* (Cambridge: Cambridge University Press, 2000); James Morgan Read, *Atrocity Propaganda, 1914–1919* (New Haven, CT: Yale University Press, 1941); David Monger, *Patriotism and Propaganda in First World War Britain* (Liverpool: Liverpool University Press, 2012); Stewart Halsey Ross, *Propaganda for War: How the United States Was Conditioned to Fight the Great War of 1914–1918* (Jefferson, NC:

McFarland, 1996). Ross provided especially rich and detailed archival evidence, although some of the general conclusions he drew are debatable. For a superb assessment of Progressive journalism during the war, see John A. Thompson, *Reformers and War: American Progressive Publicists and the First World War* (Cambridge: Cambridge University Press, 1987).

3. George Creel, *How We Advertised America: The First Telling of the Amazing Story of the Committee on Public Information That Carried the Gospel of Americanism to Every Corner of the Globe* (New York: Harper and Brothers, 1920), 5 (subsequent references cited parenthetically as *HWAA* in text).

4. For an innovative study that focused on Progressive families during the war, see Eric Rauchway, *The Refuge of Affections: Family and American Reform Politics, 1900–1920* (New York: Columbia University Press, 2001), 123–153. See Daniel H. Borus, *Twentieth-Century Multiplicity: American Thought and Culture, 1900–1920* (Lanham, MD: Rowman and Littlefield, 2009), 225–273, for an excellent discussion of the debates and misgivings surrounding American intervention.

5. David M. Kennedy, *Over Here: The First World War and American Society* (New York: Oxford University Press, 1980), 24.

6. The two fullest treatments of the CPI remain James R. Mock and Cedric Larson, *Words That Won the War: The Story of the Committee on Public Information 1917–1919* (Princeton, NJ: Princeton University Press, 1939); and Stephen Vaughn, *Holding Fast the Inner Lines: Democracy, Nationalism, and the Committee on Public Information* (Chapel Hill: University of North Carolina Press, 1980). Vaughn focused strictly on the domestic side of the CPI, offering useful ideological analyses of the committee's various publications. Like Vaughn, I will confine myself in this chapter to exploring the CPI on the home front, although later in this book I will return to the CPI to discuss some implications of its activity abroad. For a more recent general account of the agency, which is marred by a tendency to accept Creel's own self-satisfied explanations at face value and by a dearth of counterbalancing archival research, see Alan Axelrod, *Selling the Great War: The Making of American Propaganda* (New York: Palgrave Macmillan, 2009).

7. George Creel, *Rebel at Large: Recollections of Fifty Crowded Years* (New York: Putnam's, 1947), 44 (subsequent references cited parenthetically in text).

8. Box OV 4: Scrapbooks, n.d., George Creel Papers, Manuscript Division, Library of Congress, Washington, DC. For a discussion of similar ventures in participatory democracy during this decade, including adult education courses, tent meetings, community forums, and the social centers movement, see Kevin Mattson, *Creating a Democratic Public: The Struggle for Urban Participatory Democracy During the Progressive Era* (University Park: Pennsylvania State University Press, 1998).

9. William James, "The Moral Equivalent of War," February 25, 1906, www.constitution.org/wj/meow.htm.

10. Randolph S. Bourne, *War and the Intellectuals: Collected Essays, 1915–1919*, ed. Carl Resek (New York: Harper and Row, 1964), 144 (subsequent references cited parenthetically in text).

11. Kennedy, *Over Here*, 150. See also Ronald Schaffer, *America in the Great War: The Rise of the War Welfare State* (New York: Oxford University Press, 1991), 176–177. In general Schaffer's work is more critical of Wilson's wartime administration than is Kennedy's remarkably nuanced analysis, which remains unsurpassed.

12. Bourne, *War and the Intellectuals*, 71.

13. George Creel, "Military Training for Our Youth," *Century Magazine* 92 (May 1916): 20–26.

14. George Creel, "Universal Training and the Democratic Ideal," *Proceedings of the Academy of Political Science in the City of New York* 6, no. 4 (July 1916): 570–575.

15. Ibid., 151.

16. George Creel, *Woodrow Wilson and the Issues* (New York: Century, 1916), 57, 8.

17. Arthur Bullard, *Mobilising America* (New York: Macmillan, 1917), 25. For Bullard's influence in the founding of the CPI, see Vaughn, *Holding Fast the Inner Lines*, 7–14. Early on, Creel hired Bullard, who came to play an important propaganda role in Russia. See Creel, *How We Advertised America*, esp. 379.

18. Quoted in Ross, *Propaganda for War*, 218.

19. Ibid., 221.

20. John Morton Blum, *Public Philosopher: Selected Letters of Walter Lippmann* (New York: Ticknor and Fields, 1985), 65–66. In this letter to House, Lippmann recommended three men to help run the publicity bureau that Wilson was about to create, including a suggestion for chair, Vance McCormick.

21. Ibid., 60–61.

22. "Public Opinion in War Time," *New Republic* 12, no. 151 (September 22, 1917): 204–207.

23. By this I mean that Lippmann surely knew that writing personal letters directly to President Wilson would be far more effective than trying to convince an amorphous public, even a more coherent one such as the readers of the *New Republic*, to speak out for or against particular matters of war policy.

24. Box 1, n.d., George Creel Papers, Manuscript Division, Library of Congress, Washington, DC.

25. George Creel, "Public Opinion in War Time," *Annals of the American Academy of Political and Social Science* 78 (July 1918): 187.

26. Mark Sullivan, "Creel—Censor," *Collier's Weekly* 60 (November 10, 1917): 13, 36–37. For his later, more favorable view of Creel as a propaganda "artist," see Mark Sullivan, *Our Times: Over Here* (New York: Scribner's, 1933), 5:423–440. See also a scathing *New York Times* editorial of April 16, 1917, which criticized the selection of Creel as CPI chair, casting doubt in particular on his ability to deal fairly with reporters, as cited in Ross, *Propaganda for War*, 223.

27. Sullivan, "Creel—Censor," 13; Creel, *Rebel at Large*, 143.

28. Carl Schmitt, *The Concept of the Political*, trans. George Schwab (New Brunswick, NJ: Rutgers University Press, 1976), 28, 37, 35.

29. Ibid., 42.

30. For three studies examining various aspects of this suppression, see Ernest Freeberg, *Democracy's Prisoner: Eugene V. Debs, the Great War, and the Right to Dissent* (Cambridge, MA: Harvard University Press, 2008); Christopher Capozzola, *Uncle Sam Wants You: World War I and the Making of the Modern American Citizen* (New York: Oxford University Press, 2008); and Jay Feldman, *Manufacturing Hysteria: A History of Scapegoating, Surveillance, and Secrecy in Modern America* (New York: Pantheon, 2011). Feldman does not seem to be aware that his book title matches one of the chapter titles from Creel's 1916 campaign book, which championed Wilson's neutrality stance.

31. Quoted in Geoffrey R. Stone, *Perilous Times: Free Speech in Wartime* (New York: Norton, 2004), 137.

32. For an interesting discussion of Holmes's reasoning, see R. Jeffrey Lustig, *Corporate Liberalism: The Origins of American Political Theory, 1890–1920* (Berkeley: University of California Press, 1982), 116–120.

33. Capozzola, *Uncle Sam Wants You*, 59, 69.

34. Ray Stannard Baker praised the *Survey*'s "clear and honest reporting of actual conditions that will inform or convince public opinion," with that "or" modulating neatly between advocacy and information in a characteristically Progressive approach to public opinion. Quoted in Thompson, *Reformers and War*, 27.

35. George Creel, "How 'Tainted' Money Taints," *Pearson's Magazine* 33 (March 1915): 289–297. Reacting to Creel's essay in a letter to Kellogg, feminist social reformer Florence Kelley deemed *Pearson's* guilty of "criminal libel." See Kathryn Kish Sklar and Beverly Wilson Palmer, eds., *The Selected Letters of Florence Kelley, 1869–1931* (Urbana: University of Illinois Press, 2009), 201.

36. For one such analysis, see Shelton Stromquist, *Reinventing "the People": The Progressive Movement, the Class Problem, and the Origins of Modern Liberalism* (Urbana: University of Illinois Press, 2006), 178–182. As early as 1895, Rockefeller's philanthropy had been derided as "tainted," causing him to hire a publicity agent. See Scott M. Cutlip, *The Unseen Power: A History of Public Relations* (Hillsdale, NJ: Erlbaum, 1994), 55.

37. Paul Kellogg, "Letting George Do It," *Survey* (February 13, 1915): 541–542.

38. Walter Lippmann, "Paul Kellogg Muckraked," *New Republic* 2 (February 20, 1915): 60–61. For the animosity between Lippmann and Creel, see Ronald Steel, *Walter Lippmann and the American Century* (Boston: Little, Brown, 1980), 143.

39. Howard Zinn, *The Politics of History, with a New Introduction* (Urbana: University of Illinois Press, 1990), 79. Zinn observed that Wilson's sending in federal troops to help control the violence in Colorado coincided precisely with the US military occupation of Veracruz, Mexico, suggesting an interesting interplay between the president's domestic and foreign agendas to establish order by force. For an overview of the strike, see Thomas G. Andrews, *Killing for Coal: America's Deadliest Labor War* (Cambridge, MA: Harvard University Press, 2008). For Creel's role, see David C. Duke, *Writers and Miners: Activism and Imagery in America* (Lexington: University Press of Kentucky, 2002), 21–23.

40. Leon Stein and Philip Taft, eds., *Massacre at Ludlow: Four Reports* (New York: Arno/New York Times, 1971). For the role of the Walsh Commission, see Graham Adams Jr., *Age of Industrial Violence 1910–1915: The Activities and Findings of the United States Commission on Industrial Relations* (New York: Columbia University Press, 1966), 146–175.

41. Creel's comment about public opinion as "killed" was quoted in Thompson, *Reformers and War*, 280.

42. George Creel, "The High Cost of Hate," *Everybody's Magazine* 30 (June 1914): 755–770.

43. Box OV 5: Scrapbooks, n.d., George Creel Papers, Manuscript Division, Library of Congress, Washington, DC.

44. George Creel, "Poisoners of Public Opinion: Part I," *Harper's Weekly* (November 7, 1914): 436–438. One war account right next to Creel's essay was titled "Plain Hell,"

while another article nearby, authored by Amos Pinchot, compared conscription to slavery.

45. Upton Sinclair, *The Brass Check: A Study of American Journalism* (Pasadena, CA: self-published, 1920), 297. For a detailed account largely sympathetic to Lee's campaign, see Kirk Hallahan, "Ivy Lee and the Rockefellers' Response to the 1913–1914 Colorado Coal Strike," *Journal of Public Relations Research* 14, no. 4 (2002): 265–315. See chapters 4 and 5 for further discussion of Lee after the war.

46. On the complexities of scapegoating, see Kenneth Burke, "Dialectic of the Scapegoat," in his *A Grammar of Motives* (Berkeley: University of California Press, 1945), 406–408; Jacques Derrida, "Plato's Pharmacy," in his *Dissemination*, trans. Barbara Johnson (Chicago: University of Chicago Press, 1981), 61–172.

47. George Creel, "Poisoners of Public Opinion: Part II," *Harper's Weekly* (November 14, 1914): 465–466.

48. It was unsettling to discover that this same phrase was invoked by Hitler on the eve of Germany's 1933 federal elections, when he vowed to "destroy democracy by the weapons of democracy." Quoted in Frederic V. Grunfeld, *The Hitler File: A Social History of Germany and the Nazis, 1918–1945* (New York: Random House, 1974), 109. For a more benign usage referring to "public opinion" as one of the president's "weapons," see Herbert Croly, *Progressive Democracy* (New York: Macmillan, 1914), 348.

49. George Creel, Edwin Markham, and Benjamin B. Lindsey, *Children in Bondage* (New York: Hearst International Library, 1914; rpt., New York: Arno and New York Times, 1969) (subsequent references cited parenthetically in text). A note at the beginning of the book indicated that the passages cited were written by either Creel or Lindsey. In 1913 Creel scripted *Saved by the Juvenile Court*, a movie featuring the iconic Progressive reformer Lindsey, known as "the kid's judge."

50. George Creel and Benjamin B. Lindsey, "Measuring Up Equal Suffrage: An Authoritative Estimate of Results in Colorado," *Delineator* 77 (February 1911): 85–86, 151–152. See also George Creel, "What Have Women Done with the Vote?," *Century Magazine* (March 1914): 663–671.

51. Judith Schwarz, *Radical Feminists of Heterodoxy* (Norwich, VT: New Victoria, 1986), 28. This was one of many lectures Creel gave on behalf of suffrage between 1912 and 1916. Newly wedded to the actress Blanche Bates, Creel was quoted in the *San Francisco Chronicle* (November 30, 1912) as saying, "all my life has been a battle for the freedom and independence of women." See box OV 4: Scrapbooks, 232.

52. Lippmann kept quiet, but it is easy to imagine his consternation upon learning that Wilson (and House) ignored his suggestions and instead picked Creel to head the CPI, although he already might have had an inkling before the appointment since Creel, Lippmann, Baker, and some other writers got together in New York on April 5, 1917, to discuss the war crisis. Creel would not have been shy about announcing his intentions. This meeting was mentioned in Baker's diary, according to Thompson, *Reformers and War*, 180.

53. George Creel, "Our 'Visionary' President: An Interpretation of Woodrow Wilson," *Century Magazine* 89 (December 1914): 192–201.

54. Box 1, n.d., George Creel Papers, Manuscript Division, Library of Congress, Washington, DC. Stuart Ewen surmised that the muckraker's anti-business credentials would have appealed to Wilson in order to placate labor interests, but this is dubious

logic, given the far louder outcries from conservatives (including cabinet members like Lansing) who were worried about what they took to be Creel's radical socialism. See Stuart Ewen, *PR! A Social History of Spin* (New York: Basic, 1996), 110.

CHAPTER 3: The Conscription of Thought

1. Woodrow Wilson, *The Papers of Woodrow Wilson*, vol. 42, ed. Arthur S. Link (Princeton, NJ: Princeton University Press, 1983), 55.

2. For an unfavorable view deriding Creel's pushiness and his "socialistic tendencies," see Robert Lansing, *War Memoirs of Robert Lansing* (Indianapolis, IN: Bobbs-Merrill, 1935), 322–324.

3. Quoted in Kriste Lindenmeyer, *"A Right to Childhood": The U.S. Children's Bureau and Child Welfare, 1912–46* (Urbana: University of Illinois Press, 1997), 24.

4. Quoted in Alice Boardman Smuts, *Science in the Service of Children, 1893–1935* (New Haven, CT: Yale University Press, 2006), 95.

5. George Creel, "General Correspondence," n.d., Record Group 63, CPI 1-A1, National Archives and Records Administration, College Park, MD.

6. One key exception was the CPI's endorsement and close financial ties with the American Alliance for Labor and Democracy, an ostensibly independent organization with Samuel Gompers as its president, which shared publicity with the CPI, suggesting the importance for Creel of winning the hearts and minds of laborers.

7. Creel, *How We Advertised America: The First Telling of the Amazing Story of the Committee on Public Information That Carried the Gospel of Americanism to Every Corner of the Globe* (New York: Harper and Brothers, 1920) (references cited parenthetically in text).

8. James R. Mock and Cedric Larson, *Words That Won the War: The Story of the Committee on Public Information 1917–1919* (Princeton, NJ: Princeton University Press, 1939), 6.

9. Gabriel Tarde, "Opinion and Conversation," in *On Communication and Social Influence*, ed. Terry N. Clark (Chicago: University of Chicago Press, 1969), 297–318; Benedict Anderson, *Imagined Communities: Reflections on the Origins and Spread of Nationalism* (London: Verso, 1991).

10. Mock and Larson, *Words That Won the War*, 6–8.

11. George Creel, *Complete Report of the Chairman of the Committee on Public Information, 1917, 1918, 1919* (1920; rpt., New York: Da Capo, 1972), 10.

12. Harold D. Lasswell, *Propaganda Technique in the World War* (1927; rpt., New York: Garland, 1972), 22.

13. Mock and Larson, *Words That Won the War*, 48.

14. David M. Kennedy, *Over Here: The First World War and American Society* (New York: Oxford University Press, 1980), 120.

15. John M. Jordan, *Machine-Age Ideology: Social Engineering and American Liberalism, 1911–1939* (Chapel Hill: University of North Carolina Press, 1994), 94, 102.

16. For a fascinating account of the relationship between high British modernism and propaganda, see Mark Wollaeger, *Modernism, Media, and Propaganda: British Narrative from 1900 to 1945* (Princeton, NJ: Princeton University Press, 2008).

17. For an excellent account of the role of academics during the war, see Carol S. Gruber, *Mars and Minerva: World War I and the Uses of the Higher Learning in Amer-*

ica (Baton Rouge: Louisiana State University Press, 1975). See also George T. Blakey, *Historians on the Homefront* (Lexington: University Press of Kentucky, 1970). Given the importance of Ford for the CPI, it is surprising that Creel gave him such scant attention in *How We Advertised America.*

18. Guy Stanton Ford, "General Correspondence," n.d., Record Group 63, CPI 3-A1, box 15, National Archives and Records Administration, College Park, MD.

19. Carl Byoir, "General Correspondence," n.d., Record Group 63, CPI 1-A4, National Archives and Records Administration, College Park, MD. This NEA press release (dated April 12, 1918) was found in Byoir's files, which suggests that he worked on the project.

20. On Byoir, see Scott M. Cutlip, *The Unseen Power: A History of Public Relations* (Hillsdale, NJ: Erlbaum, 1994), 531–588.

21. Stuart Ewen, *PR! A Social History of Spin* (New York: Basic, 1996).

22. See John Dos Passos, *Mr. Wilson's War* (Garden City, NY: Doubleday, 1962), 301.

23. Byoir, "General Correspondence," CPI 1-A4, box 3.

24. Box 2, n.d., George Creel Papers, Manuscript Division, Library of Congress, Washington, DC. Wilson may have been thinking specifically about his refusal to intervene to protect blacks in the aftermath of race riots that hit East St. Louis in July 1917. See Kennedy, *Over Here*, 282–283.

25. Creel, *Complete Report of the Chairman of the Committee on Public Information*, 10–12.

26. For an interesting analysis of these posters, see Ewen, *PR! A Social History of Spin*, 120–124. See also Eric Van Schaack, "The Division of Pictorial Publicity in World War I," *Design Issues* 22, no. 1 (Winter 2006): 32–45.

27. To help disseminate this material the CPI also set up in June 1917 a Division of Production and Distribution. See Creel, *Complete Report of the Chairman of the Committee on Public Information*, 19–21.

28. See also ibid., 12–15.

29. Robert A. Emery, "The *Official Bulletin*, 1917–1919: A Proto–*Federal Register*," *Law Library Journal* 102, no. 3 (2010): 441–448.

30. Creel, *Complete Report of the Chairman of the Committee on Public Information*, 29–30. The three national directors of the 4MM were Ryerson (through June 1917), William McCormick Blair (through August 1918), and William Ingersoll (until the program ended in December 1918).

31. I focus on the program's administration, but for a full-length treatment that includes a discussion of the content of these speeches, see Alfred E. Cornebise, *War as Advertised: The Four Minute Men and America's Crusade 1917–1918* (Philadelphia: American Philosophical Society, 1984).

32. On the rich and important topic of World War I films and propaganda, see Larry Wayne Ward, *The Motion Picture Goes to War: The U.S. Government Film Effort During World War I* (Ann Arbor, MI: UMI Research Press, 1985); and Leslie Midkiff DeBauche, *Reel Patriotism: The Movies and World War I* (Madison: University of Wisconsin Press, 1997). The 4MM program quickly expanded to other public venues beyond movie theaters, including schools and churches, although movie audiences remained the primary target. For instructions about singing, see *4MM Bulletin* 38 (discussed in Cornebise, *War as Advertised*, 144–147).

33. Mock and Larson, *Words That Won the War*, 113. See also Carol Oukrop, "The Four Minute Men Became National Network During World War I," *Journalism Quarterly* 52 (1975): 632–637. It is especially interesting to consider how the 4MM restored and affirmed the power of the unmediated live voice on a massive scale of dissemination a full forty years after its initial mechanical reproduction (Edison's 1877 phonograph).

34. Lisa Mastrangelo, "World War I, Public Intellectuals, and the Four Minute Men: Convergent Ideals of Public Speaking and Civic Participation," *Rhetoric and Public Affairs* 12, no. 4 (2009): 607–634.

35. Carol Byerly, "The U.S. Military and the Influenza Pandemic of 1918–1919," *Public Health Reports* 125 (Suppl. 3) (n.d.): 82–91.

36. "Four Minute Men News," n.d., Record Group 63, CPI 11-A2, National Archives and Records Administration, College Park, MD. All direct quotations below are from this archive.

37. In addition to matching audiences and speakers along ethnic and racial lines, the program also allowed women to train as Four Minute Men. See Mary Yost, "Training Four Minute Men at Vassar," *Quarterly Journal of Speech Education* 5 (May 1919): 246–253. There were many junior youth 4MM programs as well.

38. For an ambitious treatise on political theory arguing for the democratic potential between neighborhoods and the nation, which gave as an illustration how the Council of National Defense interacted with local chapters precisely along the lines of the coordination between local and national for the 4MM, see M. P. Follett, *The New State* (New York: Longmans, Green, 1918), 246–247.

39. William H. Ingersoll, "The Future of the Four Minute Men," *Quarterly Journal of Speech Education* 5 (October 1919): 175–178.

40. John Dewey, *Characters and Events: Popular Essays in Social and Political Philosophy*, vol. 2 (New York: Henry Holt, 1929), 467.

41. Ibid., 570.

42. Ibid., 561, from the essay "America and War."

43. Randolph S. Bourne, *War and the Intellectuals: Collected Essays, 1915–1919*, ed. Carl Resek (New York: Harper and Row, 1964), 57, "Twilight of Idols" (subsequent references cited with the titles of specific essays parenthetically in text).

44. Dewey, *Characters and Events*, 589.

45. Ibid., 518–519.

CHAPTER 4: **Searching for a Public (to Educate)**

1. Woodrow Wilson, *The Papers of Woodrow Wilson*, vol. 42, ed. Arthur S. Link (Princeton, NJ: Princeton University Press, 1983), 181.

2. John Patrick Diggins, *The Promise of Pragmatism: Modernism and the Crisis of Knowledge and Authority* (Chicago: University of Chicago Press, 1994), 339.

3. See "Introduction," in John Dewey, *The Public and Its Problems: An Essay in Political Inquiry*, ed. Melvin L. Rogers (1927; rpt., University Park: Pennsylvania State University Press, 2012), 15. This is a valuable introduction to Dewey's political theory, even if Rogers misrepresented Lippmann's career and ideas in accepting the stale notion that he occupied an "elitist" (16) position in the "debate" (5) between the two.

4. Michael Schudson, "The Lippmann-Dewey Debate: And the Invention of Walter

Lippmann as an Anti-Democrat 1986–1996," *International Journal of Communications* 2 (2008): 1031–1042; Sue Curry Jansen, "Phantom Conflict: Lippmann, Dewey, and the Fate of the Public in Modern Society," *Communication and Critical/Cultural Studies* 6 (September 2009): 221–245. Jansen thoroughly documented the scholarship on this so-called debate.

5. Walter Lippmann, *A Preface to Politics* (New York: Mitchell Kennerley, 1913), 116.

6. John Dewey, *Democracy and Education*, in *The Collected Works of John Dewey*, 37 vols., ed. Jo Ann Boydston (Carbondale: Southern Illinois University Press, 1969), MW 9:338. Subsequent citations in the text from this multivolume edition will designate specific works as early (EW), middle (MW), and late (LW), followed by the volume number and page.

7. Both Lippmann and Dewey frequently invoked the phrase "the Great Society" to refer to modernity's complex social, political, economic, and cultural transformations. See Graham Wallas, *The Great Society* (London: Macmillan, 1914).

8. Given the large number of texts I will be examining, space does not permit me to discuss works by Lippmann or Dewey published after 1927, even if some continue to bear on the question of a public.

9. Quoted in Neil Coughlan, *Young John Dewey* (Chicago: University of Chicago Press, 1975), 98.

10. Alan Ryan, *John Dewey and the High Tide of American Liberalism* (New York: Norton, 1995), 43.

11. I should note that Dewey originally published this piece in the *Political Science Quarterly*, the same journal that published in 1887 Woodrow Wilson's famous article on the science of administration (discussed in my introduction). The phrase *agencies of clamor* is on 77.

12. Quoted in Robert B. Westbrook, *John Dewey and American Democracy* (Ithaca, NY: Cornell University Press, 1991), 88.

13. Ibid., 95.

14. Matthew Festenstein, *Pragmatism and Political Theory: From Dewey to Rorty* (Chicago: University of Chicago Press, 1997), 24.

15. I am not especially interested in tracing influence, but it is surprising to me that neither Festenstein nor Westbrook cited Emerson even once in their studies, and Jay Martin took the astonishing step of explicitly disavowing the influence of Emerson on Dewey's thinking. See Martin, *The Education of John Dewey: A Biography* (New York: Columbia University Press, 2002), 42–43. But in 1903 Dewey published a crucial essay, "Emerson—The Philosopher of Democracy" (MW 3:68–77), which quoted extensively from Emerson and celebrated his precursor's willingness to break down boundaries of thought. In particular I would argue that Emerson's notion of a transcendental over-soul, a vast intelligence uniting individuals, is pivotal for understanding how Dewey construed collective association, although Dewey's philosophy of democracy increasingly became more grounded in secular bonds of sociality. I should also point out that Dewey gave Emerson the last word in *The Public and Its Problems*.

16. Quoted in Westbrook, *John Dewey and American Democracy*, 55.

17. The phrase *race-experience* echoes a passage in "My Pedagogic Creed" that referred to "the inherited sources of the race" (EW 5:87).

18. For one notable exception, see John Dewey, *How We Think* (Boston: Heath, 1910), especially the chapter "Language and the Training of Thought," which offered a conventional account of linguistic signs.

19. For an informative comparison of key twentieth-century theories of communication (including the ideas of Lippmann and Dewey), see John D. Peters, *Speaking into the Air: A History of the Idea of Communication* (Chicago: University of Chicago Press, 1999), 1–33.

20. I should note that Dewey did not explicitly acknowledge these thinkers in his rehearsal of social psychology. For an interesting account of Dewey's ideas of collective association in relation to other Progressive theorists of group behavior (such as Mary Parker Follett and Herbert Croly), see R. Jeffrey Lustig, *Corporate Liberalism: The Origins of American Political Theory, 1890–1920* (Berkeley: University of California Press, 1982), 120–148.

21. Twain's Connecticut Yankee, who declares "training is everything," as I discuss in the first chapter, is not really engaging in education, as far as Dewey would be concerned, since Sir Boss is simply imposing a scheme of indoctrination without the willing participation or understanding of King Arthur and his subjects.

22. For a wonderful analysis of the implications of Mead's complex social psychology for theories of democracy, see Ruth Leys, "Mead's Voices: Imitation as Foundation; or, The Struggle Against Mimesis," *Critical Inquiry* 19 (Winter 1993): 277–307.

23. John Dewey, *Democracy and Education* (New York: Macmillan, 1916).

24. "'Traffic in Absolutes,' an Extract from John Dewey, with a Review, and a Footnote," *New Republic* 3 (July 17, 1915): 281–285. This was not the first time Dewey appeared in the *New Republic*. See John Dewey, "A Policy of Industrial Education," *New Republic* 1, no. 7 (December 19, 1914): 11–12.

25. For conventional views of these two books, see Ronald Steel, *Walter Lippmann and the American Century* (Boston: Little, Brown, 1980); Charles Forcey, *The Crossroads of Liberalism: Croly, Weyl, Lippmann, and the Progressive Era, 1900–1925* (New York: Oxford University Press, 1961). Forcey went so far as to call Lippmann's views in *A Preface to Politics* "puerile" and "dangerous" (117). For a more sympathetic reading of Lippmann's first book, see D. Steven Blum, *Walter Lippmann: Cosmopolitanism in the Century of Total War* (Ithaca, NY: Cornell University Press, 1984), 27–34.

26. For a memorable discussion of the daily activity of corrupt aldermen that was anything but invisible from the perspective of their grateful benefactors, see Jane Addams, *Democracy and Social Ethics* (New York: Macmillan, 1907), chapter 7. As early as 1897, Robert La Follette decried the domination of politics by the "invisible hand" of corporations. See David P. Thelen, *Robert M. La Follette and the Insurgent Spirit* (Madison: University of Wisconsin Press, 1986), 28. On La Follette, see also Nancy C. Unger, *Fighting Bob La Follette: The Righteous Reformer* (Chapel Hill: University of North Carolina Press, 2000).

27. Quoted in Maureen A. Flanagan, *America Reformed: Progressives and Progressivism, 1890s–1920s* (New York: Oxford University Press, 2007), 135. Numerous sources (mainly on the Internet) cite the origin of this passage as an April 19, 1906, speech that Teddy Roosevelt gave, with the verb *to befoul* substituting for the verb *to dissolve*. That spring 1906 date is intriguing, coming only weeks after the president's attack on muckrakers. But I have been unable to confirm such a speech, and I suspect that the false

NOTES TO PAGES 110–116   191

attribution stems from a sound recording Roosevelt made in 1912 in which he quoted the passage but used "to befoul" instead of "to dissolve."

28. John Dewey, "Index," in *The Collected Works 1882–1953*, ed. Jo Ann Boydston (Carbondale: Southern Illinois University Press, 1981).

29. For an interesting discussion that distinguished between *organization* and *organism* as pertaining to arrangements of social intelligence, see Wallas, *The Great Society*, 249–251.

30. Hilary Putnam, "A Reconsideration of Deweyan Democracy," in *Pragmatism in Law and Society*, ed. Michael Brint and William Weaver (Boulder, CO: Westview, 1991), 217–243, quotation on 222. Later in this essay Putnam quoted a passage from Dewey's 1932 edition of *Ethics* (LW 7:3–462, co-authored with James Hayden Tufts) that did explicitly invoke *power* in a striking way: "All special privilege narrows the outlook of those who possess it, as well as limits the development of those not having it. A very considerable portion of what is regarded as the inherent selfishness of mankind is the product of an inequitable distribution of power—inequitable because it shuts out some from the conditions which direct and evoke their capacities, while it produces a one-sided growth in those who have privilege" (232). Note that by still emphasizing growth, the powerful are just as stunted as the powerless in Dewey's view.

31. Walter Lippmann, *Drift and Mastery* (New York: Mitchell Kennerley, 1914), 64 (subsequent references cited parenthetically in text).

32. Forcey, *Crossroads of Liberalism*, 265. For a harsher assessment of the *New Republic* liberals (including Dewey) that emphasized how the Wilson administration mostly ignored their advice, see Christopher Lasch, *The New Radicalism in America: The Intellectual as a Social Type* (New York: Knopf, 1966), 181–224. Lasch concluded that "they were the victims of their own propaganda" (216). For another important analysis, which credited the *New Republic* editors with presenting "the country with the first statement of a general theory to replace classical liberalism" (197) but did not discuss their views about the war, see Lustig, *Corporate Liberalism*, 195–226.

33. On Dewey and Bourne, see Westbrook, *John Dewey and American Democracy*, 233–235. Westbrook recounted the unsavory story of Dewey getting Bourne fired as a political contributor to the magazine the *Dial* (his main source of income at the time) because of Bourne's attacks on Dewey's pro-war stance.

34. Quoted in John Morton Blum, *Public Philosopher: Selected Letters of Walter Lippmann* (New York: Ticknor and Fields, 1985), 74.

35. Lippmann's differing views on free speech during the war can partially be explained by a difference in venues, since a personal letter to Colonel House is quite a different rhetorical context than an article published in the *New Republic*.

36. Walter Lippmann, *U.S. Foreign Policy: Shield of the Republic* (Boston: Little, Brown, 1943), 36–37.

37. Sue Curry Jansen, *Walter Lippmann: A Critical Introduction to Media and Communication Theory* (New York: Peter Lang, 2012), both quotations on 79. In an even crankier letter to House dated August 31, 1918, Wilson wrote, "I am very much puzzled as to who sent Lippmann over to inquire into matters of propaganda. I have found his judgment most unsound." Quoted in Steel, *Walter Lippmann and the American Century*, 146.

38. Quoted in Forcey, *Crossroads of Liberalism*, 291.

39. Walter Lippmann, *The Stakes of Diplomacy* (New York: Henry Holt, 1915), 198.

40. Westbrook, *John Dewey and American Democracy*, 266–268.

41. Walter Lippmann and Charles Merz, "A Test of the News," *New Republic* (Special suppl.) (August 4, 1920): 1–42, quotation on 2. For an excellent discussion of "A Test" and *Liberty and the News*, see Jansen, *Walter Lippmann*.

42. Walter Lippmann, *Liberty and the News* (New York: Harcourt, Brace and Howe, 1920), 4–5 (subsequent references cited parenthetically in text).

43. Walter Lippmann, *Public Opinion* (New York: Harcourt, Brace, 1922), 81 (subsequent references cited parenthetically in text).

44. On the matter of mental pictures, Lippmann's mentor Graham Wallas would also seem to be an important influence. For example, in a chapter on the psychology of the crowd, he referred to "the picture formed in our mind (with the help of descriptive reporting and newspaper photographs) of our distant fellows." Wallas, *The Great Society*, 143.

45. Lippmann also was responsible in 1947 for popularizing the phrase "the cold war" in a series of articles attacking George Kennan's containment thesis.

46. Jürgen Habermas, *The Structural Transformation of the Public Sphere: An Inquiry into a Category of Bourgeois Society*, trans. Thomas Burger (1962; rpt., Cambridge, MA: MIT Press, 1989); Michael Warner, *The Letters of the Republic: Publication and the Public Sphere in Eighteenth-Century America* (Cambridge, MA: Harvard University Press, 1992). See also Russ Castronovo, "Propaganda, Prenational Critique, and Early American Literature," *American Literary History* 21 (Spring 2009): 183–210.

47. Walter Lippmann, *The Phantom Public* (New York: Macmillan, 1925), 20 (subsequent references cited parenthetically in text).

48. On the "bewildered herd," see Steel, *Walter Lippmann and the American Century*, 213. Largely because this unfortunate phrase appeared in Lippmann's definitive biography, it has subsequently been taken out of context and cited over and over again as proof that Lippmann was an elitist by folks such as Noam Chomsky who do not seem to have actually read much Lippmann, judging by their ill-informed labeling, which ironically confirms Lippmann's own arguments about how stereotyped and misleading impressions publicly circulate and linger. See Chomsky, *Media Control: The Spectacular Achievements of Propaganda* (New York: Seven Stories Press, 1997), 16–23. Lippmann borrowed the term *herd* from Wilfred Trotter, *The Instincts of the Herd in Peace and War* (London: T. Fisher Unwin, 1916), where the word was used in a pseudo-anthropological but nonpejorative sense. Lippmann briefly cited Trotter in *Public Opinion* (52).

49. John Dewey, "Review of *Public Opinion*," *New Republic* (May 3, 1922): 286–288. I have reversed the order of these last two clauses for clarity.

50. John Dewey, "Practical Democracy (Review of *The Phantom Public*)," *New Republic* 45 (December 2, 1925): 52–54.

51. For an earlier (1908) and more conventional account of the state and civil society, see Dewey, MW 5:404–434, *Ethics*.

52. James W. Carey, *Communication as Culture: Essays on Media and Society*, rev. ed. (New York: Routledge, 2009), 60.

53. For two notable exceptions that take these early chapters seriously, see Festenstein, *Pragmatism and Political Theory*; and Melvin L. Rogers, *The Undiscovered Dewey: Religion, Morality, and the Ethos of Democracy* (New York: Columbia University Press, 2009). Rogers made the intriguing claim that the public as Dewey construed it is

"subjectless" (228), but it is difficult to see how to reconcile this possibility with Dewey's insistence later in his book that the "Great Community" depends on face-to-face interactions.

54. Dewey, *The Public and Its Problems*, LW 2:244 (subsequent references cited parenthetically in text).

55. He even cited the same passage from Samuel Tilden that he cited in his 1888 essay, "The Ethics of Democracy."

56. For a more substantive understanding of the complex dynamics between smaller-scale collective activity and the state that resisted both Dewey's brand of metaphysics and Arthur Bentley's narrow view of groups as merely special interests, see M. P. Follett, *The New State* (New York: Longmans, Green, 1918).

57. He actually said, "[I]t is outside the scope of our discussion to look into the prospects of the reconstruction of face-to-face communities" (368).

58. For brief remarks along these lines, see Carey, *Communication as Culture*, 62.

CHAPTER 5: Public Relations as Social Relations

1. Walter Lippmann, *Public Opinion* (New York: Harcourt, Brace, 1922), 345.

2. Will Irwin, "Press Agent, His Rise and Fall," *Collier's* 48 (December 2, 1911): 24.

3. *The Collected Works of John Dewey*, 37 vols., ed. Jo Ann Boydston (Carbondale: Southern Illinois University Press, 1969), MW 5:465. Subsequent citations in the text from this multivolume edition will designate specific works as early (EW), middle (MW), and late (LW), followed by the volume number and page.

4. Ray Eldon Hiebert, *Courtier to the Crowd: The Story of Ivy Lee and the Development of Public Relations* (Ames: Iowa State University Press, 1966), 29.

5. Quoted ibid., 42–43.

6. For a list of Lee's clients, see Scott M. Cutlip, *The Unseen Power: A History of Public Relations* (Hillsdale, NJ: Erlbaum, 1994), 156.

7. Quoted in Sherman Morse, "An Awakening in Wall Street," *American Magazine* 62, no. 5 (September 1906): 460.

8. Ibid., 458.

9. Ivy Lee, *Publicity: Some of the Things It Is and Is Not* (New York: Industries Publishing, 1925), 13.

10. Ivy Lee, "Indirect Service of Railroads," *Moody's* (November 1907): 580–584.

11. Ivy Lee, *Human Nature and Railroads* (Philadelphia: E. S. Nash, 1915), 7.

12. Stuart Ewen, *PR! A Social History of Spin* (New York: Basic, 1996), 74. Ewen cited a later (1916) version of the "Human Nature" speech that Lee initially gave in 1914, but I prefer to use the earlier version for reasons that will soon be apparent.

13. For the American reception of Le Bon, see Daria Frezza, *The Leader and the Crowd: Democracy in American Public Discourse, 1880–1941*, trans. Martha King (Athens: University of Georgia Press, 2007).

14. J. Michael Sproule, *Propaganda and Democracy* (New York: Cambridge University Press, 1997), 55.

15. Ewen was especially prone to dramatizing how he fell under the cunning spell of Bernays, "the master" or "virtuoso" whom he credited with "orchestrating" the entire interview Ewen conducted with Bernays late in his life. Ewen, *PR! A Social History of Spin*, 3–18. To so exaggerate the power of Bernays is to enhance the parallel power of

the scholar to demystify the craft of public relations. On the history of the lionizing of Bernays, see Cutlip, *Unseen Power*, 220.

16. Edward Bernays, *Biography of an Idea: Memoirs of Public Relations Counsel Edward L. Bernays* (New York: Simon and Schuster, 1965) (subsequent references cited parenthetically in text); Larry Tye, *The Father of Spin: Edward L. Bernays and the Birth of Public Relations* (New York: Henry Holt, 1998). Although Tye made some use of this large archive, a scholarly biography that draws fully on this material remains to be written.

17. On the relation between social communion and the spread of venereal disease in early twentieth-century America, see Priscilla Wald, *Contagious: Cultures, Carriers, and the Outbreak Narrative* (Durham, NC: Duke University Press, 2008), 84–94.

18. Edward Bernays, *Crystallizing Public Opinion* (1923; rpt., Brooklyn, NY: IG Publishing, 2011), 170 (subsequent references cited parenthetically in text).

19. Edward Bernays, *Propaganda* (1928; rpt., Brooklyn, NY: IG Publishing, 2005), 78–79 (subsequent references cited parenthetically in text).

20. Quoted in Tye, *The Father of Spin*, 28.

21. For a discussion of the suffrage pageant as a "form of argumentative persuasion," see Glennis Smith Tinnin, "Why the Pageant?," *Woman's Journal* (February 15, 1913): 50. See also Margaret Finnegan, *Selling Suffrage: Consumer Culture and Votes for Women* (New York: Columbia University Press, 1999); Mary Chapman, *Making Noise, Making News: Suffrage Print Culture and U.S. Modernism* (New York: Oxford University Press, 2014).

22. For dozens and dozens of press editorials responding to the event, some sarcastic, others amused, dismissive, or supportive, see box I:519, Scrapbook 3, n.d., Edward L. Bernays Papers, Manuscript Division, Library of Congress, Washington, DC. These editorials were triggered by a series of identical letters sent by one of the marchers, Nancy Hardin, to newspapers and women's clubs all over the country soliciting their views about the march. The fact that these boilerplate letters and their responses are part of the Bernays archives strongly suggests that he orchestrated this letter-writing campaign, which was far more important in creating buzz and stirring up public opinion than the march itself.

23. Finnegan, *Selling Suffrage*, 12, 61.

24. Ewen, *PR! A Social History of Spin*, 171.

25. Quoted in Finnegan, *Selling Suffrage*, 57.

26. Maureen A. Flanagan, *America Reformed: Progressives and Progressivism, 1890s–1920s* (New York: Oxford University Press, 2007), 195.

27. Walter Lippmann, *Drift and Mastery* (New York: Mitchell Kennerley, 1914), 67–68 (subsequent references cited parenthetically in text). Lippmann's arguments partly echoed Florence Kelley, *Some Ethical Gains Through Legislation* (New York: Macmillan, 1905).

28. Sue Curry Jansen, "Semantic Tyranny: How Edward L. Bernays Stole Walter Lippmann's Mojo and Got Away with It and Why It Still Matters," *International Journal of Communications* 7 (2013): 1094–1111.

29. For an interesting analysis of social dynamics that resembles Bernays's own, see Georg Simmel, *Conflict and the Web of Group Affiliations*, trans. and ed. Kurt Wolff (1922; rpt., Glencoe, IL: Free Press, 1955). Simmel originally published a section of this book as an essay titled "Die Kreuzung Sozialer Kreise" (1922).

30. Theodor W. Adorno, "Freudian Theory and the Pattern of Fascist Propaganda,"

in *The Essential Frankfurt School Reader*, ed. Andrew Arato and Eike Gebhardt (New York: Continuum, 1982), 118–137. For a critique of Adorno's argument, see Mark Wollaeger, "Propaganda and Pleasure: From Kracauer to Joyce," in *The Oxford Handbook of Propaganda Studies*, ed. Jonathan Auerbach and Russ Castronovo (New York: Oxford University Press, 2013), 278–297.

31. See Priscilla Wald, "The 'Hidden Tyrant': Propaganda, Brainwashing, and Psycho-Politics in the Cold War Period," in *The Oxford Handbook of Propaganda Studies*, ed. Jonathan Auerbach and Russ Castronovo (New York: Oxford University Press, 2013), 109–130.

32. See Edward A. Purcell Jr., *The Crisis of Democratic Theory* (Lexington: University Press of Kentucky, 1973); David M. Ricci, *The Tragedy of Political Science: Politics, Scholarship, and Democracy* (New Haven, CT: Yale University Press, 1984), 78–96; Robert B. Westbrook, *John Dewey and American Democracy* (Ithaca, NY: Cornell University Press, 1991), 280–293. Purcell pointed out (99) that in the late 1920s there was a revival of interest among American political scientists in Le Bon's turn-of-the-century theories, which emphasized irrational crowd behavior but were now linked to more empirical analytic techniques. It is ironic that rational methods were used to gauge the significance of irrationality.

33. See Bernays, *Biography of an Idea*, 208–216; Tye, *The Father of Spin*, 125. Whereas Bernays spent an entire chapter describing this work, Tye devoted only a single paragraph. For an interesting account of the crucial role played by Doris Fleischman in the early development of public relations, including encouraging her husband, Bernays, to pay attention to women's issues, see Susan Henry, *Anonymous in Their Own Names: Doris E. Fleischman, Ruth Hale, and Jane Grant* (Nashville, TN: Vanderbilt University Press, 2012).

34. Tye, *The Father of Spin*, 74.

35. In his excellent introduction to the IG reprint of *Propaganda*, Mark Crispin Miller also noted (18) this turn by Bernays to the civic virtues of public relations in the later chapters of his book.

CHAPTER 6: Foreign Intelligence

1. Edward Bernays, *Biography of an Idea: Memoirs of Public Relations Counsel Edward L. Bernays* (New York: Simon and Schuster, 1965), 180 (subsequent references cited parenthetically in text).

2. George Creel, *How We Advertised America: The First Telling of the Amazing Story of the Committee on Public Information That Carried the Gospel of Americanism to Every Corner of the Globe* (New York: Harper and Brothers, 1920), 266 (subsequent references cited parenthetically in text as HWAA).

3. See also ibid., where he described the incident but did not identify Bernays, referring to "the alleged authority of some member of the party whose name was not given" (404).

4. It is interesting in this context to note that Bernays's father was a grain exporter.

5. Edward Bernays, "Publicity in International Trade: How Public Opinion Abroad Was Influenced by the U.S. Government During the War," *American Manufacturing Export Association Newsletter* (April 16, 1920): 1–5. One etymology of the classical Latin roots for the term *propaganda* refers to the expansion of territory by conquest.

6. On Bullard's role, see George F. Kennan, *Russia Leaves the War* (Princeton, NJ: Princeton University Press, 1956), 46–50. Kennan pointed out that technically Bullard was a freelancer, not officially employed by the CPI, but he was a trusted acquaintance of Creel and House.

7. Ibid.; David S. Foglesong, *America's Secret War Against Bolshevism* (Chapel Hill: University of North Carolina Press, 1995).

8. For Sisson's meeting and suspicious views of Lenin, see Edgar Sisson, *One Hundred Red Days, 1917–1918* (New Haven, CT: Yale University Press, 1931), 208–209.

9. Wilson to Lansing, February 16, 1918, Sisson Documents, 1917–1921, Record Group 59, A1 1120, National Archives and Records Administration, College Park, MD; letter quoted in Kennan, *Russia Leaves the War*, 417. Wilson said the transaction made him feel "uneasy," but he still told Secretary of State Robert Lansing to go ahead.

10. Of particular note is a detailed analysis that Creel and/or State Department officials would have seen, which was authored by British intelligence and "point[ed] to the signatures being forgeries." See "Russian Letters: Report on Signatures," May 17, 1918, Sisson Documents. See also Helena M. Stone, "Another Look at the Sisson Forgeries and Their Background," *Soviet Studies* 37, no. 1 (January 1985): 90–102.

11. Quoted in Stewart Halsey Ross, *Propaganda for War: How the United States Was Conditioned to Fight the Great War of 1914–1918* (Jefferson, NC: McFarland, 1996), 242.

12. Ibid., 241.

13. Alan Axelrod, *Selling the Great War: The Making of American Propaganda* (New York: Palgrave Macmillan, 2009), 166. For a facsimile reproduction of the entire CPI pamphlet, see Sisson, *One Hundred Red Days*, 459–488.

14. For a thorough discussion of these documents, including their status as forgeries, see Kennan, *Russia Leaves the War*, 412–457. For an affirmation of their authenticity, see George Creel, *Rebel at Large: Recollections of Fifty Crowded Years* (New York: Putnam's, 1947). Creel went so far as to make the outrageous claim that the publication of the papers "brought about the first direct interference in our domestic affairs by Communist agents" (179), although precisely the reverse was true. For another view of the Russian-German connection during 1917–1918, see Arthur Bullard, *The Russian Pendulum: Autocracy—Democracy—Bolshevism* (New York: Macmillan, 1919). Bullard noted, "The Bolsheviki accepted money from the German Government, whom they hated, . . . with the full intention of betraying their benefactors at first—and every—opportunity" (102).

15. As Lippmann had similarly demonstrated in "A Test of the News" (discussed in chapter 3), the fierce animosity of most Americans toward the Soviets made objective coverage of the Russian Revolution virtually impossible.

16. Nicholas J. Cull, "Roof for a House Divided: How U.S. Propaganda Evolved into Public Diplomacy," in *The Oxford Handbook of Propaganda Studies*, ed. Jonathan Auerbach and Russ Castronovo (New York: Oxford University Press, 2013), 131–146.

17. For his defensive account of his public relations work in Guatemala, see Bernays, *Biography of an Idea*, 744–755.

18. Quoted in Scott M. Cutlip, *The Unseen Power: A History of Public Relations* (Hillsdale, NJ: Erlbaum, 1994), 53.

19. Quoted in Ray Eldon Hiebert, *Courtier to the Crowd: The Story of Ivy Lee and the Development of Public Relations* (Ames: Iowa State University Press, 1966), 248.

20. Ibid., 253.

21. Ibid.

22. Ivy Lee, *The Vacant Chair at the Council Table of the World* (New York: privately printed, 1922), 5 (subsequent references cited parenthetically in text).

23. The historian Foglesong pointed out that the American Red Cross between March and November 1917 undertook propaganda campaigns against the Bolsheviks, but there is no indication that Lee was involved in these efforts. See Foglesong, *America's Secret War Against Bolshevism*, 108.

24. Ivy Lee, *USSR: A World Enigma* (New York: privately printed, 1927), 6–7 (subsequent references cited parenthetically in text).

25. Elizabeth A. Papazian, "Literacy or Legibility: The Trace of Subjectivity in Soviet Social Realism," in *The Oxford Handbook of Propaganda Studies*, ed. Jonathan Auerbach and Russ Castronovo (New York: Oxford University Press, 2013), 67–90.

26. Hiebert, *Courtier to the Crowd*, 280.

27. On Ilgner, see Diarmuid Jeffreys, *Hell's Cartel: IG Farben and the Making of Hitler's War Machine* (New York: Henry Holt, 2008), 183–188.

28. Ibid., 194.

29. William Dodd, *Ambassador Dodd's Diary, 1933–1938* (New York: Harcourt, Brace, 1941), 74 (subsequent references cited parenthetically in text). For an interesting account of Dodd and his daughter, see Erik Larson, *In the Garden of Beasts* (New York: Crown, 2011).

30. In all fairness to Lee, in the spring of 1933 it might not have been so entirely clear if and how Hitler might moderate his views now that he was in power.

31. *Investigation of Nazi Propaganda Activities, 73rd Congress* (Washington, DC: US Government Printing Office, May 19, 1934), 262 (subsequent references cited parenthetically in text).

32. See Cutlip, *Unseen Power*, 152–153.

33. For two accounts of what Americans would have known and when, see Deborah E. Lipstadt, *Beyond Belief: The American Press and the Coming of the Holocaust, 1933–1945* (New York: Free Press, 1986); and Andrew Nagorski, *Hitlerland: American Eyewitnesses to the Nazi Rise to Power* (New York: Simon and Schuster, 2012).

34. Quoted in J. P. Stern, *Hitler: The Führer and the People* (Berkeley: University of California Press, 1975), 102.

35. Alan Bullock, *Hitler: A Study in Tyranny* (New York: Harper and Row, 1964), 162.

36. Ewen, *PR! A Social History of Spin*, 4. But later in his book (446n4), Ewen seemed to accept this story by Bernays at face value. I have been unable to locate any documents in the Bernays archives or elsewhere that would lend credence to his account, although I did discover that Bernays organized a luncheon in honor of Wiegand on September 20, 1932. See box I:8, n.d., Edward L. Bernays Papers, Manuscript Division, Library of Congress, Washington, DC.

37. Cutlip, *Unseen Power*, 540–551.

38. *Investigation of Nazi and Other Propaganda (73rd Congress)* (Washington, DC: US Government Printing Office, June 5, 1934), 33. See also *Investigation of Nazi and Other Propoganda (Report #153, 74th Congress)* (Washington, DC: US Government Printing Office, February 15, 1935), 5–6.

39. On Viereck, see Ross, *Propaganda for War*, 132–136.

40. Cutlip, *Unseen Power*, 770–771.

CONCLUSION

1. Ivy Lee, *The Problem of International Propaganda: A New Technique in Developing Understanding Between Nations* (New York: privately printed, 1934), 9, 10 (subsequent references cited parenthetically in text).

2. On the IPA, see J. Michael Sproule, *Propaganda and Democracy* (New York: Cambridge University Press, 1997), 129–177.

3. Jürgen Habermas, *The Structural Transformation of the Public Sphere: An Inquiry into a Category of Bourgeois Society*, trans. Thomas Burger (1962; rpt., Cambridge, MA: MIT Press, 1989). For a more extensive discussion of Habermas, see my "Essay on Sources."

4. See Sue Curry Jansen, "'The World's Greatest Adventure in Advertising': Walter Lippmann's Critique of Censorship and Propaganda," in *The Oxford Handbook of Propaganda Studies*, ed. Jonathan Auerbach and Russ Castronovo (New York: Oxford University Press, 2013), 312.

Essay on Sources

In examining various Progressive attitudes and practices regarding public opinion in an attempt to connect a particular period in American history with a particular mode of communication, I have relied on a range of sources. A brief historiography of Progressivism reveals two key areas of contention: the relative coherence of the era and the effectiveness of its various efforts—political, social, and economic—at transforming the United States. One of the earliest scholarly assessments of Progressivism was offered by Richard Hofstadter in *The Age of Reform: From Bryan to FDR* (1955), a highly influential work that grounded the continuity of the period between 1890 and 1920 in a sense of status anxiety shared by "Mugwump types" near the end of the nineteenth century and Progressives in the following two decades. Hofstadter consequently tended to treat the activist impulses of this era as mainly ceremonial gestures, inadequate to the task at hand despite the reformers' brightest hopes and intentions.[1]

This conclusion was challenged in the 1960s by historians such as Robert H. Wiebe and Samuel Haber, who emphasized Progressivism's preoccupation with scientific administration and efficiency.[2] Led by a new core of middle-class urban professionals seeking innovative methods to manage and control the increasing chaos of capitalist industrialization, Progressivism in this view was both a symptom and a response to modernity, its organizing principle being the search for order itself. But with the collapse of consensus models of history in the following decade, scholars began to challenge whether the "Progressive Movement" (now set off in quotation marks) was even unified enough in purpose or ideas or actors to either succeed or fail as a sustained historical development. Pronouncing Progressivism a useless construct, for example, Peter G. Filene in his provocative 1970 "obituary" contended that "the movement displays a puzzling and irreducible incoherence" that could not be contained by one rubric or set of rubrics.[3] Was Progressivism primarily national in scope, or local in focus? Were Progressives in the main

1. Richard Hofstadter, *The Age of Reform: From Bryan to F.D.R.* (New York: Vintage, 1955).
2. Samuel Haber, *Efficiency and Uplift: Scientific Management in the Progressive Era, 1890–1920* (Chicago: University of Chicago Press, 1964); Robert H. Wiebe, *The Search for Order, 1877–1920* (New York: Hill and Wang, 1966).
3. Peter G. Filene, "An Obituary for 'the Progressive Movement,'" *American Quarterly* 22 (1970): 20–34. The fact that Filene here referred to Progressivism as a "movement" (31) even as he was trying to demonstrate that it was not one suggests the difficulty of entirely dispensing with such reifying historical constructs. See also John D. Buenker, "The Progressive Era: A Search for a Synthesis," *Mid-America* 51 (1969): 175–193.

agitating for social justice across the board, for a radical redistribution of wealth, or more conservatively were they simply tinkering with the status quo? Filene concluded that even these sorts of basic questions could never be adequately addressed given the insufficient convergence of interests to define this "ism." For Filene the three decades between 1890 and 1920 in the United States lacked the distinct ideological clarity that typified earlier reformist movements, such as abolitionism.

Yet as we might have expected, reports of the demise of Progressivism were greatly exaggerated, as scholars came to grasp that the era could best be apprehended as driven by a loose set of reformist agendas and affiliations, sometimes acting in concert, sometimes at odds, rather than as a single, overarching entity. And so historians began invoking the plural instead of the singular—Progressivisms and Progressives—offering more specialized and fine-grained accounts that zeroed in on particular aspects such as race, class, ethnic communities, and gender. In a renewed effort to answer the familiar but vexed question, "Who were the Progressives?" scholars along these lines assessed the agrarian roots of reform versus urban origins, the relative influence of businessmen, workers, and women, and the impact of particular regions in setting Progressive agendas.[4] Writing just as these newer historical approaches were beginning to take off, Daniel T. Rodgers in his superb overview "In Search of Progressivism" (1982) endorsed a coalitions model as a way to approach the subject, but concluded his article by tentatively proposing three broader "clusters of ideas" or "distinct social languages" that characterized Progressivism as a whole: the rhetoric of anti-monopolism, an emphasis on social bonds, and the language of social efficiency.[5] These three clusters laid the groundwork for Rodgers's subsequent attempt at a far more ambitious synthesis, his magisterial *Atlantic Crossings: Social Politics in a Progressive Age* (1998) which went against the grain of American exceptionalism to offer a deeply informed transnational account of the multiple intersecting relations between social reform in the United States during this period and similar reform efforts in Germany, England, and France.[6] Partly thanks to Rodgers's book and to the influence

4. See, for instance, Glenda Elizabeth Gilmore, ed., *Who Were the Progressives?* (New York: Palgrave, 2002); Elizabeth Sanders, *Roots of Reform: Farmers, Workers, and the American State, 1877–1917* (Chicago: University of Chicago Press, 1999); Ellen Fitzpatrick, *Endless Crusade: Women Social Scientists and Progressive Reform* (New York: Oxford University Press, 1990); Robyn Muncy, *Creating a Female Dominion in American Reform, 1890–1935* (New York: Oxford University Press, 1991); Steven J. Diner, *A Very Different Age: Americans of the Progressive Era* (New York: Hill and Wang, 1998).

5. Daniel T. Rodgers, "In Search of Progressivism," *Reviews in American History* 10, no. 4 (December 1982): 113–132, esp. 123. Filene, "An Obituary for 'the Progressive Movement,'" also mentioned in passing a coalitions model (33). For another valuable assessment of the scholarship on Progressivism, see Richard L. McCormick, *The Party Period and Public Policy: American Politics from the Age of Jackson to the Progressive Era* (New York: Oxford University Press, 1986), 263–288; and Robert D. Johnston, "Re-Democratizing the Progressive Era: The Politics of Progressive Era Political Historiography," *Journal of the Gilded and Progressive Era* 1, no. 1 (January 2002): 68–92.

6. Daniel T. Rodgers, *Atlantic Crossings: Social Politics in a Progressive Age* (Cambridge, MA: Harvard University Press, 1998). The scholarship on Progressivism published during the past few decades is vast. For example, see Neil A. Wynn, *From Progressivism to Prosperity* (New York: Holmes and Meier, 1986); Eric Foner, *The Story of American Freedom* (New York: Norton, 1998), 139–193; Sidney M. Milkis and Jerome M. Mileur, eds., *Progressivism and the New Democracy* (Amherst: University of Massachusetts Press, 1999); John Whiteclay Chambers II, *The Tyranny of Change:*

of historians such as Thomas Bender, who argued for a return to synthetic historical narratives that aspire to tell big stories while attending to relations among different subgroups within public culture, Progressivism has continued to attract sustained attention.[7]

One other trend in scholarship that has adopted a synthetic, if somewhat partial, approach to the subject deserves mention. In the introduction to their valuable collection of primary documents from the period, editors Ronald J. Pestritto and William J. Atto "do contend, emphatically, that progressivism can be understood as a coherent set of principles with a common purpose." Reiterating the thesis of Pestritto's book *Woodrow Wilson and the Roots of Modern Liberalism* (2005), they summarized that agenda in a nutshell: Progressivism has been "an argument to enlarge vastly the scope of national government for the purpose of responding to a set of economic and social conditions which, progressives contend, could not have been envisioned at the founding and for which the founders' limited, constitutional government was inadequate."[8] Asserting that "criticism of the Constitution . . . formed the backbone of the entire movement" (3), these two neoconservative scholars posited the coherence of Progressivism, and Wilson's political thinking in particular, precisely in order to challenge it as wrongheaded, a betrayal of core American principles. Enlightenment tenets originally set up under emerging laissez-faire liberalism to protect individual rights and economic interests against the intrusions of government, so their claim went, were deliberately overturned by Progressive administrators bent on expanding the authority and reach of that very state under a new kind of modern liberalism inspired by German idealism.

But treating Progressivism as a logical "argument" overestimates the importance of political theory in shaping the often contradictory practices and values of the reformers, who had plenty of other things to worry about besides the Constitution. Acting with a pressing urgency beyond hypothetical abstractions, Progressives were driven by "a fierce discontent," to borrow Teddy Roosevelt's phrase, and felt a strong obligation to take aim against a dire sea of troubles—corrupt municipal politics, the unregulated expansion of monopolies, and divisive strife between capital and labor, among many other perceived problems. Occasionally these battles pitted Progressives against one another in their efforts to refashion citizens.[9]

America in the Progressive Era, 1890–1920, 2nd ed. (New Brunswick, NJ: Rutgers University Press, 2000); Michael McGerr, *A Fierce Discontent: The Rise and Fall of the Progressive Movement in America, 1870–1920* (New York: Free Press, 2003); Maureen A. Flanagan, *America Reformed: Progressives and Progressivism, 1890s–1920s* (New York: Oxford University Press, 2007); Jackson Lears, *Rebirth of a Nation: The Making of Modern America, 1877–1920* (New York: HarperCollins, 2009), in addition to the various studies mentioned in the introduction. At the end of his synthetic account, Lears included a valuable bibliographical note.

7. Thomas Bender, "Wholes and Parts: The Need for Synthesis in American History," *Journal of American History* 73, no. 1 (June 1986): 120–136.

8. Ronald J. Pestritto and William J. Atto, eds., *American Progressivism: A Reader* (Lanham, MD: Rowman and Littlefield, 2008), 2–3. The fact that the editors referred to "progressivism" in the present tense and with a lowercase *p* suggests that they wanted to connect the historical era of the early twentieth century with contemporary American politics. My book uses the uppercase *P* to emphasize the historical specificity of the term. See also Ronald J. Pestritto, *Woodrow Wilson and the Roots of Modern Liberalism* (Lanham, MD: Rowman and Littlefield, 2005).

9. This refashioning was a messy, complex business that frequently found influential Progressive publicists such as Lippmann, Dewey, Creel, and Jane Addams at odds with one another before, dur-

This is not to say that Progressivism lacked any ideological basis, but one would be hard put to confine those ideological agendas (plural) to the sole one of revising the Constitution.[10] Such a tendentious approach gives the philosopher Georg Wilhelm Friedrich Hegel far too much weight in influencing Wilson's conception of the state and the exercise of his own executive power; Wilson's leadership was less absolutist and more open to compromise than Pestritto would have it.[11] Influenced by Edmund Burke more than Hegel, Wilson throughout his career emphasized the need for "expediency," defining Progressivism as "the adaptation of the business of each day to the circumstances of that day as they differ from the circumstances of the day before."[12] In one small example of such pragmatism, Wilson appointed conservative businessmen, including former bankers and brokers, to help run the newly created Federal Reserve and Federal Trade Commission, early administrative efforts under his first term to establish a mixed "corporate-regulatory complex," as historian Alan Dawley described Progressive statecraft.[13]

Any discussion of public opinion during this period needs to take into account the highly influential arguments of Jürgen Habermas, who in the early 1960s offered the

---

ing, and after the First World War. And while there might have been increasing civic engagement on the part of some citizens, as Kevin Mattson suggested, the first two decades of the twentieth century also saw a decline in the percentage of eligible American voters casting ballots, as Rodgers noted. See Mattson, *Creating a Democratic Public: The Struggle for Urban Participatory Democracy During the Progressive Era* (University Park: Pennsylvania State University Press, 1998); Rodgers, *Atlantic Crossings*, 116–122. Mattson's historical analysis is flawed by his tendency to fall back on overly judgmental norms of right and wrong that assume municipal grassroots efforts to organize a public are invariably better than top-down attempts; for example, he read Mayor Tom Johnson's desire to impose his own reformist "goals and agendas" on Cleveland government as a betrayal of democracy (46). But social justice and social control during this period cannot be so neatly disentangled as Mattson supposed. What he saw as an unfortunate "waning" of a democratic public during the First World War can be regarded as having a strong continuity with Progressive practices and attitudes carried over from the previous decade. How else to explain the enthusiastic embrace of war by most Progressives?

10. For a skeptical account situating Progressive ideas within wider ideologies of progress, see Christopher Lasch, *The True and Only Heaven: Progress and Its Critics* (New York: Norton, 1991), 329–368.

11. Pestritto's insistence on the impact of Hegel on Wilson failed to account for other Progressives, such as Teddy Roosevelt, who were even more committed to the nation-state but were not necessarily so influenced by German idealism. It also ignored the differences between Hegelian teleology and American Christianity, which had a far sharper sense of innate sin, especially for a devout Presbyterian like Wilson. And such ideological accounts neglected the pragmatic complexities of bureaucratization itself. For an excellent account of such practicalities, see Stephen Skowronek, *Building a New American State: The Expansion of National Administrative Capacities, 1877–1920* (Cambridge: Cambridge University Press, 1982); and for a more theoretical comparative treatment, see Marc Stears, *Progressives, Pluralists, and the Problems of the State: Ideologies of Reform in the United States and Britain, 1909–1926* (Oxford: Oxford University Press, 2002). See also his later work, which discussed Progressivism as a positive model for contemporary politics from a perspective far different than Pestritto's: Marc Stears, *Demanding Democracy: American Radicals in Search of a New Politics* (Princeton, NJ: Princeton University Press, 2010), 21–55.

12. Quoted in John Milton Cooper Jr., *The Warrior and the Priest* (Cambridge, MA: Harvard University Press, 1983), 185. On Wilson's embrace of expediency, see also 53–56, 91, 95, 122, 172, 184, 253, 265.

13. Alan Dawley, *Struggles for Justice: Social Responsibility and the Liberal State* (Cambridge, MA: Harvard University Press, 1991), 141–171.

most fully articulated historical analysis of the public and publicness, or *Öffentlichkeit*. This German term was translated into English decades later via a reifying spatial metaphor that is a bit misleading: "the public sphere." Habermas's thesis in *The Structural Transformation of the Public Sphere: An Inquiry into a Category of Bourgeois Society* is so familiar as to require little elaboration, but let me briefly summarize. He argued that around 1680 and for two centuries thereafter, private persons belonging to the emergent middle class began to engage in critical-rational debate about political matters that had previously been under the domain of the state, and through these vibrant channels of public opinion (coffeehouses, newspapers, novels) these bourgeoisie helped "put the state in touch with the needs of society."[14] In subsequent works Habermas developed this essentially historical analysis into a robust theory of deliberative democracy.

Receiving a great deal of attention, Habermas's account of the public sphere has occasioned criticism on a variety of fronts: that his model of communicative action based on speech act theory presupposes a dubious linguistic stability (Jacques Derrida); that his privileging of rationality ignores the dynamics of complex systems (Niklas Luhmann); that his rendering of constitutional democracy is skewed in favor of law at the expense of more unbounded political activism (Bonnie Honig); that he ignores the crucial role of gender in structuring a public (Nancy Fraser, among others); that he fails to allow for multiple publics and counterpublics, especially a plebeian public (Oskar Negt and Alexander Kluge); that his faith in rational consensus (not compromise) downplays how power operates under a more pluralistic and antagonistic concept of the political (Chantal Mouffe, drawing on Carl Schmitt); and that his account oversimplifies and idealizes (nearly everybody, including Habermas himself).[15] Despite these challenges and perceived inadequacies, the Habermasian version of the public sphere remains highly compelling, although perhaps less convincing as a normative ideal than as an ambitious synthesis of social and intellectual history, filled with illuminating discussions of Rousseau, Kant, Hegel, Marx, Mill, and other thinkers, tracking one key aspect of the Enlightenment and its legacies up to the twentieth century.[16]

Another problem (generally less noted by the critics cited above) is found at the tail end of his argument, or rather, arguments, since Habermas in his book offered two

14. Jürgen Habermas, *The Structural Transformation of the Public Sphere: An Inquiry into a Category of Bourgeois Society*, trans. Thomas Burger (1962; rpt., Cambridge, MA: MIT Press, 1989), 31 (subsequent references cited parenthetically in text).

15. For an array of these critiques, see Jostein Gripsrud et al., eds., *The Idea of the Public Sphere: A Reader* (Lanham, MD: Rowman and Littlefield, 2010); Lasse Thomassen, ed., *The Derrida-Habermas Reader* (Chicago: University of Chicago Press, 2006); Craig Calhoun, ed., *Habermas and the Public Sphere* (Cambridge, MA: MIT Press, 1992). Although dated, Calhoun's introduction (1–48) remains a useful overview; see also Habermas's further reflections and the volume's concluding remarks (421–479).

16. For other rich historical analyses of public opinion, see Hans Speier, *The Truth in Hell and Other Essays on Politics and Culture, 1935–1987* (New York: Oxford University Press, 1989), 143–161; John D. Peters, "Historical Tensions in the Concept of Public Opinion," in *Public Opinion and the Communication of Consent*, ed. T. L. Glasser and C. T. Salmon (New York: Guilford, 1995), 3–32; Hanno Hardt and Slavko Splichal, eds., *Ferdinand Tönnies on Public Opinion: Selections and Analyses* (Lanham, MD: Rowman and Littlefield, 2000), 1–110; Kirk Wetters, *The Opinion System: Impasses of the Public Sphere from Hobbes to Habermas* (New York: Fordham University Press, 2008).

distinct accounts of public opinion, one historical and the other focused on his present (mid-twentieth-century) state of affairs. First, he provided a narrative of the rise and downfall of publicness that closed near the end of the nineteenth century. This moment of decline was marked for Habermas by a decisive turn away from deliberative politics, which was triggered in part by a growing state interventionism that began "to adopt the interests of civil society as its own" (142). Second, in the final two sections of his study, Habermas offered an analysis of the contemporary scene, which he found rather dreary, with the concept of public opinion now "liquidated," dispersed into vapid social and psychological registers that signaled modern democracy's failure to sustain itself amid the onslaught of manufactured mass culture under late capitalism.

Here Habermas (in 1962) revealed his allegiance to a distinctly Cold War ethos about the threat of the burgeoning mass media and mass consumption—television, advertising, commercial book clubs, and other modes of coercive communication that now prevented citizens from thinking for themselves. A similar contempt for mass culture was expressed by Frankfurt School theorists such as Theodor Adorno (a strong influence on Habermas), along with most American intellectuals after the Second World War. In contrast to his highly nuanced earlier historical analysis, this section of the book is surprisingly reductive, with Habermas making categorical assertions such as "the world fashioned by the mass media is a public sphere in appearance only" (171), thus assuming a total divide between appearance and "reality." But in the absence of a public assembled into one body in one place, a dubious proposition even in the eighteenth century, in order to debate and share opinions, citizens invariably must rely on mediated representation.[17] Habermas likewise offered other simplistic binaries such as "critical publicity is supplanted by manipulative publicity" (178), as if there were no middle ground between the two. In other words, he fully accepted the post-1920 derogatory assumptions about the top-down, inevitably staged deceit of propaganda as spawning nothing but false consciousness. Once "mass" replaced "public" as the adjective modifying "opinion," it was all over for Habermas.[18]

17. For this argument, see John D. Peters, "Realism in Social Representation and the Fate of the Public," in *Public Opinion and Democracy:Vox Populi, Vox Dei?*, ed. Slavko Splichal (Creskill, NJ: Hampton, 2001), 85–102. Other essays in the collection are also valuable, especially the historical accounts by Splichal (21–53) and Paul Beaud and Laurence Kaufmann (55–84). See also Michael Warner, *Publics and Counterpublics* (New York: Zone, 2005). In his compelling updating and refining of Habermas, Warner got around this soft spot in the original argument by defining a *public* as an imagined relation among strangers constituted by discourse and brought into being by mere attention (65–124). Warner's seven propositions regarding the circulation and reception of texts did not directly address the scope or scale of a public (could it be a solitary "you" or an implied reader?). But in an earlier essay, first published in the Calhoun collection and reprinted in Warner's *Publics and Counterpublics* (159–186), Warner did centrally engage "the mass public" and "the mass subject," suggesting that a "double movement of identification and alienation" remained "the legacy of the bourgeois public sphere's founding logic, the contradictions of which become visible whenever the public sphere can no longer turn a blind eye to its privileged bodies" (182–183). In the main, I adhere to the classical liberal understanding of the public as a site of (privileged) impersonality.

18. Habermas's later works, which ambitiously engaged theories of communication, law, morality, and deliberative democracy were less historically specific than *The Structural Transformation*, but traces of his earlier thinking remained. See, for instance, Jürgen Habermas, *The Theory of Com-*

The difficulty is that his earlier history of rise and decline cut off just as it got most interesting, jumping suddenly from the late nineteenth century to the middle of the twentieth century without considering the transformation from "critical" to "manipulative" publicity that clearly did not take place overnight, but gradually occurred between 1890 and the First World War (and beyond). Habermas gave short shrift to this key transitional period of Progressive thought and action. Although he was carefully attuned to the incremental rise and evolution of the bourgeois public sphere, if a bit nostalgic and glowing in his assessment at times, he seemed less interested in tracing the historical subtleties of its erosion. In place of detailed analysis, he provided a kind of theological fall that rested on Manichaean antitheses, so that the public in effect had to wither and die for the sin of consuming the apple of mass culture.

Asserting that "public opinion" became a "problematic entity in the final quarter of the nineteenth century," for example, Habermas quoted a German treatise from 1879 that bemoaned the people's incessant need for "diversions" as opposed to a century prior, when a "social principle" "placed an obligation upon each individual" (240). Perhaps, but could this simply be a yearning for a golden past, and even if not, what would be the way forward from this point? Habermas did not say, other than to briefly allude to Gabriel Tarde, whose subtle and complex analyses of "mass opinion" (in relation to newspaper reading, for instance) at the turn of the twentieth century Habermas dismissively skimmed over because this opinion was "separated from the functional complex of political institutions" (240). While Kant merited fifteen pages of discussion, Tarde was dispensed with in two sentences.[19]

Habermas also displayed a distinctly Eurocentric bias. It is striking, for example, that Walter Lippmann or John Dewey did not appear anywhere in his study, despite their pioneering analyses of public opinion that predated his own by four decades. In one of the largest and most important collections of essays dedicated to the German philosopher's theories, *Habermas and the Public Sphere* (1992), edited by Craig Calhoun, these two Progressive intellectuals were also conspicuously absent, meriting only a passing nod to Dewey, which was buried in a single footnote (431n15). Since the late 1980s and early 1990s (when his work was translated into English), Habermas has dominated academic discussions about the public sphere, but my study makes clear that thinkers such as Lipp-

municative Action, Lifeworld and System: A Critique of Functionalist Reason, vol. 2, trans. Thomas McCarthy (Boston: Beacon, 1987), 301–331 (on Weber and legitimation); and Jürgen Habermas, *Between Facts and Norms: Contributions to a Discourse Theory of Law and Democracy*, trans. William Rehg (Cambridge, MA: MIT Press, 1996), where he discounted a public sphere that could be "manufactured" at will (364). But, for example, depictions of gay men and lesbians on mainstream network television in the United States (such as sitcoms) over the past three decades have arguably been more influential in shaping the growing public acceptance of gay rights and marriage equality than other less mass manufactured forms of communication, such as newspaper editorials.

19. Habermas was also dismissive of modern empirical techniques such as polling that attempt to gauge public opinion, suggesting that although these increasingly approved measures might accurately forecast election results, they are essentially tautological by definition in that they do not tell us much about how such opinions are formed in the first place. For a similar critique that argued that the very asking of such questions presupposes consensus, see Pierre Bourdieu, "Public Opinion Does Not Exist," in his *Communication and Class Struggle*, vol. 1: *Capitalism, Imperialism*, ed. A. Mattelart and S. Siegelaub (New York: International General, 1979), 124–130.

mann and Dewey well before him voiced similarly deep concerns about the viability of a democratic public.

Scholars who have examined publicity practices during the Progressive Era have tended to follow the lead of Habermas by continuing to take a dim view of mass persuasion, whether practiced by the state (Creel's Committee on Public Information) or public relations counsels like Bernays. Social historian Stuart Ewen is perhaps the most prominent. Bernays occupied pride of place in Ewen's *PR! A Social History of Spin* (1996), a wide-ranging and perceptive study of American publicity as it developed throughout the twentieth century. Dramatizing the magnetic personality of Bernays, whom he met late in life, Ewen bought into the publicist's claims about the entrancing sway of his craft, even as he tried to distance himself from this seductive power by imputing bad faith to it. In his summation, Ewen admitted that Bernays had some democratic inclinations, but then went on to emphasize the dark side of his propagandizing: "This Bernays was the painter of mental scenery, the fabricator of captivating 'pseudo-environments' designed to steer the public mind furtively toward the agendas of vested power. He was a master of stagecraft, shaping 'news' and 'events' with a hidden hand. Beside the democrat stood the demagogue, a nimble master of illusions, a man who sought to colonize the public sphere on behalf of entrenched managerial interests."[20]

Ewen's eloquent if overheated critique was fueled by a puritan anti-theatrical bias, condemning all show, combined with a conspiratorial Marxism that automatically assumed that entrenched authority, particularly corporate, will inevitably be put to evil use. By treating this hidden mastery as virtually unchecked, Ewen and other scholars of his ilk (like Noam Chomsky) have bolstered the significance and virtue of their own righteous demystifying of these elitist propaganda wizards. When Ewen discussed other figures also close to vested power, such as Lippmann (who coined the term *pseudo-environment*), he arrived at basically the same set of conclusions.

But people in positions of power might actually help direct the public toward a greater egalitarianism, as many Progressives believed. In another highly informative history of American propaganda, which appeared a year after Ewen's, J. Michael Sproule (a scholar of communications) offered a more sympathetic account of Bernays along these very lines. Bernays, Sproule explained, "described the chief social value of public relations as its opposition to suppression of minority views. In fact, dissident ideas gained the most from wide publicity since otherwise they could never overcome established conceptions."[21] Yet Bernays was being shifty here, using the term *minority* in a strictly numerical sense to refer to small cadres of the powerful as well as to marginalized, oppressed groups, as if the two would inevitably share common interests, when they clearly would not. Bernays simply cannot be taken at face value, as Sproule tended to do in his descriptions of the arguments advanced by publicists promoting the significance of their work.

Propagandists tend to be cagey rhetoricians (if not always masterfully so); their slippery rhetoric needs to be closely interrogated and treated with some skepticism, but also

20. Stuart Ewen, *PR! A Social History of Spin* (New York: Basic, 1996), 400.
21. J. Michael Sproule, *Propaganda and Democracy* (New York: Cambridge University Press, 1997), 58.

with some serious respect, so as not to dismiss their ideas (and practices) too quickly as simply false consciousness, all smoke and mirrors. For a collection of essays that tries to reorient the field by moving beyond pejorative value judgments, see *The Oxford Handbook of Propaganda Studies* (2013), which I co-edited with Russ Castronovo, including the introduction, "Thirteen Propositions About Propaganda."[22]

22. Jonathan Auerbach and Russ Castronovo, eds., *The Oxford Handbook of Propaganda Studies* (New York: Oxford University Press, 2013).

Index